AN APPRAISAL OF THE REGULATION OF MEDICAL PRACTICE IN CAMEROON

AN APPRAISAL OF THE REGULATION OF MEDICAL PRACTICE IN CAMEROON

Roland Djieufack
Michel Mbetiji Mbetiji
Grace Mary Nkafu Tazanu

GALDA VERLAG 2026

Bibliografische Information der Deutschen Nationalbibliothek
Die Deutsche Nationalbibliothek verzeichnet diese Publikation in der Deutschen Nationalbibliografie; detaillierte bibliografische Daten sind im Internet über https://dnb.de abrufbar.

ISBN 978-3-96203-534-1 (Print)
ISBN 978-3-96203-535-8 (E-PDF)

If you have any questions about product safety, please contact us at the following e-mail address : contact@galda.com

TABLE OF CONTENTS

CHAPTER FOUR: REMEDIES FOR VIOLATION OF MEDICAL PRACTICE IN CAMEROON

DEDICATION

To our beloved families

PREFACE

The primary objective of this book is to raise the general awareness of the respect of the rights of patients in Cameroon. Patients under medical acre are a group of persons that are vulnerable because ill-health of a human being comes with so many challenges. It is on this premise that this study sets out to examine the effectiveness of existing regulatory instruments governing medical practice in Cameroon. The research assumes that the supervision and control of the activities of medical practitioners is ineffective. This study therefore aims at pointing out the hurdles that beset the protection of the rights of patients in health establishments in Cameroon from a legal right-based approach. In an attempt to establish this fact, this study strongly reveals that persistent malpractices by medical practitioners violate the rights to health of patients. It also establishes that apart from the negligence of medical practitioners, government ineptness also contributes to medical malpractices. The sanction of violation of medical practice through litigation is hampered by the inability of victims to adduce sufficient expert evidence to inculpate medical practitioners, with the result that most of them go unpunished. The remedies available to victims of malpractices which are mostly compensatory damages are inadequate. Judicial malfunctioning discourages victims of medical malfeasance from seeking legal redress, and the consistent laxity with which medical practitioners are supervised, greatly restraint regulatory efforts. There is therefore an urgent need for a more stringent implementation of existing legislative and regulatory instruments governing medical practice in Cameroon. This is compounded by the fact that mindful of their rights which are enshrined across different international and domestic statutes, the effective protection of their rights as prescribed under Cameroonian Law in particular is a call for concern.

Adopting both qualitative and quantitative research methodology, involving in-depth content analysis of primary and secondary data, this study advocates for an enhanced enforcement of the laws in place in order to adequately guarantee and enforce the rights of patients exposed to medical practice in Cameroon. The emphasis today in Cameroon in particular, is towards the respect of dignity and welfare of patients with through the effective implementation of existing legal instruments. By the findings registered by this study, cases of victims of medical practice on patients in Cameroon are incessantly flooding the courts and other concerned administrative structures. Despite the existence of legislations governing their rights in Cameroon, there is still an urgent need for stakeholders concerned with the conditions of patients to adequately exercise their responsibilities; and it is in response to this duty that this book has been written. This is clearly an indication that Cameroonians particularly those affected medical practice are becoming more conscientious and that the Cameroonian government is, to some extent, responding adequately to their preoccupations. In this book, the authors have carefully discussed their viewpoints from a legal perspective. This current study is a clear reflection of the efforts put in by the authors during years of Doctorate research as we have drawn from existing literature on insolvency law in general in Cameroon as well as from other jurisdictions, analyzed the relevant statutes and elucidated on material drawn from extensive field research work conducted in Cameroon.

The book is structured in seven chapter and it is a useful source of reference for students of Medical Law and Human Rights Law, legal practitioners, magistrates and judges, health workers who actively are involved in the welfare of patients. This study will definitely go a long way to enhance understanding to existing regulations on Medical Law in Cameroon.

Roland Djieufack, Ph.D
Michel M. Mbetiji, Ph.D
Grace Nkafu, Ph.D
Cameroon

ACKNOWLEDGEMENTS

This study indeed would not have been conducted without the assistance of many persons who in various ways aided to shape our ideas. We actually had the assistance of some staff working in the decentralized services of the Ministry of Public Health, Ministry of Labour, Ministry of Social Affairs, Ministry of Women's Empowerment and the Family, Ministry of Justice, found in the major cities of Bafousam, Bamenda, Buea, Douala and Yaoundé in Cameroon. We also register our gratitude to some associations concerned with the welfare of patients for responding positively to our questions and provided useful information. We humbly accept and take responsibility for all errors and omissions in this book.

LIST OF LEGAL INSTRUMENTS

National Instruments

Decrees / Decisions

Circulars

International Instruments

Conventions/Charters/Declarations

Principles and Guidelines

TABLE OF CASES

Cameroonian Cases

Foreign Cases

ABBREVIATIONS

AfMA:	Africa Medical Association
AFCHPR:	African Charter on Human and Peoples Right
CENAME:	Centrale Nationale D'approvisionnement en Médicaments et Consommables Médicaux Essentiels
CEDAW:	Convention on the Elimination of All Forms of Discrimination against Women
CERD:	Convention on the Elimination of All Forms of Racial Discrimination
CONAC:	Commission Nationale Anti-Corruption
CMC:	Cameroon Medical Council
CME:	Continuing Medical Education
CRC:	Convention on the Rights of the Child
CRPD:	Convention on the Rights of Persons with Disabilities
ICESCR:	International Covenant on Economic Social and Cultural Right
ICCPR:	International Covenant on Civil and Political Rights
IATSIC:	International Association for Trauma and Intensive Care
LANACOME :	Laboratoire Nationale de Contrôle de Qualité des Médicaments et d'Expertise
MINSANTE :	Ministère de la Sante Publique du Cameroun

NDRA: National Drug Regulatory Authority

NGO: Non-Governmental Organization

OECD: Organization for Economic Co-operation and Development

T I: Transparency international

TI-C: Transparency International Cameroon

UNO: United Nations Organization

WFME: World Federation for Medical Education

WHA: World Health Assembly

WHO: World Health Organization

WMA: World Medical Association

CHAPTER ONE

General Introduction

1.1 Background to the Study

The practice of medicine has been subject to regulation from time immemorial. Control of physician action through medical legislation and ethics has a long history and is not unique to modern society. Before legal regulation, there was self-regulation as typified by the Hippocratic oath(460-370BC) introduced by Hippocrates who is considered the father of modern medicine, for medical practitioners in the art of healing. It states; "I will abstain from intentional wrong doing and harm, especially from abusing the bodies of man or woman, bond or free". The oath also states;" I will impart precept, oral instruction, and all other instruction to my own sons, the sons of my teacher, and to indentured pupils who have taken the Healer's oath, but to nobody else", this created the medical 'closed shop', restricted to a selected group[1]. The 'closed shop' became formalised with the rise of the Guilds[2], Association of Specialist Workers who oversaw the practice of their trade and determined who could join. Barber-surgeons' guilds emerged in Paris and London in the 1300s as both trades used sharp instruments. The apothecaries were originally allied with grocers' guilds because they both used and sold spices[3].

---

1 Green, B., (2017) "Use of the Hippocratic or other Professional Oaths in UK Medical Schools in 2017: Practice, Perception of Benefits and Principlism", *BMC Research Notes* at http://10;777 doi.org/10.1186/s13104-017-3114-7 (accessed on the 6th day of December2024).

2 Elliott, A.K., *Death of the Guilds. Professional, States, and the Advance of Capitalism, 1930 to the Present.* (Yale University Press, 1999).

3 *Ibid.*

In the early 1500s in the United Kingdom, many physicians were working with no formal training or knowledge. Physicians therefore petitioned parliament to ask that nobody without appropriate qualification be allowed to practise medicine, stating that unqualified practitioners caused "great harm and slaughter of many men"[4]. In 1511, a statute placed regulation of the medical profession in the hands of bishops. The church was apparently considered the one institution whose influence was extensive and potent enough to be effective in supressing quacks and licencing the members of the medical profession[5]. The purpose of the 1511 statutes was to eliminate unqualified practitioners, and to that end it provided for a financial reward for those who reported them.

In 1518, the Royal College of Physicians of London was granted a royal charter and it took over licensing of doctors in London. In 1704, Apothecaries were recognised as practising doctors, and in 1745, a Bill was passed forming the Royal College of Surgeon in England, thus the medical profession was officially divided into three classes; physicians, surgeons, and apothecaries. In 1815, the Apothecary Act was passed which introduced compulsory apprenticeship and formal qualification for apothecaries, in modern terms general practitioners, under the license of the society of apothecaries[6].

The 1858 Medical Act marks the start of the modern period of medical regulation in the United Kingdom[7]. The UK General Medical Council was finally established with aim to create a register of all licensed medical practitioners, oversee undergraduate medical schools, provide professional guidance, remove practitioners from the register if their peers decided. The 1950 medical act introduced disciplinary boards, a compulsory year of training for doctors after their university qualification. The Medical Act 1983 provide the current statutory basis for the General Medical Council function. The Council is bound by laws that that implement a European Directive on mutual recognition of Professional qualifications from European Countries.

In the USA and Canada, modern health care regulation emerged in the 19th Century, influenced by a variety of stakeholders responding to local

---

4 Raach, J.H., (1944), "English Medical Licencing in the Early Seventeenth Century", *Yale Journal of Biology and Medicine*, 16(4), pp.267-288.

5 *Ibid.*

6 Loudon, I. S., (1982), "The Origin of the General Practitioner", James Mackenzie Lecture, *J R Coll Gen Pract*, 33(246), pp 13-23.

7 Roberts, M.J.D., (2009), "The Politics of Professionalization: MPs, Medical Men, and the 1858 Medical Act", *Med Hist*, 53(1), pp.37-56.

concerns for healthcare quality, access and professional training[8]. Organised professionals were empowered to by the state to govern their own affairs especially entry into practice and the conduct of professional practice[9]. In western Europe, professional regulation was more state directed[10]. Regulatory practices changed over the course of the 20th and 21st Centuries in response to changing stakeholders and shifting interests[11].

During World War II the British Medical Association (BMA) had been the focal spot at which doctors of all the allied nations congregated from time to time to discuss problems of medical practice and to compare the conditions of medical service and education in their respective countries. In 1944, an informal meeting of doctors from several countries convened at BMA house in London to initiate plans for an international medical organisation to replace the "*Association Professionnelle Internationale des Médecins*" (APIM)[12] which was founded in 1925, with a membership of 23 countries and had suspended operations with the advent of World War II[13]. Subsequently, an International Medical Conference was organised in London in 1946 by APIM and BMC, the twenty-nine National Medical Organisations which were represented at this International Medical Conference became the founder associations[14]. It was decided during this conference that the name of the association should be the World Medical Association, thus the WMA came into being on September 1947. This organisation was created to ensure the independence of physicians, and to work for the highest possible standards of ethical behaviour and care by physician at all time[15]. Attempts at updating the Hippocratic oath to align it with the practice and language of modern medicine saw the adoption of the Geneva Declaration in 1948 by the General Assembly of the World

8 Adams, T.L., (2020), "Health Professional Regulation in Historical Context: Canada, the USA and the UK (19thCentury to present)", *Hum Resour Health,* 18 (72) at https://doi.org/10.1186/s12960-020-00501-y (accessed on the 6th day of December *2024)*

9 Gidney, R D. *et al, Professional Gentlemen: The Professions in Nineteenth-Century Ontario* (Toronto, University of Toronto Press; 1994), p. 78.

10 Howell, C. D., (1981), "Reform and the Monopolistic Impulse", *Acadiensis,* 11(1), pp.3-22.

11 See *supra* note 8.

12 Foreign Doctors: A Meeting at B.M.A. House. *British Medical Journal,* Dec.2, 1944, p.732.

13 Association Professionnelle Internationale des Medecins. Suplement to the British Medical Journal, 4 September 1937 at htpps://www.jstor.org/stable/25367152 (accessed on the 7th day of December 2024).

14 Australia, Austria, Belgium, Canada, Czechoslovakia, Denmark, Egypt, Eire, Finland, France, Great Britain, Greece, Iceland, Iraq, Luxembourg, Netherlands, New Zealand, Norway, Palestine, Iran, Poland, Portugal, South Africa, Spain, Sweden, Switzerland, Turkey, United States.

15 The World Medical Association, at https://www.wma.net (accessed on the 7th day of December 2024).

Medical Association[16]. The Geneva Declaration spells out a physician's moral obligations to his patients, and an explicit commitment to the humanitarian goals of Medicine[17]. This Declaration has been adopted as the International Code of Medical Ethics[18]. This declaration has gone a step further as it hinges on the commitment of the medical doctor to maintain the noble profession of the medical tradition.

The Africa Medical Association (AfMA) was established in 2004 to act as the representative voice of physicians, and where appropriate patients. It influences policy and launches and participates in projects with the goal of improving healthcare in Africa. It aims at achieving the highest quality of health to patients in the continent through advocacy and action, and the highest possible standard of ethical behaviour and care by physicians at all times[19].

In Cameroon before the advent of science-based medicine, traditional medicine was the dominant medical system for the local people until the arrival of the European. This herbal medicine was generally not adequately researched, and was weakly regulated[20]. During the mandate period, a health care system that was coordinated from Nigeria was established in the territory of Southern Cameroons[21]. Public health in Southern Cameroons during the Mandate period, was therefore the preserve of the Director of Medical and Sanitary Services (DMSS) who was based in Lagos, Nigeria[22]. Under him were medical doctors, dispensaries attendants, nurses, dressers, vaccinators and sanitary inspectors whose role was to ensure the functioning of the health care system in Nigeria and Cameroons. The two department were later on separated. The Southern Cameroons medical department was directly responsible to the medical headquarter in Lagos, Nigeria. The DMSS in Nigeria issued regulations and instructions on medical and health matters

---

16 The Geneva Declaration is an adaptation of the Oath of Hippocrates by the World Medical Association to bring it in line with the practice and language of modern medicine.

17 *Ibid.*

18 This Code was first formulated by the World Medical Association in 1949. It was subsequently amended by the World Medical Assembly in 1968, 1983 and 2006 in Sydney, Venice and Pilanesberg respectively.

19 Africa Medical Association, at htpps://africama.net (accessed on the 7th day of December 2024).

20 Enang, A.E., (2019), "An Appraisal on the Evolution of Medicine in Cameroon", *2nd International Conference on Research in Social Sciences*, p.86.

21 Ngwa, A.C. *et al*, (2020), "British Southern Cameroons Health Services as an Appendage to Nigerian Health Sector, 1922-1961", *International Journal of Scientific Research and Management*, 8(3), p.638.

22 Forkusam, A.L., (1978), "The Evolution of Health Services in the Southern Cameroons under British Administration 1916-1945", DES Dissertation in History, University of Yaoundé

to the Southern Cameroons resident in Buea for onward transmission to the medical department in Victoria[23].

The medical department in Southern Cameroons was headed by a Senior Medical Officer (SMO) who was stationed in Victoria and was charged with the implementation of decisions taken by the DMSS in Lagos, Nigeria[24]. It was the responsibility of the SMO to design medical policies for the territory, supervise all aspects of medical works, and ensure the conduct of research and training. The SMO was also responsible for producing comprehensive reports on the healthcare situation of Southern Cameroons and forward to the DMSS in Lagos, Nigeria.

In 1946, Southern Cameroons was part of the British Cameroon that became a Trust Territory of the United Nations under the administration of Britain[25]. Britain accepted the responsibility of providing medical care as a statutory service. The Medical Service Department was reorganised. The Richards Constitution of 1947 divided Nigeria into three Administrative Regions namely; Northern, Western and Eastern Regions of Nigeria, Southern Cameroons was administratively attached to the Eastern Region, Thus the SMO was now directly answerable to Director of Medical Services for the Eastern Region who was stationed in Enugu[26].

In 1949, the structure of the medical department saw changes, Southern Cameroons was reorganised into two provinces (Cameroon province and Bamenda province) with each having three divisions. This administrative division affected the administrative structure of the medical services. The territory that was formerly administered medically by the SMO now became the responsibility of the Principal Medical Officer still with headquarters in Victoria[27]. There were two senior medical officers stationed in the two provinces. Bamenda and Victoria gained the status of provincial medical administrative headquarters, there were now six medical districts in Southern Cameroons which was beneficial to the improvement and extension of medical services and staff in the territory.

In 1954, Southern Cameroons ceased to be part of the Eastern Region and acquire a semi-autonomous status as a Quasi Region. This came at a time

---

23 NAB, File No. Sc/1928/3, Hospital fees: General Correspondence for the Procedure in Medical Correspondence.

24 *Ibid.*

25 See *supra* note 21 at p. 641.

26 *Ibid* p. 640.

27 *Ibid.*

when the medical authorities in the Eastern Region at Enugu were reflecting on putting in place Hospital Advisory Boards (HAB) born out of a Senior Medical Officers' Conference held at Enugu on 29th March 1954. This was intended to ease the liaison between the public and hospital management[28]. The Director of medical services, Enugu, released a medical circular instructing that all hospitals should have a HAB for the purpose of improving the relationship between the hospitals and their patients, and to encouraged the public to take a healthy interest in their local hospitals. When Southern Cameroons gained a Quasi Status, the principal medical officer for the territory took measures to create HABs in the six divisions the territory had at the time. The Advisory Boards comprised the District Officer of the area where the hospital was located as chairperson, the Medical Officer as secretary, the most Senior Nurse, the Pharmacist and four representatives of the local population. The HAB role was to advise the hospital administration on the improvement of the medical services provided by the hospital, answer questions and criticisms from the public arising out of the administration of the hospital and to advise on any other matter which may be referred to it by a member of the public[29].

In 1955, due to allegation of corruption and extortion amongst the staff of government hospitals, Hospital Visiting Committees (HVCs) were instituted[30]. This Committees were made up of members drawn from local population willing to take interest in the affairs of the hospital, particularly the welfare of the patient. The committee had to meet with the medical doctor in charge from time to time and bring to his attention any unsatisfactory state of affairs which he might be in a position to change.

The health policy in French Cameroon was geared at building health infrastructures, reinforcing health regulation and reorganising health services[31]. The French colonial masters saw in health policies a means to preserve their lives rather than an obligation towards the indigenous population[32]. The first health system was instituted by Order of 16 November 1916 "Le Service Medical" (The Medical Service) which comprised the central and the external services. The mission of the Medical Service was later elaborated as dealing with health care and administrative or general control

---

28 NAB, File No. B.3/30, Minutes of Senior Medical Officers' Conference, Enugu, 29 March 1954.

29 See *supra* note 27 at p.642.

30 *Ibid.*

31 Kontchou, L.F., « *Evolution des Politiques Sanitaires au Cameroun (1919-2000) : Approche Historique* », Université de Yaoundé 1, Mémoire en vue de l'obtention d'un DEA, Année Académique 2008-2009, p.1.

32 *Ibid.*

attributions[33]. In 1938, the Order of 7th June 1938 changed the Medical Services to the Health Service (Le Service de Sante). The centre services were ruled by general and specific stipulations. In the various Regions, Regional Centres and mobile units were put in place[34]. They were managed by medical doctors who had as prerogatives to control the procurement of medicine, ensure hygiene and sanitation and oversee the execution of legal instruments. The medical doctor for the mobile unit had to ensure health education, and provide health care to patients amongst others[35].

In 1939, French Cameroon had 150 medical centres and 50 doctors[36]. Nurses had to be trained in Senegal where the French colonial administration created a medical school, or in France, after their graduation from the nursing school. In 1959, private doctors were authorised to go operational[37].

Today in Cameroon, the Ministry of Public Health is responsible for the maintenance and implementation of health services. The health system is decentralised and divided into three levels; Central (Strategic level) is represented by the central service of the Ministry of Public Health, the Intermediary (Technical level) represented by the 10 regional delegates of public health that coordinates health activities in the regions, and the Peripheral (Operational level) represented by district health services, they are in charge of the implementation of health programmes[38]. The health service is provided through a decentralised health system including 10 Regional Delegations of Health, 181 Health Districts, 2260 Public Health Facilities, 4 General Hospitals, 3 Central Hospitals, 14 Regional Hospitals, 164 District Hospitals, and 155 Sub-Division Medical Centres[39]. The health facilities of the health system are divided into seven main categories; General Hospitals, Central Hospitals, Regional Hospitals, District Hospitals, District Medical Centres, Integrated Health Centres, Ambulatory Health Centres. Some challenges facing the Cameroon health system include; corruption, outdated

33 Ndong, O., (1995), « Le Droit Camerounais a la Protection de la Sante et de la Salubrité Publique de 1916 à 1978 », Tome 1 : Les Administrations Sanitaires, p.13.

34 Tegna, E M., (1989), « Historique de Politique de Sante au Cameroun : De la Promotion Sanitaire Allemande au Politique Sectorielle Actuel », *Review Scientifique de L'école Des Science de la Sante de L'université Catholique D'Afrique Central,* No.4, p.145.

35 See *supra* note 31.

36 Martin du Gard, M., (1939), *L'appel Du Cameroun, Paris* : Flammarion,, pp.71-72.

37 Law No. 10 of 23 February 1959

38 Kibu, O., (2019), "Health System Decentralisation as a Critical Deriver for Better Care", *Nkafu Policy Institute,* p. 2, at https://www.nkafu.org. (Accessed on the 7th day of December 2024)

39 Ministry of Public Health, at http://www.minsante.com (Accessed on the 7th day of December 2024)

equipment, and patients paying for approximately 70 percent of health services out of pocket[40].

Cameroon is a member of WMA and AfMA. Cameroon developed its first Health Sector Strategy in 2001-2015. The legal and institutional framework of the health system is characterised by a multitude of regulatory instruments. There is for example, Decree No. 83/166 of 12 April 1983 on the Code of Medical Ethics in Cameroon, Law No 90/036 of 10th August on the Organisation and Practice of Medicine in Cameroon, institutionally there is; the Cameroon Medical Association[41], the Cameroon National Association of Dental Surgeons[42], the Cameroon Nursing Society[43], etc. The duty of these bodies is to protect members of the public by ensuring that doctors and other health care givers are properly qualified, that they perform their services with diligence, and that they observe at all times, high moral and ethical standards[44].

Medical legislation (rules, policies and regulation) has continuously evolved to regulate the practice of Medicine. The fundamental objective is to protect the right to health, safeguard the standards of the profession and to protect the public against unskilled practitioners. As someone licensed and authorized by law to prescribe drugs and use devices for the treatment of sick and injured human beings, the role of medical practitioners in the pursuit of good health cannot be over- emphasized. In the case of *Smith v. Lane*[45] it was held that "the practice of medicine… includes the application and use of medicines and drugs for the purpose of curing, mitigating, or alleviating bodily diseases …". By virtue of Section 2(1) of the Law relating to the Organization and Practice of Medicine in Cameroon, "persons engaged in the practice of medicine shall be subject to registration with the Medical Association". Thus, within the exercise of his duties, a doctor shall be bound by the rule of law,

---

40 *Ibid.*

41 Law No 80/7 of 14 July 1980 establishes the Cameroon Medical Association. Part 11 of Law No 90/036 of 10th August 1990 relating to the Organization and Practice of Medicine enumerate on the Organization and function of the Association.

42 Law No 90/034 of 10 August 1990 on the Practice and Organization of Dental Surgeon in Cameroon.

43 Founded in 1992 in accordance with law No. 90/053 of 19 December 1990 on Freedom of Association.

44 Section 19-21 of Law No 90/036 of 10th August 1990 on the Organisation and Practice of Medicine in Cameroon provides that; the Cameroon Medical Association established in Section 1 of law No. 80/7 of 14 July 1980, shall comprise all physicians practicing their profession in Cameroon. The Association shall ensure compliance with the principles of moral conduct and devotion essential to the practice of medicine as well as observance of the rules prescribed by the Code of Ethics.

45 *Smith v. Lane*, 24 Hun (N.Y.) 633.

professional secrecy, the Code of Ethics adopted by the Cameroon Medical Association[46] and approved by the Supervisory Authority.[47]

In Cameroon, frequent medical malpractices have become disturbing, especially in public health institutions. The proliferation of institutions imparting medical care with inadequate infrastructure and human resources, has adversely affected the standard of medical care given to some patients[48]. Increase commercialization has resulted in a decrease in ethical values in this field as the quest for profit maximization seems to override the interests of patients.

1.2 Contextualising the Problem

There exist legislative and regulatory safeguards monitoring the activities of conventional medical practitioners in Cameroon. This notwithstanding malpractices has become a recurrent issue. These malpractices are marked by poor patient care,[49] misdiagnosis[50], wrong treatment methods, abandonment of patients, prescription errors, surgical errors, exorbitant billing, etc., which continue to endanger the lives of patients. Some every day emergencies have ended in fatality because some hospitals request down payment before treatment is administered[51]. A recent glaring example in Cameroon is the case with *Marie O Polyclinic* in Douala which was closed down by the Minister in charge of Public Health[52] for issuing an exorbitant bill of XAF six million to the family of a COVID-19 patient, in violation of Decree No. 041/CAB/PM of 20 April 2020 which defines free treatment of such patients[53]. Moreover, there

---

46 *Ibid.*

47 The Minister of Public Health.

48 Bauer, A., (2014) "Illegal Health Clinics in Cameroon", *Borgen Magazine*, at https://www. borgen maga zine.com /illegal-health-clinics-cameroon/ (accessed on 19th day of April 2022).

49 A case in point is the experience of recovered Corona Virus patients who were confined at the Olembe Isolation Center in Yaoundé, reported by Fabiola Kemegni in Cameroon Post in May 2020. They testified that the two weeks that they were confined were two weeks of uncertainty and agony. That the medical team only came by once for screening, and that they received no specific medical treatment rather they were kept aside and ask to wait until the virus disappears.

50 Misdiagnoses and delayed diagnosis aggravate patients' conditions. For example, a stage-4 breast cancer condition which is misdiagnosed as a huge boil spells doom for the patient.

51 The France 24 Observers, on the 15 march 2016, report of a case which occurred in March 13, 2016, in the Lanquintinie hospital in Douala, where a woman used a razor blade to slice open her pregnant sister's belly (Monique koumateke) in a bid to save her unborn twins in front of the hospital where her sister was unattended to, because she did not have the down payment required by the doctor. The woman and her twins eventually died.

52 By Decision No. 30-255/l/Minsante/cabon May 14, 2020.

53 Bilong C., (2020), "Cameroun : La Clinique Marie O Fermée Pour Non-Respect de Règlementaire

have been reports of wrong diagnoses since the outbreak of the COVID-19 pandemic with dire consequences for medical practitioners[54].

The above notwithstanding, there has been a sharp decline in the regulatory standards of the profession and which can be attributed to the overwhelming impact of commercialization of medical services in violation of Article 7 of Decree No. 83/166 of 12 April 1983 on the Code of Medical Ethics. There are more than a thousand hospitals and training centers operating illegally in violation of Section 2 of Law No. 90/036 of 10 August 1990[55], consequently, posing a threat to public health. Such illegal institutions are often responsible for the death and worsening medical conditions of innocent patients[56]. A good example is the case of the death of a 5-year-old child who was administered an overdose of anesthesia during a surgical operation conducted to correct her hearing complications in *Polyclinique Archangel*, in Bonapriso, Douala on the 27th of April 2022.

1.3 Justification for the Study

The work is informed by the prevalence of medical malpractice in Cameroon. Often, doctors violate the Ethics of the profession with impunity. Patients without enough or sufficient financial resources wait long hours in corridors; some die in pain under the passive watch of the professionals, while financially viable patients skip queues and obtain prompt, careful, and effective care[57]. Again, most patients at the public hospitals, after paying the consultation fee and waiting for hours are later told that the doctor is not

en Vigueur et Atteinte à la Moralité Publique, *Echos Sante,* at https://echosante.info (Accessed on the 6th day of December 2024).

54 Cameroon Radio Television (CRTV) News of May 15, 2020, reported of many scandals that have ensued following the outbreak of Covid-19. On May 2, 2020, a medical doctor was assaulted by family members of a woman who died in a private clinic in Douala for wrong diagnosis. This woman was diagnosed COVID positive whereas the family said she was suffering from hypertension. It is reported that no COVID test was conducted on her, coupled with the fact that and the doctor delayed attending to the woman.

55 Some operate without a license while others are run illegally from private homes, some are even run by laboratory technicians and nurses.

56 Statement of Biwola Sida, the National Health Inspector of the Ministry of Public Health, to the Borgen Magazine, in 2014.

57 Yamb B. & Bayemi O., (2017), "Corruption and Discrimination in Douala Metropolis Public Hospitals of Cameroon", Journal *of Economics Library* 4(4), p.502-513.

on seat[58]. One author[59] concluded that absenteeism of healthcare workers is ubiquitous because public hospitals do not have systems to monitor and sanction staff who fail in their public responsibilities. The culture within public hospitals is highly tolerant towards absenteeism.

Medical malpractice clearly violates the right to health. Patients experience physical and psychological trauma in the hands of some unscrupulous doctors. To compound it all, most victims are unable to, unwilling, or ignorant of their rights to complain. Even those who are aware of the right face financial constraints. Moreover, the legal procedural hurdles associated with instituting claims in court remain daunting.

The main focus of this work is on medical law with specific emphasis on issues relating to medical practice in Cameroon. The work is also limited to medical practice within the conventional medical field.

The work is geographically limited to Cameroon, a country in Central Africa with an area of 475,440 square kilometres, and a population of about 25,640,965[60]. She is bordered by Nigeria to the Northwest, Chad to the Northeast, the Central African Republic to the East, the Republic of Congo to the Southeast, Gabon and Equatorial Guinea to the South, and the Atlantic Ocean to the Southwest[61]. The country is made up of a union of two former United Nations Trust Territories; French Cameroon, and British Southern Cameroon, operating two legal systems, the civil law and the common law respectively. There are two official languages in Cameroon; the French language is spoken by almost 80 per cent of the population, and the English language by about 20 percent[62]. This research will be conducted from 2017 to date.

---

58 Direct observation at the Regional Hospital Bafoussam on 13/10/2020, where some pregnant women upon paying the consultation fee to see the gynaecologist, were later told after several hours of waiting that the doctor was unavailable.

59 McPake B., *et al.*, (1999), "Informal Economic Activities of Public Health Workers in Uganda: Implications for Quality and Accessibility of Care", 49, *Soc Sci Med*, pp. 849–65.

60 Cameroon Country Profile, National Geographic at https://kids.nationalgeograhic.com. (accessed on the 6th day of July 2022).

61 *Ibid.*

62 Nathan Ferdinand, (2010), la langue français dans le monde en 2010 at ISBN 2098824076.

CHAPTER TWO

The Need for the Regulation of Medical Practice in Cameroon

2.1 Introduction

Regulation has grown in importance as a tool for government to monitor the quantity, quality, safety and distribution of services in health systems[63]. It has as objective the protection of patients' fundamental human rights, that is, the right to health. Regulation also confers certain advantages to the profession with respect to recognition, credibility, and political influence[64]. The notion that doctors have complete professional freedom has long been a fantasy[65]. Medical practitioners are directly involved with the life of the people, there is therefore need to establish checks and balances of medical practice to ensure that physicians not only respect their ethical and fiduciary duty towards their patients, but most importantly uphold fundamental human rights, especially the right to health which is so fundamental to sustain life. Good quality medical care and respect for patient autonomy demand that care be managed ethically.

---

63 Clarke, D., "Law, Regulation and Strategizing for Health", Chapter 10 in: Schmets G et al, editors (2016), *Strategizing National Health in the 21st Century: A Handbook, Geneva*: World Health Organization.

64 Aldridge, S., (2008), "The Regulation of Health Professionals: An Overview of the British Colombia Experience", *Journal of Medical Imaging and Radiation Sciences,* 39(1), pp.4-10.

65 Samanta, A. and Samanta, J., (2004), "Regulation of the Medical Profession: Fantasy, Reality and Legality", *Journal of The Royal Society of Medicine,* 97(5), pp.211-218.

The regulation of the medical profession is for the most part done by the profession itself (self- regulation) through professional medical boards or councils as is the case with Cameroon. However, self-regulation in general, allows wide latitude in dealing with problems within the profession, and it has been roundly condemned in favour of statutory regulation, which has been repeatedly endorsed as an appropriate regulatory mechanism since it carries the force of law, and also provides a proper foundation for the contract of the medical profession with society[66]. Globally, there is a move from the premise that the profession is self-regulating, which is increasingly seen as protecting its own interest, to a model of co-regulation in partnership with the public to better protect the public interest[67]. The regulation of medical practice in Cameroon is state-sanctioned self-regulation[68] characterized by a certain degree of professional autonomy; the State granting the profession the right to regulate its conduct by developing rules that it oversees and enforces with powers derived from legislation.

The regulation of medical practice in Cameroon is necessitated by the obligation of the State to fulfil its international human right obligation to respect, protect and fulfil the right to health, which cannot be fully enjoyed unless it is fully protected and regulated. Moreover, economic complications, unavailability of human and material resources, and lack of basic infrastructures, greatly contribute to violation of ethical standards justifying rigorous regulation. Again, medical practitioners are more often than not driven by economic factors to indulge in unprofessional conduct. Regulation is therefore imperative to enable patients with low economic power to access medical care.

The first part of this Chapter analyses human rights consideration for regulating medical practices and the second part evaluates institutional and economic considerations necessitating the regulation of medical practices in Cameroon.

---

66 *Ibid.*

67 Yam, C., *et al*, (2016) "Medical Regulation: Ten Key Trends Emerging from an International Review", *JMed Regul*, 17-28, p.102.

68 See *supra* note 44, Section 20(3).

2.2 Human Rights Considerations for Regulating Medical Practice in Cameroon

The right to health is a constant concern for the international community. It is the economic, social, and cultural right to a universal minimum standard of health to which all individuals are entitled[69]. The Constitution of the World Health Organization[70] defines the right to health as "the enjoyment of the highest attainable standard of health," which is a fundamental right of every human being without distinction of race, religion, political belief, economic or social condition. Health is in turn defined positively in the Preamble of same Constitution as "a state of complete physical, mental and social well-being and not merely the absence of disease or infirmity"[71]. Indeed, this right has been endorsed in numerous instruments, adopted both at the international, Regional and National levels[72]. It is reported that just about 52 per cent of African citizens have access to health care, and the quality of health services in the continent is generally poor[73]. Each year, approximately 97 million Africans incur appalling health care cost, which plunges them further into poverty[74]. In Cameroon, the doctor to patient ratio is one doctor per 50.000 persons[75]. This ratio greatly affects the quality of services provided to patients. Regulating medical practices will significantly improve on accessibility and the quality of medical services.

States are committed to uphold and respect the right to health, which cannot be achieved without the effective control and supervision of medical practice. It is in pursuance to this that there is need to regulate the activities of medical institutions and professionals in order to ensure that this right is

---

69 Right to health at en.m.wikepedia.org (accessed on the 17th day of December 2024)

70 Constitution of the World Health Organization 1946, this Constitution marks the first formal demarcation of a right to health in International Law. The objective of WHO, as defined in Article 1 of its Constitution, is "the attainment by all peoples of the highest possible level of health".

71 *Ibid.*

72 These include; the Universal Declaration of Human Rights, Article 12(1) of the International Covenant on Economic, Social and Cultural Rights, Article 5(iv) of the Convention on the Elimination of All Forms of Racial Discrimination (CERD) Articles 10(h), 11(1)(f) ,12, 14(2)(b) and 16(1)(e) of the Convention on the Elimination of All Forms of Discrimination Against Women (CEDAW) , Articles 24 and 25 of the Convention on the Rights of the Child (CRC), and Articles 23(1)(c) and 25 of the Convention on the Rights of Persons with Disabilities (CRPD).

73 Cullian, K., (2021), "Universal Health Coverage: Only Half of Africans have Access to Health Care", *Health Policy Watch*, at http://www.healthpolicy-watch.news (accessed on 11th day of July 2022).

74 *Ibid.*

75 Sina,K N., "Public Health: Over 35000 Health Care Workers Needed", *Cameroon Radio Television News*, July 2020.

not violated in the day-to-day practice of medicine, more so because health policies and practices may inadvertently violate human rights. Moreover, the duties owed by health professionals to their patients are frequently in consonance with those demanded by human rights guidelines.

This section will examine some general principles underpinning the right to health. It also considers respect of the right to health under International Human Right Laws, and National laws.

2.2.1 The Right to Health as a Common Concern for Humanity

The phrase common concern for humanity refers to humanity as a whole. Matters of common concern requires a global, and humanitarian response. International law scholar Dinah Shelton explains that "issues of common concern are those that inevitably transcend the boundaries of a single State and require collective action in response[76], it is "the notion of common concerns or a global set of values and interests independent of the interests of states[77]. Health is one of such values. Health is a fundamental value which must be recognize as a common concern and safeguarded through laws and regulation, especially superior norms of constitutional law.

In the seventies, the political and economic conditions of the international community were difficult. Against the backdrop of urbanization and political uncertainty, health disparities between developed and developing countries and even within countries became so great that people found them politically, socially and economically unacceptable[78]. In 1977, the World Health Assembly (WHA) proposed a primary social target for all governments, international organizations and the global community: "To enable all of the world's citizens to enjoy by 2000 a level of health that would allow them to lead a socially active and economically productive life". This social target of "Health for All" (abbreviated "HFA") emphasizes the attainment of the highest possible level of health by societies a basic human right, and observing ethical principles in health policy making, health research and service provision[79]. It advocated for Formulation of policies and strategies guided by principles of equity and

---

76 Shelton, D., (2009) "Common Concern of Humanity", *Environmental Law and Policy* 39(2), p.83.

77 *Ibid.*

78 Basic Principles of Healthy Cities: Health for All, Department of Health, March 2009, at http://www.chp.gov.hk/files/pdf/hcp-health-for-all-en.pdf. (accessed on the 25th day of April 2021).

79 *Ibid.*

solidarity. In September 1978, the World Health Organization (WHO)'s First International Conference on Primary Health Care was held in Alma-Ata, former USSR. Representatives signed the Alma-Ata Declaration which reaffirmed that health is a fundamental human right and that primary health care was the key to attaining "Health for All". After the Alma-Ata meeting, health promotion movements were initiated in many countries[80].

States parties are referred to the Alma-Ata Declaration which proclaims that the existing gross inequality in the health status of the people, particularly between developed and developing countries, as well as within countries, is politically, socially and economically unacceptable and is, therefore, of common concern to all countries.

Under the International Covenant of Economic Social and Cultural Right (ICESCR)[81], States parties are called upon to recognize the essential role of international cooperation and comply with their commitment to take joint and separate action to achieve the full realization of the right to health. States parties are to ensure that the right to health is given due attention in international agreements and, that these agreements do not adversely impact upon the right to health. Similarly, States parties have an obligation to ensure that their actions as members of international organizations take due account of the right to health. Accordingly, States parties which are members of international financial institutions, notably the International Monetary Fund, the World Bank, and Regional Development Banks, should pay greater attention to the protection of the right to health in influencing the lending policies, credit agreements and international measures of these institutions.

Indeed, all members of society; individuals, including health professionals, families, local communities, intergovernmental and non-governmental organizations, civil society organizations, as well as the private business sector, have responsibilities regarding the realization of the right to health.

2.2.1.1 Respect of the Rights to Health under International Human Rights Laws

The right to the highest attainable standard of health, referred to as "the right to health" is affirmed in several human rights instruments. The Universal Declaration of Human Rights (UDHR) adopted by the United Nations

---

80 *Ibid.*
81 Article 12 of the ICESCR.

General Assembly in 1948, provides in part that every person has the right to a standard of living adequate for the health and well-being of his or her family, including food, clothing, housing, medical care and necessary social services[82]. Therefore, there is a right to health guaranteed under the Universal Declaration of Human Rights from which a patient's right is derived. While not a treaty creating a set of binding obligations, it is universally accepted as a fundamental human rights document, inspiring the formulation of some other crucial instruments[83]. One of such instruments is the International Covenant on Economic, Social and Cultural Rights (ICESCR) 1966, which is widely considered as the legal instrument of protection for the right to health. It recognizes "the right of everyone to the enjoyment of the highest attainable standard of physical and mental health"[84].

Under the ICESCR, each State Party undertakes to take steps, individually and through international assistance and co-operation, especially economic and technical, to the maximum of its available resources, with a view to achieving progressively the full realization of the right to health recognized in the Covenant by all appropriate means, including particularly the adoption of legislative measures[85]. This implies that the rights under the Covenant are subject to "progressive realization" having regard to the limited resources that may be available within the particular State[86]. The progressive realization of the right to health imposes an obligation on States parties to guarantee equal treatment without discrimination[87] and to take reasonable steps within a short time after entry into the Covenant to achieve these rights progressively.

---

82 Article 25(1) of the Universal Declaration of Human Rights, 1948.

83 The International Covenant on Civil and Political Rights 1966, the United Nations Convention on the Rights of the Child 1989, Article 24 states: (1) States parties recognize the right of the child to the enjoyment of the highest attainable standard of health and to facilities for the treatment of illness and rehabilitation of health. State parties shall strive to ensure that no child is deprived of his or her right of access to such health care services, and the ICESR 1966.

84 Article 12 ICESCR 1966.

85 *Ibid*, Article2 (1).

86 Article 12 of ICESCR at para 47, states: "A State which is unwilling to use the maximum of its available resources for the realization of the right to health is in violation of its obligations under article 12. If resource constrains render it impossible for a State to comply fully with its Covenant obligations, it has the burden of justifying that every effort has nevertheless been made to use all available resources at its disposal in order to satisfy, as a matter of priority, the obligations outlined above."

87 Article 2(2) of ICESCR provides the States Parties to the present Covenant undertake to guarantee that the rights enunciated in the present Covenant will be exercised without discrimination of any kind as to race, colour, sex, language, religion, political or other opinion, national or social origin, property, birth or other status.

Indeed, since the right to health is subject to progressive realization, what is expected of a State will vary over time. At such, States need devices to monitor and measure these variable dimensions of the right to health. Not all aspects of the right to health under the Covenant can or may be realized immediately, but at a minimum, States must show that they are making every possible effort, within available resources, to better protect and promote all rights under the Covenant.

The Committee on Economic, Social and Cultural Rights is charged with the task of monitoring the rights and obligations undertaken by States parties to the International Covenant on Economic, Social and Cultural Rights. It has expanded upon the scope of the right to health (notwithstanding the principle of progressive realization in terms of resource constraints) to include underlying determinants of health and reinforced the importance of *minimum core obligation*[88].

The minimum core obligations imposed on States parties are taken as a minimum standard of a right which individuals under any circumstance are entitled to enjoy, and in which the State party cannot compromise regardless of the economic measure in operation. The Committee has imposed three levels of obligation on states parties viz: the obligation to respect, protect and fulfil[89]. The obligation to respect requires States to refrain from interfering directly or indirectly with the enjoyment of the right to health, the obligation to protect requires States to take measures that prevent third parties from interfering, and the obligation to fulfil requires States to adopt appropriate legislative, administrative, budgetary, judicial, promotional and other measures towards the full realization of the right to health. Indeed, it emphasized the importance of access to judicial remedies for the rights considered justiciable in accordance with national legal system operating in States parties for the enforcement of the violation of the right to health[90].

---

88 *Ibid*, Article 12, para.43 provides: In General Comment No. 3, the Committee confirms that States parties have a core obligation to ensure the satisfaction of, at the very least, minimum essential levels of each of the rights enunciated in the Covenant, including essential primary health care.

89 General Comment No.14 at para. 33.

90 General Comment No.14, at para 59, states: Any person or group victim of a violation of the right to health should have access to effective judicial or other appropriate remedies at both national and international levels. All victims of such violations should be entitled to adequate reparation, which may take the form of restitution, compensation, satisfaction or guarantees of non-repetition. National ombudsmen, human rights commissions, consumer forums, patients' rights associations or similar institutions should address violations of the right to health.

Other International human rights instruments containing provisions protecting the right to health, includes; The United Nations Principles for the Protection of Persons with Mental Illness and the Improvement of Mental Health Care 1991[91], the United Nations Convention on the Rights of Persons with Disabilities 2007[92], and the Convention on the Elimination of All Forms of Discrimination against Women (CEDAW)1981.. Indeed Article 10(h) of CEDAW provides for access to specific information to help to ensure the health and wellbeing of families, including information and advice on family planning. The right to health is also encapsulated in regional treaties; these include amongst others; the European Convention on Human Rights (ECHR) 1953[93], and the American Convention on Human Rights 1969, which provides that everyone shall have the right to health, understood to mean the enjoyment of the highest level of physical, mental and social wellbeing[94].

The African Charter on Human and Peoples' Rights 1981[95], also known as the Banjul Charter is an international human rights instrument that is intended to promote and protect human rights and basic freedoms in the African continents. It provides that every individual shall have the right to enjoy the best attainable state of physical and mental health. It goes further to provide that States parties shall take the necessary measures to protect the health of their people and to ensure that they receive medical attention when they are sick. It also enjoins the States parties to the Charter to recognize the rights, duties and freedoms enshrined therein and to undertake to adopt legislative or other measures to give effect to them[96] within their jurisdiction. Therefore, not only did the charter awards rights to individuals and people, but also includes duties incumbent upon them. This Charter does not provide for any right of derogation for the States parties in public emergencies. In fact, in *Commission Nationale des Droits des l'Homme et des Libertes v. Chad*[97],

91 Principle 8(1) states that every patient shall have the right to receive such health and social care as is appropriate to his or her health needs. It further provides that every patient shall be protected from harm, including unjustified medication, abuse by other patients, staff, or other acts causing mental distress or physical discomfort.

92 Article 17 provides that every person with disabilities has a right to respect for his or her physical and mental integrity on an equal basis with others.

93 Recognition of the right is indirect; it is limited to civil and political rights. However, the European Court of Human Rights established that deprivation of a 'duty to take care' amounted to a violation of socio-economic rights in *Airey v Ireland* [1979] ECtHR 3.

94 See Article 10(1) of the American Convention of Human Rights 1969.

95 See Article 16(1)(2) of the African Charter of Human and Peoples; Rights 1981.

96 *Ibid.*, Article 1.

97 African Commission on Human and Peoples' Rights, Comm. No.74/92 (1995) para 21, decision taken at the 18th Ordinary Session, October, 1995, at http://www.hrlibrary.umn.edu/africa/

the commission stated that The African Charter, unlike other human rights instruments, does not allow States parties to derogate from their treaty obligations during emergency situations. Thus, even a civil war in Chad cannot be used as an excuse for the State to violate or permit the violation of rights enshrined in the African Charter.

Other provisions[98] in the African Charter on Human and Peoples' Rights also impact on the right to health by reinforcing its protection from different perspectives[99]. In *International Pen & Ors v Nigeria*[100], a complaint was lodged on behalf of Ken Saro Wiwa, a writer, environmentalist and president of the Movement for the Survival of the Ogoni People (MOSOP). While he was in detention awaiting execution with others, his health condition deteriorated and his requests for medical attention were denied. The Commission held the Nigerian government liable for violating the complainant's right to health under Article 16 of the African Charter.

It is significant to note that the Cameroon Constitution recognizes the government's commitment to uphold human rights pursuant to these international treaties[101]. This therefore, places an obligation upon Cameroon as a member State, to provide medical healthcare that meet the basic minimum standards as a right, for the citizens to enjoy the highest attainable standard of health. However, frequent breaches of these minimum standards are the cause of increased medical malpractice in the country, there is therefore need to effectively regulate medical practices in order to minimize the infringement of these standard and also for Cameroon to fulfil its international obligations.

---

comcases/74-92.(accessed on 1st day of October 2020).

98 Protocol to the African Charter on Human and Peoples' Rights of Women in Africa (2005), Article 62 states: Every state party shall undertake to submit every two years, from the date the present Charter comes into force, a report on the legislative or other measures taken with a view to giving effect to the rights and freedoms recognized and guaranteed by the present Charter.

99 In *Free Legal Assistance Group & Ors v Zaire* (Comm. Nos.25/89, 47/90, 56/91, 100/93) 1995, the complainants alleged varying degree of human rights abuses, amongst which is the failure of the government to provide basic services such as; safe drinking water, electricity and shortage of medicine. The Commission held that the failure to provide basic health services constituted a violation of Articles 4, 5, 6, 7, 8, 16 and 17 of the African Charter.

100 (1998) Comm. Nos.137/94, 139/94, 154/96 and 161/97.

101 The Preamble to the Revised 1996 Constitution of Cameroon, this includes the African Charter on Human and Peoples 'Rights, the Universal Declaration of Human Rights and the United Nations Charter. Article 45 of the Revised 1996 Constitution declares that: "Duly approved or ratified treaties and international agreements shall, following their publication, override national laws, provided the other party implements the said treaty or agreement" .

2.2.2 The Right to Health as a State Responsibility

International human rights law establishes that States have the primary obligation to *respect, protect,* and *fulfil* human rights in health[102]. The obligation to *respect* requires States not to interfere, directly or indirectly, with the enjoyment of this right. States should also ensure that there are laws and regulations in place that ensure that health care services are affordable, accessible, acceptable, and of good quality[103]. Under the obligation to *protect,* States are required to take measures that prevent third parties from interfering with the guarantees under the right to health. This implies that laws and regulations are appropriately implemented and that violations of human rights that occur in health settings are properly investigated, redressed, and prevented[104]. Finally, the obligation to *fulfil* requires the State to adopt appropriate legislative, administrative, budgetary, judicial, promotional, and other measures for the full realization of the right to health[105].

States fulfil these obligations through legislation that provides functioning public and private health care facilities, and making these facilities accessibility for all sections of the population. The services provided in these facilities must respect medical ethics, be scientifically and medically appropriate and of good quality. In fact, States must make every possible effort within available resources, to realize the right to health without delay. States are to make regulations compelling hospitals and other health institutions to adopt appropriate measures for the protection of their patients' lives" and provide "an effective independent judicial system to prosecute and punish medical personnel who indulge in medical malpractices[106]. Indeed, the Inter-

---

102 United Nations Committee on Economic, Social and Cultural Rights, Economic and Social Council. General Comment No. 3. The Nature of States Parties' Obligations. E/1991/23.1990,at http://www.refworld.org/docid/4538838e10.html. (accessed on the 26th day of April 2021).

103 United Nations Committee on Economic, Social and Cultural Rights, Economic and Social Council. General Comment No. 3. The Nature of States Parties' Obligations. E/1991/23. 1990, at http://www.refworld.org/docid/4538838e10.html. (accessed on 26th day of April 2021).

104 United Nations Committee on the Elimination of Discrimination Against Women. General Recommendation No. 24: Article 12 of the Convention (Women and Health). A/54/38/Rev 1, chap.I. 1999.

105 United Nations Committee on Economic, Social and Cultural Rights, Economic and Social Council. Twenty-second session. General Comment No. 14: The Right to the Highest Attainable Standard of Health (Art. 12 of the International Covenant on Economic, Social and Cultural Rights). E/C.12/2000/4. 2000, at http://tbinternet.ohchr.org/_layouts/treatybodyexternal/Download.aspx?symbolno=E%2FC.12%2F2011%2F1&Lang=en. (accessed on the 26th day of April 2021).

106 Bañez, X A. & Dekanosidze, T., (2017), "The State's Obligation to Regulate and Monitor Private

American Court of Human Rights has also established that "the duty of the State to regulate and supervise the institutions which provide health care services, is a necessary measure aimed at the due protection of the life and integrity of the individuals under their jurisdiction[107].

States have primary obligation to protect and promote human rights norms. The protection of these rights compels states not only to refrain from intentional violation of these rights, but also inflicts the positive obligation to take appropriate measures in order to ensure the effective protection of these standards within the state[108]. Thus, these international human rights obligations indirectly compel the government to regulate medical practice in Cameroon. Cameroon has ratified some of these international commitments, especially the Ouagadougou Declaration on Primary Health Care and Health Systems in Africa 2008 which reaffirms the principle of the 1978 Alma Ata Declaration on health as a fundamental human right and the responsibility of government to cater for the health of their population.

Human rights obligations are also defined and guaranteed by International Customary Law[109] and International Human Right Treaties, creating binding obligations on the State that has ratified them to give effect to these rights. This is embodied in the principle of state responsibility. Under article 2(1) of ICESCR, a country is obliged to take steps 'to the maximum of its available resources, with a view to achieving progressively the full realization' of the rights recognized in ICESCR. The UN Committee on Economic Social and Cultural Rights has stated that this provision is 'a necessary flexibility device, reflecting the realities of the real world and the difficulties involved for any country in ensuring full realization of economic, social and cultural rights'.

However, the Committee has also stated that 'the phrase must be read in the light of the overall objective of the Covenant which is to establish clear obligations for States parties in respect of the full realization of the rights in question', and that 'it thus imposes an obligation to move as expeditiously and effectively as possible towards that goal'. The Committee has stated that, notwithstanding the progressive realization provision, there are two obligations that are of immediate effect. They are the guarantee in Article

Health Care Facilities: The Alyne Da Silva Pimentel and the Dzebniauri Cases". *Public Health Rev.*, 38(17), at https://doi.org/10.1186/s40985-017-0063-6. (accessed on the 2nd day of April 2021).

107 Inter-American Court of Human Rights. *Ximenes Lopes v. Brazil.* Judgment. 2006. Series C.149.

108 Shelton, D., (2007), "Human Rights, Health and Environmental Protection: Linkages in Law and Practice", *Hum. Rts.& Int'l Legal Discourse,* 1, p.9.

109 Customary law is evidence of a general practice of states accepted as law and followed out of a sense of legal obligation.

2(2) of ICESCR that the rights under the Covenant will be exercised without discrimination of any kind and the obligation under article 2(1) to 'take steps'. This means that steps towards realization of the rights under the Covenant must be taken within a reasonably short time after the country becomes party to the Covenant and that the steps should be deliberate, concrete and targeted as clearly as possible towards meeting the obligations under the Covenant.

2.2.2.1 Regulating Medical Practice as a Guarantee of the Right to Health in Cameroon

The Preamble to the Constitution of the Republic of Cameroon confirms the sacred and inalienable character of individual liberties and the State's attachment to the fundamental rights set out in the Universal Declaration of Human Rights, the United Nations Charter, the African Charter on Human and Peoples' Rights and all the related International Agreements[110] that Cameroon has duly ratified[111]. Article 45 of the Cameroon Constitution stipulates that in case of conflict with national legislation, the international treaties shall be overriding. Therefore, as a State party Cameroon has obligation under these international instruments, both moral and legal, to fulfil its commitment to protect and promote health rights of the citizens, which compels it to regulate medical practices in order to guarantee right to access medical and health care services, respect of medical ethics, and right to an effective remedy in case of violations of these rights.

Cameroon has made some strides towards the realization of the right to health. This can be gleaned from numerous legislative instruments enacted for this purpose[112]. However, the most important obstacle to the right to health at the national level is the non-functioning and poor regulation of public institutions, with the result being "health according to finances" philosophy which impede access to health services.

---

110 This includes the ICESCR 1966, Convention on the Elimination of all forms of Discrimination against Women 1979, Convention on the Right of the Child 1989, ICCPR.

111 Paragraph 2 of the Preamble of Cameroon revised 1996 Constitution.

112 Amongst which are Decree No. 83/166 of 12 April 1983 on Code of Medical Ethics, Law No. 90/036 of December 1990 organizing the Medical profession, Decree No. 95/13 of 7 February 1995 relating to the organization of Basic Health Services in Health District on the enforcement of the "Declaration of the National Policy on The Reorientation of Primary Health Care, Law No. 96/3 of 4 January 1996 relating to the Framework Law on Health, Decree No. 2000/686 of 13 December 2000 relating to the organization of Health Boards, Law No. 2003/6 of 22 December 2003 governing Blood Transfusion.

a) Right to Access Health Services and Facilities

The regulation of medical practices is in line with the state's responsibility to respect the rights to health. In this light under the obligation to respect, states are to ensure that functioning public health and health-care facilities, goods and services, as well as programs, are available in sufficient quantity within the State[113]. This includes, however, the underlying determinants of health, such as safe and potable drinking water and adequate sanitation facilities, hospitals, clinics and other health-related buildings, trained medical and professional personnel receiving domestically competitive salaries, and essential drugs.

These health facilities, goods and services are to be accessible to everyone without discrimination, within the jurisdiction of the State. They must be within safe physical reach for all sections of the population especially vulnerable or marginalized groups such as ethnic minorities and indigenous population[114]. Moreover, the health facilities, goods and services must be affordable for all. Payment for health-care services, as well as services related to the underlying determinants of health, has to be based on the principle of equity, ensuring that these services, whether privately or publicly provided, are affordable for all, including socially disadvantaged groups. The state should also create conditions that will assure to all, medical service and medical attention in the event of sickness"[115]. Increasing affordability and access to health care services can better be achieved where there is an efficient monitoring system to ensure that medical practitioners do not involve in practices that tend to limit access to health;(for instance, charging high consultation fees, corrupt practices, prescription of drugs that are not cost effective in relation to the patient's economic situation, and ordering unnecessary medical examination, etc.).

Even though the Cameroon government has gradually extended the health map with the setting up of new health areas, the construction of hospitals and health centres in both rural and urban areas, equipping of some health facilities, and the deployment of quality staff, the low rate of accessibility to health indicates that much is still to be done. In Cameroon access to health care services is often hampered by unethical attitude of medical practitioners which violates the right to health. Instead of the humane and appropriate

---

113 The Right to Health, World Health Organization, Fact Sheet No. 31, Office of the United Nations High Commission for Human Right.p.4.

114 *Ibid.*

115 See Art. 12.2 (d) of ICESCR.

health care expected, patients in Cameroon encounter a variety of abuses that are an affront to basic human dignity and jeopardize health outcomes. These abuses range from pervasive violations of patients' rights to informed consent, confidentiality, privacy, treatment, and non-discrimination to more egregious abuses, including extortion, neglect, torture and cruel, inhuman, and degrading treatment especially in psychiatric facilities, and drug rehabilitation centres.

Moreover, there is still doctor-patient ratio imbalance[116], desertion of posts by medical and paramedical staff in service in isolated and remote rural areas, inadequate financial resources for prevention and health care, high cost of some drugs, remoteness of some health centres from the homes of rural populations, difficult provision of emergency health care to poor patients, persistent corruption in some hospitals, absence of a legal framework for the protection of the rights of the sick, and ineffective repressive measures for the sale of street drugs, are some of the ill inhibiting the enjoyment of the right to health in Cameroon.

b) Right to Medical Information

Every health care provider is ethically and legally required to maintain patient treatment record[117]. This record is a legal document which serve to protect the legal interests of all participants in the health care delivery system, and this record is a confidential document. Under early common law, the physician had absolute ownership rights to the records of her patients[118]. The traditional school of thought held that physicians viewed their patients' medical records as a personal diary and, therefore, the physician owned the record and could do with it as she pleased[119]. As patients' autonomy emerged, however, a legal recognition that patients had a property right to the information within the record developed[120].

116 According to WHO the doctor patient ratio in Cameroon is 1 doctor per 50.000 inhabitants instead of the WHO recommended ratio of 1 doctor per 10000 inhabitants.

117 Rosenman, H., (1997), "Patient's Right to Access their Medical Record: An Argument for Uniform Recognition of a Right to Access in United State and Australia", *Fordham International Law Journal*, 21(4), p.1506.

118 See *McGarry v. J.A. Mercier Co*, 272 Mich. 501 (Mich. 1935) (holding that in absence of agreement to contrary, X-ray negatives, which are part of clinical record, are property of physician or surgeon rather than of patient).

119 Henry, P F., (1993), "Legal Issues Relating to Access to Medical Records", *Nurse Practitioner Forum*, 4, p. 120.

120 Roach, W H. *et al*, (1985), *Medical Record and The Law*, Maryland, Aspen Publication, p.59.

Today, the generally accepted notion is that the hospital owns the hospital medical record, subject to the patient's interest in the information it contains[121]. Thus the patient has the right to access the medical record at reasonable times and upon reasonable notice. Indeed, access to medical record will lead to better medical care and will protect patients against the indiscretion of physicians. It will also enhance patient doctor communication[122]. Providing individuals with easy access to their health information empowers them to be more in control of decisions regarding their health and well-being.

In most health facilities in Cameroon, the patient does not have access to his medical record, even when discharged from the hospital, what the patient has is just his consultation booklet. Besides, the diagnosis process and procedures are not documented accurately and precisely and this generate incomplete and inadequate medical records. In such a situation the patient cannot have access to the information on his/her ailment. This act of physicians is a violation of the patient's right to information. In effect, the unwillingness of physicians to provide adequate medical record, limit the possibility to audit the quality of medical services rendered to patience.

Patients also have the right to know the risks and benefits of accepting or declining certain therapies, as well as any alternative treatments available. Physicians need to communicate this information to their patients in culturally sensitive and understandable language, as well as offer full disclosure of test results, unless requested otherwise by the patient. However, where the physician determines that full disclosure would cause severe psychological harm to the patient, it may be reasonable to postpone disclosure of full diagnosis to a patient.

The Cameroon legislation uphold this right by providing in its Code of Medical Ethics[123] that a doctor may lawfully conceal a serious prognosis from his patient, and a fatal prognosis may not be divulged to the patient except with the greatest prudence; it may be divulged to the family, unless the patient is already so aware or he has appointed a third party to be informed.

---

121 See *supra* note 172 at p.1510.

122 Carter, M., (1998), "Should Patients Have Access to Their Medical Records?", *Med J Aust*, 169, pp.596-597.

123 Section 27(1)(2) of Decree No 83/166 of 12 April 1983 on Code of Medical Ethics in Cameroon.

c) Right to Confidentiality

Confidentiality is one of the core obligations of medical practice. It requires health care providers to keep a patient's personal health information private unless consent to release the information is provided by the patient. Public policy dictates that physician maintain confidentiality of their interchanges with their patients, and of their records. Physicians are well advised not to divulge information or acknowledge the doctor-patient relationship without a patient's consent[124]. From the ethical point of view, respect for the principles of beneficence, non-maleficence and also autonomy is recognized as a major justification for maintaining patient confidentiality, based upon a fundamental consideration for persons[125]. Health information is not only based on objective observations, diagnoses, and test results, but also subjective impressions about the patient, their lifestyle, habits, and recreational activities. The improper disclosure of such highly sensitive information could harm patients' reputation or result in lost opportunities, financial commitments, and even personal humiliation[126].

The doctor is legally and ethically obligated to keep patients' medical information, including information disclosed by the patient to the physician, confidential, and may only break this confidentiality in particular settings. If the patient loses capacity, health information should be disclosed according to the patient's best interest (e.g., the physician may disclose relevant health information to friends, family, or the health care proxy to help guide medical decisions). The physician in certain circumstances, may override his duty of confidentiality to patients and clients if it's done to protect their best interests or the interests of the public. This means he may override his duty if he has information that suggests a patient or client is at risk of harm, or is posing a risk of harm to someone else.

Medical practitioners must exercise discipline in not discussing patient specifics with their family members or in social gatherings and social media. They should make their best efforts to ensure the safety of patient information, even within the hospital setting. Generally speaking, patients have the right to refuse to see anyone not connected to a hospital or connected to the hospital but not directly involved in their care and treatment, and they

---

124 Hirsh, B D., (1989), "The Patient's Right to Confidentiality", *J Med Pract Manage*, 4(3), pp. 204-9.

125 Christina, M. *et al*, (2016), "Confidential Breaches in Clinical Practices: What Happens in Hospitals?", *BMC Medical Ethics*, 17(52), at http://bmcmedethics.biomedcentral.com/articles/10.1186/s12910-016-0136, (accessed on the5th day of May 2021).

126 *Ibid.*

have the right to be protected from having details of their condition made public[127].

Section 4 of the Code of Medical Ethics[128] in Cameroon provides that; "Professional secrecy shall be binding on all doctors, unless otherwise provided by law, provided that in all conscience it is not harmful to the interests of the patient". In addition, Section 4 of the Law regulating Medical Practice[129] provides that a physician in service in the administration or in the private sector is subject to professional secrecy, to the code of ethics of the profession adopted by the Doctors Council, as duly approved. This entails that all information received by medical practitioners in the exercise of his profession must be treated with confidence. The main purpose of this provision is to protect the patients right to confidentiality. However, where the secrecy of the information proves to be harmful to the public or the patient, the doctor will be released of his obligation under this section.

However, there has been conflict between human rights and medical ethics where the rule of law, an essential part of democratic society, requires medical confidentiality to be breached. Patients expect confidentiality to be absolute, otherwise they would not trust doctors with their intimate details, and medical ethics require that this information be protected as far as possible. Human rights, however, demand that justice takes priority, and doctors know that, despite great reluctance, they may be obliged to disclose confidential information in court. Thus, issues of social justice, the punishment of those who have committed a serious crime, outweigh medical confidentiality[130].

d) Right to Remedy in the Event of Malpractice

Under the obligation to *protect* State needs to ensure that laws and regulations are appropriately implemented and that violations of rights to health are properly investigated, redressed, and prevented. This imposes the obligation on States to create judicial or other remedies that enable their holders to invoke their protection in court or before another similarly independent authority when a person required to observe them fails to do so. States have obligations to provide Simple, Prompt, and

---

127 See *supra* note 179.

128 Decree No 83/166 Of 12 April 1983 on Code of Medical Ethics in Cameroon.

129 Law No 90/036 of 10 August 1990.

130 Peel M., (2005), "Human Right and Medical Ethics", *Journal of The Royal Society of Medicine,* 98(4), pp.171-173.

Effective Remedies in case of violation[131]. Any person or group victim of a violation of the right to health should have access to effective judicial or other appropriate remedies at national levels. All victims of such violations should be entitled to adequate reparation, which may take the form of restitution, compensation, satisfaction or guarantees of non-repetition. Non judicial mechanisms should be mechanisms which are inter alia legitimate, accessible, predictable, equitable, transparent and rights-compatible; that is, in line with internationally recognized human rights[132]. National ombudsmen, human rights commissions, consumer forums, patients' rights associations or similar institutions should address violations of the right to health.

The incorporation in the domestic legal order, of international instruments recognizing the right to health can significantly enhance the scope and effectiveness of remedial measures, and should be encouraged in all cases. Incorporation enables courts to adjudicate violations of the right to health, or at least its core obligations, by direct reference to the Covenant. Judges and members of the legal profession should be encouraged by States parties to pay greater attention to violations of the right to health in the exercise of their functions. States parties should respect, protect, facilitate and promote the work of human rights advocates and other members of civil society with a view to assisting vulnerable or marginalized groups in the realization of their right to health.

Civil and or Criminal proceedings can be initiated where there is a complaint from victims of medical malpractice in Cameroon, but unfortunately such complaints hardly come up. This is partly because victims have lost confidence in judicial processes in the country. Delays and high cost of judicial proceedings makes the whole process burdensome for victims of medical malpractices. Moreover, the judicial mechanisms for the protection of the right to health, which is an economic and social right is inadequate. The traditional common law remedies were conceived for the protection of conventional civil and political rights. All in all, a lack of adequate and effective

---

131 Inter American Commission on Human Right, "Access to Justice as a Guarantee of Economic, Social, and Cultural Rights: A Review of the Standards adopted by the Inter-American System of Human Rights". Online at http://www.cidh.oas.org/countryrep/accesodesc07eng/accesodescv.eng.htm. (accessed on the 6th day of May 2021).

132 "Access to Legal Remedies for Victims of Corporate Human Rights Abuses in Third World Countries", 2019, Paper Requested by European Parliament Sub Committee on Human Right, P.11, at Https://Www.Europarl.Europa.Eu/Regdata/Etudes/STUD/2019/603475/EXPO_STU(2019)603475_EN.Pdf. (accessed on the 5th day of May 2021).

remedies in the domestic law of a state for the protection of economic, social and cultural rights is an infringement of the rules contained in international human rights instruments, which enshrine the right of access to such remedies and, consequently, to those rights[133].

All in all, Human rights principles require that services to patients meet standards set out in International and Regional Human Rights Norms and Agreements[134]. The provisions of these international human right agreements have been interpreted by human right bodies to prohibit numerous forms of abuse in health settings. States are to make regulations compelling hospitals and other health institutions to adopt appropriate measures for the protection of their patients' lives" and "an effective independent judicial system which is well empowered and capable of determining and holding medical practitioners responsible for the cause of death of patients under their care, whether in the public or the private sector[135].

Cameroon's moral and legal obligation to fulfil its commitment to respect, protect and fulfil the right to health is wanting. This is evidenced by repeated manifestation of medical malpractices in the country, and what is more is that the perpetrators are hardly prosecuted and punished. This reveals the need for more effective commitment, through the control of medical services.

2.3 Administrative Considerations for Regulating Medical Practice in Cameroon

Medical malpractices in Cameroon thrive on administrative malfunctioning. Government's ineptness in controlling its borders through which there is influx into the country of substandard pharmaceuticals and medical equipment, coupled with inefficient quality control mechanisms, and its inability to provide the necessary financial, human and material resources to enable medical personnel perform their duties rigorously, are factors militating against proper medical practices in the country thus creating a

---

133 Peel, M., (2005), "Human Right and Medical Ethics", *Journal of The Royal Society of Medicine*, 98(4), pp.171-173.

134 These standards are set out in major treaties such as; the ICCPR, ICESCR, Convention Against Torture, ACHPR, Convention on the Elimination of All Forms of Discrimination Against Women, Convention on the Right of the Child, Convention on the Right of Persons with Disability, International Convention on the Elimination of All Forms of Racial Discrimination.

135 Bañez,, X A and T. Dekanosidze, T., (2017) "The State's Obligation to Regulate and Monitor Private Health Care Facilities: the Alyne Da Silva Pimentel and the Dzebniauri Cases". *Public Health Rev.* 38(17). at https://doi.org/10.1186/s40985-017-0063-6. (accessed on 2nd day of April 2021).

need for monitoring and control of medical practitioners' activities. This is the focus of this part of the work.

2.3.1 Porous Trans-National Borders

Africa's porous border remained a major challenge as it aids smuggling of prohibited items and irregular migration as well as other trans-national organized crimes and human trafficking[136]. It is almost impossible for weak state institutions, small armies and poorly funded police forces to control[137]. Africa imports 70 per cent of its pharmaceutical products[138]. The trafficking of inert or substandard medication into West Africa is not generally reckoned as a major organized crime activity, but its ramifications are grave and extend beyond the region. Aside from the loss of life among those who unwittingly leave their illnesses untreated, low-potency medication facilitates the development of drug-resistant strains of malaria, tuberculosis, and other infectious diseases[139]. Regulation is therefore essential to control the influx of these substandard medical products.

The porous nature of borders with neighbouring countries like Nigeria, Chad, Gabon, and Equatorial Guinea remain a major problem in Cameroon. Cameroon's border with Nigeria spans 1690km[140] and are highly porous. Thus, unscrupulous traders have created clandestine routes to avoid custom duties. Therefore, goods which are banned from importation into the country are smuggled into the markets. Drugs such as tramadol are smuggled into Cameroon through neighbouring Nigeria. Coupled to these, the lack of human and material resources hinders the effective regulation of smuggled goods[141].

Indeed, the World Health Organization (WHO) states that the use of counterfeit drugs in hospitals are suspected of leading to over 200,000

---

136 Obah, N G. *et al*, (2020), "Porous Borders and National Integration in Africa", *Journal of African Foreign Affairs*, 7(3), p89.

137 Somerville, K., (2013), "Africa's Borders: Porous, Unprotected and Blocking Trade and Economic Development", *African Arguments*, at https://Africanarguments.Org. (accessed on 1st day of May 2022).

138 Pheage, T., (2017), "Dying From Lack Of Medicines", *Africa Renewal*, at Https://Www.Un.Org. (accessed On 2nd day of May 2022).

139 Keziah, N., (2022), "Illegal Drugs: Cameroon Suffers Tax Losses, Health Threats" Cameroon Radio Television February, at https://www.crtv.cm> 2022/02 (accessed on 2nd day of May 2020).

140 *Ibid.*

141 Funwie, B N., (2019), "Border Protection: Officials Delve on the Issue of Smuggling", *Cameroon Radio Television*, at Https://Www.Crtv.Cm. (accessed On 1st of May 2022).

deaths worldwide each year. Cases involving blood transfusion infections, counterfeit malaria drugs, antibiotics and tuberculosis drugs have left patients either severely ill or dead, especially in Cameroon[142]. Some of the vendors of these banned medical products actually diagnose, prescribe and administered some of these drugs to patients in their medicine stores. This is done with no medical supervision. Indeed, the poor quality of storage of these drugs and their mode of delivery render them even more dangerous[143].

2.3.2 Ineffective Quality Control System

In Cameroon, drug procurement is organized around the National Essential Drugs and Medical Consumables Procurement Centre (CENAME). The National Drug Regulatory Authority (NDRA) is in charge of controlling drugs. However, some administrations other than the Ministry of Public Health, have health facilities and are customers of CENAME, whose drugs are not always controlled by NDRA. There is therefore a vast network of illicit supplies that feeds the market of street drugs[144]. Drug donation is also a source of procurement which is integrated into the system, but their quality is not always controlled.

The drug quality assurance system in Cameroon is based on several pillars namely; laboratory quality control, pharmaceutical inspection and market supervision, approval, pharmaco-vigilance, control on imports, rigorous selection during the acquisition process, proper storage of drugs, the fight against fake drugs and illicit trafficking pharmaceutical products. As exhaustive as these processes might be, most of them are poorly implemented. Deficiencies in the quality control of drugs have led to the development of the informal sector of drug sales that represents 25 percent of the market[145].

The National Laboratory for the Quality Control of Drugs and Valuation (LANACOME) is the structure in charge of quality control of drugs. However, this control is not systematic for imported drugs and only a small proportion of batches circulating are controlled. As a result, counterfeit medicines, and illicit drug trafficking has developed, and this sector represents about 30 per

142 Martez, M., (2014), "Illegal Hospitals In Cameroon", Voice of America, World Health Organization, at Https://Borgenproject.Org/Illegal-Hospitals-Cameroon/ (accessed On 19th Day Of April 2022).

143 Aurore, B., (2020), "Unsafe Roadside Medication Risks Public Health in Cameroon", at Https://Www.Aa.Com.Tr. (accessed On 2nd day of May 2022).

144 Ministry of Public Health, Health Sector Strategy 2016-2027.

145 Rapport d'inspection et de Supervision MINSANTE 1er semestre2015.

cent of the pharmaceutical market in Africa[146]. Inspections and controls of pharmaceutical services are insufficient due to the lack of logistics, equipment and qualified financial and human resources to cover the national territory[147].

Furthermore, administrative structures in charge of organizing and regulating laboratory and blood transfusion activities are not sufficiently equipped in terms of human, material and financial resources to optimally fulfil their duties. The availability of quality blood products remains rare in Cameroon. The country needs about 400,000 secure blood bags per year for medical and surgical care of patients, however, less than 50 per cent of these needs are met, (a total of 147,034 blood bags were collected in 2022)[148]. The inadequacy of safe blood products contributes significantly to maternal mortality (bleeding complications), and to many deaths of under 5 children due to anemia[149]. It is also responsible for the insufficiency in the management of surgical cases and patients with chronic diseases whose treatment depends on blood products such as the hemodialysis and hemophiliacs[150].

The assessment of the competence of medical practitioners is at best haphazard and inadequately done. The requirements are minimal frequently consisting of a declaration by the physician that he or she has paid his /her annual contribution to the Cameroon Medical Council, has taken an insurance policy covering occupational hazards and a statement by the doctor testifying that he/she has continued in the active practice of medicine and suffers from no known physical or mental impediments to the practice of medicine[151].

While the Cameroon Medical Council does not have a rigorous policy to continually assess physician competence, the problem of deficient standard continues. Moreover, after graduating from medical school, doctors are not compelled to take up refresher courses to renew the license to practice. Medicine evolves constantly and so should practice. There is no expiration date of the Cameroon medical license and doctors in Cameroon could essentially practice forever without any form of re-evaluation and re-examination of

146 Fondation Chirac, L'appel du Cotonou, 2009.

147 "Agenda for the Transformation of the Cameroonian Health System: Time to Act", at https://www.minsante.cm. (accessed on 12th day of May 2022).

148 Revelation by the Minister in Charge of Public Health, Manaouda Malachie, on June 7th 2023 in a Press Conference he granted at the Emergency Management Unit of the Ministry of Public Health in Yaoundé in prelude to the World Blood Donor Day which was celebrated on 14 June 2023.

149 *Ibid.*

150 See *supra* note 201.

151 See Section 6 of Law No 90/036 of 10 August 1990 relating to the Organization of the Practice of Medicine in Cameroon.

their skills[152]. This is worrisome because without any form of updated medical knowledge, experience is usually based on outdated knowledge. "The so-called "seniors" who trained in the 1970s and have not updated their knowledge are a big obstacle to evidence-based medicine especially in Cameroon and other lower-income countries"[153].

The idea that one can be licensed and certified as a young person and that this will guarantee competence for the rest of one's career is no longer tenable to ensure the quality and standards of care expected by patients. This is due in part to rapid changes in practice brought on by advances in medical science, but it also reflects the recognition that skills may not be maintained indefinitely or may deteriorate over time[154], and when this happen the patient will be at the mercy of the practitioner.

It is true that the Cameroon National Medical Council organizes medical conferences yearly during which selected subjects are presented by colleagues and discussed. The medical conference also provides a space for presentation of scientific works. This goes a long way to strengthen the skills of the participants. However, participation is not obligatory. In developed countries[155] a new system called revalidation has also begun that requires doctors to renew their license to practice every five years. The purpose of this new approach is to ensure that licensed doctors are up to date and fit to practice.

The doctor's unofficial private activities (private practice in health facilities) though expressly forbidden in Cameroon[156], persist, and have a considerable influence on the hours of work spent by personnel at their duty post, and are a diversion of human resources and potential revenue, because these activities help to "lure away" patients who are subsequently treated in relatively informal private facilities at high cost[157]. Given the fact that in the

---

152 Remarks made by Dr. Dzekem in a Twitter Chat Hosted by the Clinical Research Education Networking and Consultancy on December 6, 2011.at https://Keafon.Com/Continuing-Medical-Education-Cme-In-Cameroon (accessed on 8th day of September 2020).

153 *Ibid.*

154 Cruess, S R. *et al*, (2005), "The Medical Profession and Self-Regulation: A Current Challenge", *AMA Journal of Ethics Virtual Mentor,* 7(4), Pp.320-324.

155 The United Kingdom for example.

156 Section 13 of the 1990 law Organizing the Practice of Medicine in Cameroon states; subject to special enactments, civil servants and government contract employees who are in active service or employed persons in general shall not be authorized to practice medicine on a private basis.

157 Vinard, P. & Djateng F., (2007), "Anti-corruption Strategy and Governance Indicators in the Health Sector in Cameroon", Washington, D.C.: World Bank Group.p.22 at http://documents.worldbank.org/curated/en/167021468232168697/Cameroon-Anticorruption-strategy-and-governance-indicators-in-the-health-sector-in-Cameroon-mission-of-March-24-April-12-2007.

Cameroon health sector, there are several networks that are united by common specialties or studies, the use of umbrella protection is an oft-cited problem and under these conditions, it is very difficult to enforce a ban on private activities outside and even within the hospital. Penalty procedures exist in the public service; however, they are onerous to implement, and are particularly difficult to enforce where the director lacks strong political support. A hospital official can only be effective if he or she has strong political backing. Unfortunately, this support is dependent on his or her level of cooperation[158].

In Cameroon, today it is difficult to distinguish between a legal and illegal practitioner, mainly due to weak regulation[159]. Most doctors serving in public hospitals are owners of some of these illegal clinics[160] while others do part time there. Even though the Cameroon Medical Council Disciplinary Board is empowered to warn, suspend or dismiss a medical practitioner found guilty of professional misconduct[161], a matter maybe referred to the Disciplinary Board only by the supervisory authority, the legal department or a licensed doctor[162]. Thus, access to the Disciplinary Board is limited and this narrows the ability of aggrieved patients to seek redress, and the consequences is general apathy of medical practitioners toward misconduct.

2.3.3 Infrastructural Deficiencies

The Cameroon health care system suffers from intense defects at the macro level such as a shortage of doctors and nurses, absenteeism, hostility and violence to patients, poor infrastructure, lack of resources and more which impact negatively at the micro level of care for individual patients[163]. There is gross inadequate health personnel and health facilities in Cameroon[164]. In fact, the World Health Organization estimate that the doctor patient ratio

---

(accessed on 22nd of April 2021).

158 *Ibid.*

159 Pemunta, N V. *et al*, (2020), "Self-Medication within the Context of Medical Pluralism in Yaoundé, Cameroon", *Pan African Medical Journal,* 37(14), at https://www.Panafrican-MedJournal.Com/Content/Article/37/14/Full. (accessed on 2nd day of May 2022).

160 Mostly in urban cities like Douala, Bafoussam

161 Section 48 of Law No 90/036 of 10 August 1990 on the Organization and Practice of Medicine in Cameroon.

162 *Ibid.*, Section 42.

163 Tinyami, E. *et al,* (2015), "Cameroon Public Health Sector: Shortage and Inequalities in Geographic Distribution of Health Personnel", *International Journal for Equity in Health*, Vol.14 Issue 43.

164 Soh, M., (2013), "Access to Health Care Vis a Vis Women's Reproductive Health in Cameroon", *Journal of International Women's Studies*, 9(1), pp. 117-134.

in Cameroon is close to one doctor per 50.000 inhabitants instead of the recommended one doctor per 10000 inhabitants in a country of more than 25 million[165].

The health system is under-manned; there are inadequate numbers of doctors and nurses, leading to deficiencies in the quantity and quality of medical services delivered. To compound the problem, the proportion of the state budget allocated to health is between 6-8 per cent[166]. This is well below the commitment made by African leaders during the Abuja Summit in 2001 where it was recommended that 15 per cent of the national budget should be allocated to health[167]. This underperformance can be attributed to insufficient political will, low capacity to mobilize resources and poor use of available funds.

There is poor distribution of hospitals and staff. Over 55 per cent of all physicians in the country practice in the Center, Littoral and West Region, against only 10 per cent for East, Adamawa, North West, and South Regions[168], where only 18 per cent of the overall population lives[169]. Where all the experts or specialists are concentrated at the center, patients in the periphery are at risk in case of complications. For example, putting to birth without trained attendants implies that complications such as postpartum haemorrhage[170] may not be well managed. Indeed, in 2015, the Director of the Kumba District Hospital[171] lamented that the institution was suffering from an acute shortage of staff and infrastructure to handle the thousands of patients that seek treatment at the facility[172]. He said the number of patients consulted annually at the health facility rose from 25,000 in 2013, to over 33,000 in 2014. He maintained that this figure greatly out-numbered the ratio

165 Kindzeka, M E., (2016), "Death of Pregnant Woman Provokes Debate on Cameroon's Health Care", *Voa News*.

166 Chongwang, J., (2022), "Cameroon : Update on the State of Implementation of the Abuja Declaration" , at https://www.africanconstituency.org (accessed on the 5th day of October 2023)

167 Health Sector Strategy 2016-2027.

168 Ministry of Health, RGPS, 2011.

169 World Bank, (2013), Better Access to Health Care for All Cameroonians, at http://www.worldbank.org/en/country/cameroon/publication/better-health-care-access-for-all-cameroonians. (accessed on 29th day of April 2022).

170 Tita, A T. *et al*, (2005) "Evidence-Based Reproductive Health Care in Cameroon: Population-Based Study of Awareness, Use and Barriers", *Bulletin of The World Health Organization*, 83, pp.895–903.

171 Dr. Zachs Ebongo Nanje.

172 Fokwen, M., (2015), "Acute Staff Infrastructure Shortage hits Kumba District Hospital", *Cameroon Post*, at https://cameroonpostline.com/acute-staff-infrastructure-shortage-hits-kumba-district-hospital/%E2%80% 8B. (accessed on 25th day of April 2022).

of workers required. Needless to say, such a huge number has the potential to overburden the doctor which in turn may compromise his ability to work optimally.

Generally, Cameroon has one of the most deplorable healthcare systems in the world, ranking the 150th position of 187 countries in the Human Development Index[173]. The existing healthcare facilities in Cameroon are often short of essential drugs, immunization supplies, beds, and medical-emergency equipment[174]. Institutionally, hospitals are often poorly run, and understaffed. The lack of adequate beds and space, leads to early discharge of patients from hospitals before they have fully recovered[175]. The lack of a power supply, lack of blood, delayed referral, delayed decision making, and the patient's inability to pay bills, compounded by the lack of essential medical products, is striking. These factors have a strong bearing on the causes of malpractices in Cameroon.

Administrative structures in charge of organizing and regulating laboratory and blood transfusion activities are not sufficiently equipped in terms of human, material and financial resources to optimally fulfil their duties. The equipment available in most hospitals are inadequate as compared to the workload. Most laboratories do not have an efficient maintenance system with the result that equipment is largely obsolete[176].

Insufficient government expenditure largely explains why the few available healthcare facilities have limited qualified healthcare workers and is often short of essential materials such as drugs, beds, and modern medical equipment. Cameroon has the highest per capita health expenditure in sub-Saharan Africa, \$61 per person compared to \$51 for sub-Saharan Africa as a whole. On the contrary, government expenditure on health is limited and comprises of about 27per cent of the total healthcare burden, with the rest financed by citizens and international donors[177]. These infrastructural deficiencies have led to an upsurge of unauthorised clinics and the sale of drugs by road side vendors.

---

173 Nzima, V. (2014), "Health Sector Strategy and Economic Development in Cameroon: History, Challenges and Perspectives" (Master's Theses), Georgia State University, Atlanta, GA. at https:// pdfs.semanticscholar.org/7c52 /39080dbc8c67b76ec85cb97b9c496c9ccc9b.pdf. (accessed on 29th day of April 2022).

174 United Nations International, Cultural, and Educational Fund. (2011). the State of the World's Children 2011- Executive Summary: Adolescence an Age of Opportunity. Unicef.

175 Ako, S., (2015), Reproductive Health in Cameron", at www.gmfer.ch.Endo/Reprod-health/ cameroon/NetReproduction Cameroon.htm. (accessed on the 29th day of April 2022).

176 See *supra* note 200, at p. 88.

177 See *supra* note 230.

What emerges from this is a picture of official neglect from the highest quarters, coupled with poor standards of health delivery at institutional levels. This problem can be curtailed by regular control of medical services in these areas. A particular piece of medical equipment or a particular medical product may not have been available when the patient/plaintiff was receiving medical care in the hospital. The patient may claim that this lack of availability constituted negligence on the part of the hospital, whereas the hospital argues that it did not have sufficient funds to purchase the relevant item. Thus, a patient who dies because he/she does not receive a blood transfusion may have lost his/her life in circumstances where the hospital cannot be successfully sued for negligence as the question of resource allocation from the Ministry of Public health has such a political component as to place it outside the remit of the duty of care[178].

2.3.4 Inaccessibility to Remote Areas

The inadequacy of healthcare personnel and healthcare facilities is further compounded by inaccessibility to remote areas and villages. Inaccessibility to remote areas has two consequences; it hinders and discourages doctors from taking up duty posts in these areas, and at the same time prevents patients in these areas from getting the much-needed medical attention. The pro-urban uneven distribution of the available health workforce due to inaccessibility and poor social amenities in the rural areas is consequently of major concern. For example, in Cameroon, a physician in the Center Region catered for 5,449 persons as opposed to 26,726 persons to a physician in the Adamawa region[179].

This uneven distribution of health personnel has seen a departure in the provision of sufficient, fair and quality health-care services to the population. In the Northern Regions for instance, which are amongst the least represented with health personnel for instance, it was observed that an estimated 61 per cent of births were unattended and ≥35 per cent of children died of diarrheal[180]. These shortages highlight the need for regulation in order to improve, and develop accessibility to remote areas, and increase availability of doctors and other health personnel to the population of rural poor, and vulnerable regions.

---

178 Obafemi, K A. R, (2017), "Medical Negligence Litigation in Nigeria: Identifying the Challenges and Proposing a Model Law Reform Act", (A PhD thesis), at http://www.tara.tcd.ie. (accessed on 2nd day of May 2022).

179 Ministry Of Public Health Cameroon, Department of Human Resource. General Census Report of Health Personnel, Yaoundé 2012.

180 Amani A. (2010) "The Health Workers Crisis in Cameroon", (Master's Thesis), 2010, Institute of Public Health, Georgia State University.

Lack of road infrastructure also hinders transportation to these areas. As a result, patients have to go long distances to hospitals with limited means of transportation means making the reception of timely treatment difficult[181]. These distances, especially for pregnant women, reduces their motivation to attend prenatal visits as required[182], and cause them to seek delivery assistance from traditional birth attendants.

To compound the problem, the current armed crisis in the North West and South West Regions of the country has made access to health care services and facilities in some of these areas almost impossible. Trained medical practitioners and nurses working in remote areas in these regions left their duty posts and fled for their lives as the tension heightened. Attacks on health personnel and facilities are common[183]. Patients are abandoned in the hospitals with no medical attention. Some with complication have to brave the risk and trek for days to seek medical attention. Even in urban areas in these regions obtaining treatment is a challenge. It is extremely difficult for patients to get to hospitals if there is a medical emergency on a Monday, which has been declared a lockdown for some time now. According to the United Nations close to one in five health care facilities is no longer functioning in these Regions due to the ongoing crisis[184].

2.4 Economic Considerations for Regulating Medical Practice in Cameroon

Regulation of medical practices is also necessitated by the desire to mitigate the economic situation of both the medical practitioners and the patients with relation to efficiency, accessibility and affordability to medical services. Cameroon is a lower-middle- income country. In 2020 the Covid-19 pandemic aggravated the already poor economic condition of the country, and caused a significant deterioration in economic activities. Household and

181 Morales L S. *et al*, (2002) "Socio Economic, Cultural and Behavioural Factors Affecting Hispanic Health Outcomes", *Journal of Health Care for the Poor and Underserved*, 13, pp. 477-503.

182 Edie, G. E. H. E. *et al*, (2015), "Perceptions of Antenatal Care Services by Pregnant Women Attending Government Health Centers in the Buea Health District, Cameroon: A Cross Sectional Study". *Pan African Medical Journal*, 21(1) at Https://Www.Panafrican-Med-Journal.Co. (accessed on 2nd day of May 2022).

183 Recently, on the night of the 8th of June 2022, the District Hospital in Mamfe, South West Region, was burnt to ashes as a result of the armed conflict.

184 Access to Health Care in Cameroon Severely Limited as Violence and Unrest Rule", *Medicins Sans Frontierre*, July 2021 at https://www.org. (accessed on 2nd day of May 2022).

business income is on the decrease, in fact, it is estimated that the pandemic increased the extreme poverty rate from 24.5 percent in 2019 to 25.3 per cent in 2021[185]. This adverse economic situation also has a toll on medical practices, as medical practitioners are indulging in all forms of unethical practices in a bid to meet up with the rising cost of living. More so, patients/consumers purchasing power has decreased, rendering them vulnerable, and unable to access medical services.

2.4.1 Low and Irregular Income

It is no secret that public health workers expressed dissatisfaction with working and living conditions due to low salary, overwork burden, no professional autonomy, limited opportunities for career progress and lack of sufficient as well as modern equipment for smooth and effective practices in Cameroon[186]. In Cameroon, the period set from recruitment to a complete integration of a staff to reception of first salary could last for 36 months or more, while the personnel is expected to be at work during this period, a situation said to be complex and confusing[187]. Indeed, the unsuitable living and working environments, including salary cuts, among other factors prompted many public health personnel in Cameroon to migrate to other sectors or abroad for better conditions[188]. Some of them, when posted to remote areas prefer to remain in big cities and work with two or more private clinics where the salaries are far better. The rate of absenteeism in public hospitals in Cameroon varies between 2 and 37 per cent[189]. This is caused *inter alia* by the quest for additional income. Regulating the activities of medical practitioners therefore seek to ensure that medical doctors in public hospitals do not abandon their duty post in order to pursue private gains elsewhere.

In the public sub-sector, salaries allocated to health personnel do not motivate their retention in the system. Often there is a disparity between the

---

185 World Bank, the World Bank in Cameroon, overview, at http//www.worldbanl.org. (accessed on the 14th July 2022).

186 Fongwa, M N., (2002) "International Health Care Perspectives: The Cameroon Example", *J Transcult Nurs*, 13(4), P 325-30.

187 Ministry of Public Health Cameroon, National Policies on Human Resources for Health, Yaoundé, Cameroon, 2011.

188 Obame, A *et al*, (2003) 'La Migration du Personnel de la Sante Qualifie dans la Region Afrique : Le Cas Du Cameroun', *Health Sci Dis*, Vol 4, pp. 22 -27.

189 Tchuinguem, G., (2009), 'Ampleur, Couts, Facteurs Personnels et Occupationnels de L'absentéisme dans la Fonction Publique Hospitalière au Cameroun', (Masters Thésis), *Université De Montréal.*

personnel profile and the duty post, which partly explains low performance[190]. Low and irregular income aggravate malpractice, as in a bid to increase his pay packet, the doctor engages in numerous unethical practices, for example selling drugs to patients during consultation, which is forbidden. Increase commercialization of practice has decreased the standard and quality of care rendered in hospitals with money making being the prime motivation of the medical practitioner, rather than the life of the patient. This attitude has led to the spread of mushroom hospitals in Cameroon that are out not to safe life but to make money at the expense of patients' life. The standard of patient care is compromised in order to inflate profit margin by conducting unnecessary diagnostic test with the dubious motive of increasing medical bills.

When a patient visits a hospital for treatment, the drugs he finally consumes and the test that he undergoes are stipulated almost entirely by the doctor. Thus, doctors use this as an opportunity to make additional cash by promoting each other through prescription of certain brand of drugs, or referrals to particular laboratories in return for payment from the owners. The ultimate burden falls on the patient through excessive or costly medication, unnecessary and expensive diagnostic tests, prolonged and expensive hospitalization. These days in Cameroon, it is not uncommon for doctors to write down prescriptions, or order for examinations and suggest that the patients should goes to a named pharmacy to get the drugs, or to a particular diagnostic laboratory to do the examination. At times when the patient fails to comply, the doctor refuses to prescribe for the patient.

Regulation encourages medical practitioners to respect ethical obligations and resort to best practices. However, this is hardly achieved as low income at times pushes doctors to conspire with clients to issue fake medical certificates in exchange of huge compensation, even though this act is punishable by the Medical Code of Ethics[191] and the Cameroon Penal Code[192], doctors take the risk to indulge in it.

2.4.2 Protection of Consumers Interests

Regulation is consumerism at its height, as it is policy geared towards controlling goods and services in favour of consumers of such goods and

190 National Health Development Plan 2016-2020, published by the Ministry of Public Health, 2016.
191 See Section 21 of the 1983 Cameroon Code of Medical Ethics.
192 See Section 259 of the Cameroon Penal Code.

services. It ensures that these goods and services do not negatively impact on consumers[193]. A consumer according to *Black's law Dictionary*[194], is one who consumes, an individual who purchases, uses, maintains and disposes of products and services; user of the final product; a member of the broad class of people who is affected by pricing policies, financial practices, qualities of goods and services, credit reporting, debt collection and other practices for which the state and general consumer protection laws are enacted. From this definition patients making payment for availing health services are consumers. The same is true according to the Legal Framework on Consumer Protection in Cameroon[195] which defines a consumer as any person who uses products to meet his own needs and those of his dependents rather than to resell, process, or use them within the context of his profession, or any person enjoying the services provided[196].

Generally, in the doctor- patient relationship, the patient is the consumer of medical services, while the doctor is the provider of such services. From a public policy perspective, the rationale for the regulation of medicine is patient protection[197]. Regulation is essential to define a clear framework within which health professionals acquire and maintain the competence needed to provide health services that are of high quality, i.e., that are safe, effective and patient centered. It has as main objective the protection of consumers' interests by promoting the quality of services provided by operators and ensuring socially acceptable pricing[198].

Regulation recognizes that consumers are not always in a position to protect themselves. The relationship between consumers and service providers is unequal. This unequal relationship has led to the exploitation of consumers by the more powerful service providers[199]. Regulation thus seeks to adjust this power relation. In the provision of medical services, there is an imbalance of knowledge, resources, and power between the patient and the medical practitioner. This is a product of physicians possessing legitimized, referent, and expert power[200] and patients being reliant on them to provide the care

193 See *supra* note 64, p.13.

194 Black, M. A., (1990), *Black's Law Dictionary*, 6th ed. p.316.

195 Law No 2011/012 of 06 May 2011 Framework on Consumer Protection in Cameroon.

196 *Ibid.*, Section 2.

197 Arrow, K L., (1963), "Uncertainty and the Welfare Economics of Medical Care", *Am Econ Rev.*, 53(5), Pp.941-973.

198 See *supra* note 118.

199 See *supra* note 64, p.7.

200 Beisecker, A E., (1990), "Patient Power in Doctor-Patient Communication: What Do We know?"

they need[201]. This exposes the patient to a degree of risk, as they have little or no knowledge about the characteristic component of medicine, and are also unable to completely or objectively assess the qualifications, competency, or fitness to practice as a medical practitioner.

The use of regulation is therefore instrumental to ensure protection of consumers from unqualified, incompetent, or unsafe health care providers[202]. This is achieved through the establishment and enforcement of professional practice and education standards[203], so as to prevent doctors from misrepresenting their qualification, making unfounded claims for cures, failing to exercise due diligence in providing care, or engaging in other forms of malfeasance. This would yield large benefits by assuring patients that they are in good hands.

The traditional relationship between patient and doctor can be considered paternalistic; in such a relationship the patient takes the subordinate role because the provider is the medical expert with years of medical training. Physicians in the provision of services are thus driven by paternalistic attitudes, according to which they know better what is best for the patient. They believed that because of patients' limited abilities or seemingly lack of knowledge, they are not able to know what is best for them. Thus, patient's dignity, well-being[204], and their right to decision making are often undermined.

2.4.3 Taxation of Illegal Medical Products

The taxation of illegal medical products in Cameroon leads to the inference that such products have been validated for consumption. Vendors of illegal drugs make a lot of sales and profit from their business. This is because their businesses are patronized by the vast majority of the population. The State through the Ministry in charge of Finance and the Ministry in charge of Decentralization collects taxes from these vendors. This fact alone suggests that their activities are recognized and approved by the government.

Health Commun. 1; 2(2), pp.105-22.

201 Bending, Z J., (2015), "Reconceptualising the Doctor-Patient Relationship: Recognizing the Role of Trust in Contemporary Health Care", *Bioeth Inquiry*, 12, pp.189-202.

202 See *supra* note 119.

203 *Ibid.*

204 Pūra,s D., (2016), "Report of the Special Rapporteur on the Right of Everyone to the Enjoyment of the Highest Attainable Standard of Physical and Mental Health". United Nations General Assembly, Human Rights Council. Thirty-second Session. A/HRC/32/32.4 at http://www.ohchr.org/ EN/Issues/Health/Pages/AnnualReports.aspx. (accessed on 23rd day of October 2020).

The government should not therefore cry foul when these very products are destroying the lives of citizens.

Most patients, who are unable to afford the high prices and prescriptions required in pharmacies, opt for medication of doubtful quality from unregistered operators. The control of medical practices seeks to avoid such occurrences. Indeed, Statistics from the National Gendarmerie headquarters in Yaoundé, indicate that a total of 665,352 tons of drugs were seized in 2019, and about 2000 tablets of tramadol were seized from transporters intercepted at the end of November 2021[205], because they were smuggled into the country.

2.4.4 Poverty

Poverty is another cause of malpractices in the country. Poverty related difficulties include a lack of basic infrastructure, lack of sufficient number of health care providers, absence of accountability for serious medical malpractice, and exploitation of patients[206]. It is a condition that increases disease risk and presents severe health challenges. It inhibits relations between patient and medical practitioners and pushes patients towards self-help. Poor medical care and poverty of the population usually occur simultaneously, and often amplify each other. About 80 per cent of Africans, mostly those in the middle-income bracket and below rely on public health facilities, and these public health facilities suffers from chronic shortages of equipment and drugs. The implication is that an overwhelming majority of the poor are unable to access effective healthcare services.

Financial transactions are becoming more and more the main means of obtaining even the slightest health service in Cameroon[207]. For example, because of financial constraints, 45 per cent of pregnant women wait until the second or third trimester to seek prenatal care, and by then it is often too late to adequately anticipate or arrest complications[208]. Failure to attend prenatal visits may increase the risk of maternal or infant mortality, because

---

205 See *supra* note 198.

206 Begum, H., (2001), "Poverty and Health Ethics in Developing Countries". *Bioethics*,15(1), pp.50-56.

207 Moungbakou, I B M., (2018), "Commodification of Care and Its Effect on Maternal Health in the Noun Division (West Region Cameroon)", *BMC Medical Ethics*, 19(43), p.72.

208 Ajong, A B. *et al*, (2016), "Knowledge of Women in Family Planning and Future Desire to Use Contraception: A Cross Sectional Survey in Urban Cameroon", at https://Bmcresnotes.Biomedcentral.Com/Articles/10.1186/S13104-016-2155-7. (accessed on 2nd day of May 2022).

health issues like high blood pressure and Sexually Transmitted Diseases are not detected and managed sufficiently early in pregnancy[209].

2.4.5 Corruption

Corruption is an obstacle to the provision of medical services to patients. Medical personnel devise every means to extort money from patients, which aggravate their woes. Corruption in hospitals is mostly rife in the emergency units. The Coved- 19 pandemic profoundly exposed the rate of corruption in the health sector. The large sum of money required to deal with emergencies and the need for urgency in disbursing these funds form a perfect ground for corruption[210]. Government personnel diverted these funds or misappropriated these funds for private use thereby leaving the citizens without emergency aid. Stocks of medicine worth over 536 million CFA frs disappeared, with no information regarding its management. Again, the sum of 288million CFA francs set aside to purchase 15.000 rapid Covid-19 tests was misappropriated[211]. Many Covid-19 related deaths were as a result of lack of finance, even though the government announced that treatment was free. Doctors, nurses and other health personnel were not provided with enough face masks and other medical gadgets to enable them effectively render risk free services. The result was that most of these health personnel deserted the hospitals, and as a result Covid-19 patients were abandoned in isolation wards and centres to die unattended. Effective regulation entails accountability for funds received and for disbursement of such funds.

Patient's decisions to purchase counterfeit or substandard drugs on the street are not solely due to the cost of such products in formal health care institutions, but also due to the unavailability of proper medications required by patients, leading the latter to purchase drugs of doubtful quality on the streets[212].

---

209 Obasi, E Z., (2013), "A Review of the Barriers and Socio-Cultural Factors Influencing the Access to Maternal Health Care services in Nigeria", (Master's Thesis), Helsinki Metropolia University of Applied Sciences, Helsinki, Finland.

210 Transparency International, Corruption Perception Index 2020, at Https://Www.Transparency.Org. (accessed on the 4th day of May 2022).

211 Songne, M., (2022), "Cameroon: IMF Awaits New Audit on Covid-19 Fund Management ", *The Africa Report.*

212 Geest, S V D., (1988) "The Articulation of Formal and Informal Medicine Distribution in South Cameroon", *The Context of Medicines in Developing Countries,* Vol.12, as cited by Ojong N., (2020), "The COVID-19 Pandemic and the Pathology of the Economic and Political Architecture in Cameroon", *Healthcare,* 8;176, p.6.

2.5 Conclusion

Medical practitioners play an important role in ensuring that the right to health is actually enjoyed by patients, this explains why there is need to monitor and supervise their activities to curtail possible violation. While the right to health allows for progressive realization, in acknowledgement of the limits imposed by resource and other constraints, States also have obligations to guarantee that this right will be exercised without discrimination of any kind and that deliberate, concrete and targeted steps will be taken towards the right's full realization. However, there is a gap between the recognition of the right to the highest attainable standard of physical and mental health and its systematic implementation at the country level. One analysis[213] found that most of United Nations Member States' national constitutions failed to guarantee rights related to public health, medical care, or overall health.

Cameroon has made efforts in guaranteeing the right to health through regulating medical practices, but much remains to be done. The unchecked influx of defective medical products and devices into the country, poor working condition of medical practitioners, the lack of infrastructure and modern equipment, low salaries[214] amongst others, limit access to health care, and promote malpractices by health care professionals of both the public and private sectors in Cameroon, thus violating the right to health. The duty of saving life is burdensome, and where the efforts of medical practitioners are not being adequately compensated, they tend to lose interest in this life saving mission, and look for compensation elsewhere.

Regulating medical practice is therefore aimed at ensuring that patients' rights to adequate medical care is safeguarded, and the quality of medical services offered by practitioners are supervised and controlled in order to protect the public from incompetent and unscrupulous medical practitioners who are out to protect their interest over the interest of patients.

However, incessant malpractices are indicative of the fact that rules and principles of medical practices are outrightly flaunted by medical practitioners. Weaknesses in the implementation of both existing legislative and regulatory instruments governing the activities of the medical profession

---

[213] Heymann, J., (2013), "Constitutional Rights to Health, Public Health and Medical Care: The Status of Health Protection In 191 Countries", *Glob Public Health*, 8(6), Pp.639-53

[214] Mr. Sylvain Nga Onana President of CAP Health Syndicate in Cameroon in an Interview with Cameroon Radio Television on 9th July 2020.

in Cameroon are mostly responsible for such contemptuous behaviours of medical practitioners, necessitating a more rigorous regulation.

CHAPTER THREE

Compliance with Rules and Principles of Medical Practice in Cameroon

3.1 Introduction

Medical practitioners pose peculiar risks to the public health and safety[215]. They cannot be allowed to perform their services unguided. There are guiding principles and standards governing medical practices which every medical practitioner must comply with. Standards of practice refer to principles governing effective and ethical practice of medicine whether in a public or private setting. It also refers to the actual behaviour of an individual alleging to apply medical principles, or experience, for the purpose of helping others[216].

Standards of medical practice are tools which may be used to control the volume and intensity of services offered to patients without sacrificing quality[217]. They have been considered to be increasingly necessary and desirable because they provide an evaluation device to ensure proficiency and safety, and also because of the general perception that many health care professionals and systems are not performing as well as they could. Indeed, there are global

---

215 Hogan, D., (1983), "The Effectiveness of Licensing: History, Evidence and Recommendations", *Law Hum Behav*, 7, pp.117-136.

216 Dawes, R M., (2016), "Standards for Psychotherapy" in *Encyclopedia of Mental Health*, 2nd Edition, pp.219-224.

217 Walker, R D., (1994), "Medical Practice Guidelines", *West J Med*,161(1), p. 40.

concerns about the quality of professional health care practice. Economic, technological, social and demographic development, coupled with changing attitude and expectations of the public have forced the medical profession to become more openly and explicitly accountable for their decisions[218]. It is believed that complying with these standards will enhance the probability of high quality and ethical practice[219], and reduce the risk of adverse events.

These principles and standards are mostly established by national medical professional associations and international medical bodies. In Cameroon these rules and standards are set by statutory instruments particularly; the Code of Medical Ethics[220] and the Law Organizing the practice of medicine in Cameroon[221]. In fact, statutory instruments have been repeatedly endorsed as an appropriate regulatory mechanism since they carry the force of law, and also provides a proper foundation for the contract of the medical profession with society[222]. These statutes contain standards which must be strictly adhered to by the practitioner in the performance of their duties.

Apart from these legislative enactments, International Treaties, Conventions, and Declarations setting standards and rules of medical practice duly ratified by Cameroon are also applicable in the country. Ratification of these international treaties compel adherence to its standards. The power of the state to provide for the general welfare of its people authorizes it to prescribe all such norms as in its judgment will secure or tend to secure them against the consequences of ignorant and incompetent medical practitioners, as well as of deception and fraud.

Therefore, the government and professional associations are under the responsibility to ensure that the standards and rules set out in the statutory, regulatory and international instruments are observed by medical practitioners, and infringements are met with appropriate sanctions. The ultimate goal is to foster the professional practice of medicine and protect the public from unprofessional, improper and incompetent actions.

However, the persistence of medical malpractices in the country is a strong indication of the fact that the standards and rules of practices prescribes in these instruments are hardly complied with. This chapter

---

218 World Health Organization Regional Office of Europe, Meeting on Guidelines in Health Care Practice, Schloss, Velen, Broken, Germany, 26-28 January 1997.

219 *Ibid.*

220 Decree No 83/166 Of 12 April 1983 of The Code of Medical Ethics in Cameroon.

221 Law No 90/036 of 10 August 1990 relating to the Organisation and Practice of Medicine in Cameroon.

222 See *supra* note 270.

analyses the compliance to rules and principles of medical practices by medical practitioners in Cameroon. The first part will analyze compliance to general principles of medical ethics and standards set by statutory instruments in Cameroon, while the second part will analyze compliance to standards set by national and international regulatory institutions.

3.2 Compliance with General Principles of Medical Ethics

Ethics is an inherent and inseparable part of medicine. Ethics is the moral principle which attempts to verify what is morally right and what is morally wrong in human action, and it has also been described as the science of morals and rules of conduct recognized in human life[223]. Some moral norms for right conduct are common to human kind as they transcend cultures, regions religion and other group identities and constitutes common morality. Particular morality refers to norms that bind groups because of their culture, religion, profession, and include responsibilities, ideals, professional standards etc. an example of particular morality is the physician accepted role to provide competent and trustworthy service to their patients[224]. Code of Ethics in medical practice describes what is expected from medical doctors registered and licensed to practice medicine. It determines the principles that characterize good medical practice and clarify the standards of professional ethics expected from medical doctors by their professional peers, other health professionals and the community[225].

The role of ethics has become a moral, legal and basic need in almost all stages of medical practice. The United State Supreme Court in *Hawker* v. *The State of New York*[226] states that the physician is one whose relations to life and health are of the most intimate character. It is fitting, not merely that he should possess knowledge of diseases and their remedies, but also that he should be one who may safely be trusted to apply those remedies, character is as important a qualification as knowledge.

---

[223] Anup, N. *et al*, (2014), "Knowledge, Attitude & Practices Regarding Ethics & Law Amongst Medical and Dental Professionals in Rajasthan—A Questionnaire Study", *IOSR Journal of Dental and Medical Sciences*, 13(5), pp.102–109.

[224] Varkey, B., (2021), "Principles of Clinical Ethics and Their Application to Practice", *Med Princ Pract*, 30(1), pp. 17-28.

[225] Australian Medical Council: Good Medical Practice: A Code of Conduct for Doctors in Australia. July 2009.

[226] 170 U.S 189,18 S.Ct. 573, (1898).

Autonomy, beneficence, non-maleficence, and justice constitutes the four principles of medical ethics. Beneficence and non-maleficence can be trace back to the oath of Hippocrates 'to help and do no harm', while autonomy and justice evolved later and gained acceptance as important principles of ethics. Compliance to these principles will result in providing fair treatment, protecting patients from unnecessary risks, enhancing recovery, improving and increasing patient's pain tolerance level, reducing patient's anxiety, making motivation for the patient to have a better cooperation with the medical team, reducing treatment costs, increasing satisfaction and strengthening mutual trust between the physician and the patient[227].

The Code of Ethics of the Medical Profession in Cameroon encapsulates these ethical principles in its provisions which sets the normative guidelines of professional conduct to be followed by the registered physicians in Cameroon. Indeed, the Cameroon Code of Medical Ethics[228] compels every doctor, at the time of enrolment in the Cameroon Medical Association, to declare before the Council of the Association that he has cognizance of the present Code of Ethics and shall undertake, under oath and in writing, to abide by it, and any violation of the provisions of the Code attracts sanctions[229]. However, the provisions of these code are not effectively complied with by medical practitioners in Cameroon resulting to malpractices and its ensuing consequences to patients.

3.2.1 The Principle of Respect for Autonomy

The philosophical underpinning for autonomy, as interpreted by philosophers Immanuel Kant (1724–1804) and John Stuart Mill (1806–1873), and accepted as an ethical principle, is that all persons have intrinsic and unconditional worth, and therefore, should have the power to make rational decisions and moral choices, and each should be allowed to exercise his or her capacity for self-determination[230]. To violate a person's autonomy is to treat the person merely as a means, that is in accordance with the goals of others. Such treatment is a fundamental moral violation because autonomous persons are

---

227 Nasiriani, L. *et al*, (2018), "The Related Factors of Compliance to Professional Code of Ethics from Midwives' Perspective Working in Healthcare Centres of Tehran-Iran", *The Pan African Medical Journal*, 30(40), at htpps://www.ncbi.nlm.nih.gov/pmc/articles/PMC6110552/#CIT0011. (accessed on the 26th day of April 2021).

228 Decree No. 83/166 of 12th April 1983.

229 *Ibid.*, Section 62.

230 Guyer, P., (2003), "Kant on the Theory and Practice of Autonomy", *Soc Philos Policy*, 20(2), pp.70–98.

ends in themselves capable of determining their destinies. This ethical principle was affirmed in a court decision by Justice Cardozo in 1914[231]. In this case the defendant physician placed the plaintiff under anaesthesia. The plaintiff had consented to this treatment for the purpose of an examination only. While the plaintiff was unconscious, the defendant removed an abdominal tumor. In holding that the operation amounted to a trespass to person, Judge Cardozo stated:

> *Every human being of adult years and sound mind has a right to determine what shall be done with his own body; and a surgeon who performs an operation without his patient's consent commits an assault, for which he is liable in damages. This is true except in cases of emergency where the patient is unconscious and where it is necessary to operate before consent can be obtained*[232].

This principle implies that autonomous actions should not be subjected to controlling constraints by others. Individual's views and rights must be respected so long as their thoughts and actions do not seriously harm other persons. Correlative to this obligation is the right to self-determination, which supports various autonomy rights, including those of confidentiality and privacy[233].

However, the principle of autonomy does not extend to persons who lack the capacity (competence) to act autonomously because they are immature, incapacitated, ignorant, coerced, or exploited, for example; infants, irrationally suicidal individuals, drug-dependent patients. In this context, a patient is generally considered as competent where he/she is able to understand a therapy, or procedure, able to deliberate regarding major risk and benefits, and to make a decision in light of this deliberation[234]. The motive for determining incompetence is to protect patients against decisions they might make that are not in their interests.

Respect for autonomy involves treating persons to enable them to act autonomously[235]. It obligates professionals to disclose information, to probe for

---

231 See *Schlendorff v. the Society of the New York Hospital*, 211 NY 125 105 NE 92 1914

232 See *Supra* 285, at 92.

233 Beauchamp, T L. and Childress J F., (1994), *Principles of Biomedical Ethics*, 4th Edition, New York, Oxford University Press, p.126.

234 *Ibid, at* 136.

235 *Ibid*, at 125.

and ensure understanding and voluntariness, and to foster adequate decision-making. This requires that the patient have autonomy of thought, intention, and action free of coercion or coaxing when making decisions. The authority of the medical practitioner should not be used to foster or perpetuate the dependency of patients, rather it should be used to promote their autonomy, this requires equipping them to overcome their sense of dependence and achieve as much control as they desire. Medical practitioners are therefore obligated to tell the truth, respect the privacy of patients, respect confidential information, and obtain consent for any medical intervention[236].

The basic paradigm of autonomy in medical ethics is informed consent. Physicians are obliged to disclose medical information and treatment options that are necessary for the patient to exercise self-determination and supports informed consent, truth-telling, and confidentiality. Indeed, all prominent medical codes of ethics, hold that medical practitioners must obtain the informed consent of patients prior to any substantial intervention. This is needed to protect the autonomous right and welfare of patients, and encourage medical professionals to act responsibly towards patients. The patient must be competent to understand and decide, must receive a full disclosure of his/her situation, must comprehend the disclosure, act voluntarily, and consent to the proposed action[237].

The principle of patient autonomy was recognized by the Supreme Court of Nigeria in *Medical and Dental Practitioners Disciplinary Tribunal v Okonkwo*[238]. The defendant, a medical practitioner attended a patient who was a Jehovah's Witness. In the course of her treatment, she declined blood transfusion on the basis of her religious belief, she died and the defendant was charged before a medical disciplinary tribunal with infamous conduct. The Supreme Court firmly ruled, based on the principle of patient autonomy that the medical practitioner had acted appropriately. Ayoola JSC stated:

> *[I]t follows that the choice of an adult patient with a sound mind to refuse informed consent to medical treatment, barring state intervention through judicial process, leaves the practitioner helpless to impose a treatment on the patient. ... To a large extent the practitioner should be the judge of the choice that may be better in the circumstances. The choices*

---

236 *Ibid.*

237 See *supra* note 281.

238 (2002) AHRLR 159.

> *become a question of personal attitude rather than one of professional ethics. ... If a competent adult patient exercising his right to reject life-saving treatment on religious grounds thereby chooses a path that may ultimately lead to his death, in the absence of judicial intervention overriding the patient's decision, what meaningful option is the practitioner left with, other, perhaps, than to give the patient comfort?*[239].

Indeed, the law on blood transfusion in Cameroon[240] aptly encapsulate informed consent in its provisions. Blood transfusion is done with the consent written or expressed by both the donor and the donee[241], failure to obtain such consent is punishable[242].

Disclosure of information is particularly important with respect to surgery, medication, treatment, etc. The obligation to disclose information to patients is a necessary condition for valid informed consent. The law imposes obligation on doctors to make reasonable disclosure to patients on the nature of the illness or infirmity, the nature of the treatment proposed, the danger of using such treatment or alternative treatment, and then permit the patient to decide whether to submit to such treatment or not[243]. This disclosure is based on the general obligation of doctors to exercise reasonable care by giving information. Where the doctor fails to disclose, and it results in injury to the patient, he may be held liable.

There are controversies on how much of such information should be disclosed[244]. It is generally accepted, that excessive disclosure may amount to bad medical practice[245]. In certain cases, physicians often claim that nondisclosures benefit the patient, especially in case of emergency[246]. Moreover, a doctor may legitimately withhold information based on a sound medical judgement that to divulge the information would be potentially harmful to a depressed, emotionally drained or unstable patient, and may

---

239 *Medical and Dental Practitioners Disciplinary Tribunal v Okonkwo* (2002) AHRLR 159, at para 75.

240 Law No 2003/006 of 22 December 2003 on Blood Transfusion in Cameroon.

241 *Ibid,* Sections 5,7,8.

242 *Ibid,* Section 15(1).

243 Mccoid, A H., (1957), "A Reappraisal of Liability for Unauthorized Medical Treatment", *Minn L Rev*, 41, p.381

244 Prillaman, H L., (1990), "A Physician's Duty to Inform of Newly Developed Therapy", *Journal of Contemporary Health Law and Policy,* 6, pp.43-58.

245 See *William v. Menehan*, 191 Kan. 6, 379 P.2d 292 (1963).

246 *Bennan v. Parsonnet*, 83 N.J.I., 20,83 A. 948.

increase the anxiety of the patient[247]. Also, where disclosure would render the patient incompetent to consent to or refuse the treatment, disclosure may be withheld.

The Cameroon Medical Code of Ethics recognizes the principle of patient autonomy when it provides for doctors to obtain the informed consent of patients before proceeding to perform therapeutic abortion, except in the case of extreme urgency where the patient is not in a fit state to give her consent[248], however, where the patient refuses to consent, after having been duly informed, the doctor must accept such refusal. Again, the Code provides that a serious prognosis may lawfully be concealed from the patient, and a fatal prognosis may not be divulged to him except with the greatest prudence; it must normally be divulged to his family, unless the patient is already so aware or if he has appointed a third party to be informed[249].

However, most Cameroonian patients are not provided with sufficient information to enable them to make a fully informed decision as to their treatment. The process is regarded generally as one that involves obtaining signatures without providing full disclosure of risks. For the less educated patients, disclosure of several risks to treatment implies a confession of incompetence on the part of the doctor, leading to a loss of confidence in his or her abilities. A second challenge to the notion of individualistic informed consent in Cameroon is one derives from the Cameroon socio-cultural belief that the medical practitioner is all knowing and as such whatever he decides is best for the patient.

3.2.2 The Principle of Beneficence

The term beneficence is often understood to cover acts of kindness or charity that go beyond strict obligation. Beneficence here is used as an obligation to maximize possible benefits, and minimize possible harm. It supports a number of moral rules amongst which is the rule to protect and defend the rights of others, prevent harm, and remove conditions that will

247 Van Oosten, F F., (1991). "The So- called 'Therapeutic Privilege' or 'Contra-Indication': Its Nature and Role in Non-Disclosure Cases", *Medicine and Law,* 10(1), pp.31-34.

248 Section 29 (2) of Decree No 83/166 of 12 April 1983 on Code of Medical Ethics provides that; Therapeutic abortion may however be performed if such action is the only way of safeguarding the mother's life. Section 29(4) states; a doctor must, if necessary, accept the refusal of the patient, who has been duly informed. There shall be no exception to this rule, save in the case of extreme urgency, and where the patient is not in a fit state to give her consent.

249 *Ibid,* Section 27.

cause harm. This principle is at the very heart of health care. The Hippocratic Oath requires physicians to benefit their patients 'according to their best judgment'. Beneficence obliges medical practitioners to act for the benefit and welfare of the patient.

Indeed, the International Code of Medical Ethics requires doctors to deal honestly with patients, act in the best interest of patients when providing medical care, and strive to use health care resources in the best way to benefit patients. Medical practitioners owe their patients complete loyalty, and when faced with examinations or treatment that is beyond their capacity, they must refer patients to other physicians who have the necessary capacity[250].

This principle is sustained in the Cameroon Code of Medical Ethics wherein doctors are called upon to always give patients all necessary medical care within their power and to always act correctly and courteously, and show themselves sympathetic towards patients[251]. Moreover, doctors must prescribe treatment within the limits imposed by the condition of the patient, and never to give treatment to a patient with a view of profiting therefrom[252]. In effect, the Code stipulates that the doctor must always in good faith, not prescribe very costly treatment to a patient until the patient or his family have been informed of the sacrifices which it will entail, and the benefit to be derived therefrom. However, this principle is more often than not flaunted by medical practitioners in Cameroon.

3.2.3 The Principle of Nonmaleficence

The principle of nonmaleficence refers to the duty to refrain from causing harm. It underlies the medical maxim *primum non nocere*, meaning, 'above all (or first) do no harm[253]'. This principle states that one ought not to inflict evil or harm, and harm here is defined as an adverse effect on one's interest. The obligation of nonmaleficence is expressed in the Hippocratic oath as; "I will use treatment to help the sick according to my ability and judgement, but I will never use it to injure or hurt them".

---

250 WMA International Code of Medical Ethics adopted by the 3rd General Assembly of the World Medical Association London in 1949 as amended by the WMA General Assembly, Pilanesberg, South Africa in 2006.

251 See *supra* note 303, Section 22.

252 *Ibid*, Section 24(1)(2).

253 See *supra* note 288, p.189.

This principle supports several specific moral rules viz; do not kill, do not cause pain or suffering, do not incapacitate, do not cause offense, do not deprive others of the goods of life[254]. Non maleficence is the obligation of the physician not to inflict harm to the patient through act of commission or omission, and not imposing risk of harm. Providing a proper standard of care that avoids or minimize the risk of harm is supported not only by commonly held moral convictions, but by the laws of society as well[255]. This principle affirms the need for medical competence, and articulates a fundamental commitment on the part of health care professionals to protect their patients from harm.

The practical application of this principle is for the doctor to weigh the benefits against burdens of all intervention and treatments, to eschew those that are inappropriately burdensome, and to choose the best cause of action for the patient. This is particularly important and pertinent in difficult end-of-life care decisions on withholding and withdrawing life-sustaining treatment. In such situations doctors should act in accordance with the patient's interests and wishes. In Cameroon euthanasia and physician assisted suicide is not permitted. The medical practitioner is obliged to use all possible means within his/her power to keep a patient alive even where there is little chance of success. Life sustaining treatment may not thus be terminated.

3.2.4 The Principle of Justice

Justice is generally interpreted as fair, equitable, and appropriate treatment of persons. The most important aspect of justice in medical ethics is distributive justice. It refers to the fair, equitable, and appropriate distribution of health care resources determined by justified norms that structure the terms of social cooperation[256]. This requires that medical procedures uphold existing laws and are fair to all players involved. Medical benefit should be dispensed fairly such that people with similar needs and in similar circumstances should be treated with fairness in the light of expensive diagnostics, procedures and medications.

---

254 Iserson, K V., (1999), "Principles of Biomedical Ethics", *Emergency Medicine Clinics of North America*, 17(2), pp. 283-9.

255 *Ibid.*

256 Fleishacker, S., (2004), *A Short History of Distributive Justice*, Harvard University Press, at http://doi.org/10.2307/j-ctv2fcct3g (accessed on the 28th day of May 2023)

This principle seeks to eliminate discrimination in medical care. Administering medical care should not be based on sex, race, religious beliefs, and sexual orientation. indeed, the Cameroon Code of Medical Ethics[257] enjoins doctors to attend to all sick patients with the same diligence irrespective of their status, nationality, religion, reputation and the feeling they might have towards them. It further provides that in no case shall the doctor exercise his profession under conditions prejudicial to the quality of medical care and attention. Suffice to say that the practical application of this principle is wanting in Cameroon. Social status and financial prowess are used as criteria for treatment of patients especially in public hospitals. The quest for personal gain drives practitioners to discriminate especially on the basis of status and reputation. It is not uncommon to find poor patients unattended to in favour of the wealthy and renowned patients in hospitals.

With the increasing rate of malpractices in Cameroon, it can be deduced that medical practitioners in the performance of their duties are constantly violating these core ethical principles, coupled with the fact that they are not sufficiently equipped to fulfil these ethical obligations. In addition to the above four core principles of medical ethics, there are statutes enacted by the legislator in Cameroon which outline other rules which medical practitioners must comply with in the exercise of their profession.

3.3 Compliance with Rules Prescribed by Statutory Instruments

The main statutory instruments regulating the practice of the medical profession in Cameroon are Decree No. 83/166 of 12 April 1983 on the Code of Medical Ethics, and Law No. 90/036 of 10th august on the Organization and Practice of Medicine in Cameroon. This section will examine adherence to standards of practice prescribed by these statutes.

3.3.1 Compliance with Standards of the Cameroon Code of Medical Ethics

Codes often specify rules of etiquette as well as professionals' moral responsibilities. These professional codes tend to foster and reinforce member-

---

[257] Section 2(1).

identification with the prevailing values of the profession[258]. The Cameroon Code of Medical Ethics is a 1983 legislative instrument which spells out the ethical obligations of medical practitioners, and compels adherence to these standards of medical practice. Some of the ethical standards set by the Code, and the extent of their compliance by medical practitioners will be examined.

3.3.1.1 Respect for Life

The medical practitioner in the performance of his duties is compelled to respect life and to prioritize patient care over self-interest. Indeed, Section 1 of the Cameroon Code of Medical Ethics stipulates that "respect for life constitute in every instance the primary duty of a doctor", and again Section 3(2) specifically states that a doctor may not leave his patients in the event of public danger, except upon an order issued in writing by the competent authority. Most often doctors in Cameroon do not respect these provisions; delays in attending to patients during emergency, absenteeism and negligence performance of duty are outright violation of this provision.

The Code spells out the legal and ethical duty of a doctor towards the patient. Patients must be able to trust doctors with their lives, to obtain this trust the doctor must make the care of his patient his priority and must practice within standards of his profession. He/she must recognize and work within the limit of his competence. He must take prompt action if he feels that the safety dignity and comfort of his patient is being compromised. He must treat patient politely and considerately[259], in this light he is expected to support patients in caring for themselves.

It is mandatory for the doctor to make the care of his patient his first concern. He is expected to give the patient all the necessary medical care within his power, either personally or with the help of qualified third parties[260] to improve and maintain their health. To achieve this, he/she may engage with colleagues to maintain and improve the safety and quality of patient care[261].

---

[258] See *supra* note 288, p.6.

[259] Indeed, Section 22 of the Code of Medical Ethics enjoins the doctor to "always act correctly and courteously towards the patient and to show himself sympathetic towards him".

[260] *Ibid.*

[261] *Ibid.*, Section 46 provides (1) A Doctor treating a patient must suggest a consultation with a specialist whenever circumstances so require. (2) He must accept a consultation requested by the patient or his friends and relations. (3) In both cases the doctor shall propose the consultant whom he deems most qualified, but he must take the patient's wishes into account and agree, in principle, save for any serious reasons to meet any other doctor. He shall be responsible for organizing the procedure for consultation. (4) If the examining doctor considers that he should

In furtherance of his duty to give priority to his patient, and considering the devastating effect of a wrong diagnosis the Code enjoins the doctor to be very diligent in making diagnosis no matter the time that it may take, he/she must not rush in formulating diagnosis[262]. After making the diagnosis, the doctor must prescribe treatment that is affordable taking into consideration the economic status of the patient, this is adumbrated in Section 24(1) which provides "…He must in good faith not prescribe very costly treatment for a patient until the patient or his family have been informed of the sacrifices which this would entail and the benefit which they may derive from it", thereafter the doctor must ensure that the treatment prescribed is strictly carried out.

The Code forbids any act of abortion[263] except it is necessary to save the life of the mother[264]. It further spells out the procedure to be followed where therapeutic abortion is envisaged. The doctor performing the abortion must first of all obtain the written opinion of two doctors, attesting that abortion is the only remedy in the case in question. The report shall be drawn up in three copies, one given to the patient and the other two are kept by the attending physician. A report of the procedure is to be forwarded to the president of the Medical Council. However, where it is impracticable for the doctor to get the opinion of two doctors, the decision to carry out therapeutic abortion is at the discretion of the doctor who must forward a report of same to the Minister of Health and the President of the Medical Council[265].

3.3.1.2 Professional Secrecy

In order to protect patients and their interest, and to further the relationship of trust between the doctor and the patient, the duty of professional secrecy is endorsed in the Code of Medical Ethics in Cameroon. The Code makes Professional secrecy a binding obligation to all doctors in Cameroon provided it is not harmful to the patient[266]. Professional secrecy is an old traditional

not agree to the choice made, he may withdraw and shall not be obliged to explain his refusal.

262 *Ibid.*, Section 23 (1) provides: A doctor must always formulate his diagnosis with the greatest care, regardless of the time that this work may cost him. (2) After having made his diagnosis and prescribed treatment, the doctor must endeavour to ensure that this treatment is carried out, especially if the patient's life is in danger.

263 *Ibid*, Section 29(1).

264 Therapeutic abortion.

265 See *supra* note 317, Section 29.

266 *Ibid.*, Section 4.

moral precept of the health profession indicating the duty of secrecy regarding data about a third party, obtained by the medical professional through the exercise of his/her duty. Indeed, professional secrecy is simultaneously a right of the patient and a duty of the professional. The Hippocratic Oath stipulates that "whatsoever in the course of practice I see or hear (or even outside my practice in social intercourse) that ought never to be published abroad; I will not divulge but consider such things to be holy secrets"[267].

This duty is associated with the bioethical principle of autonomy, meaning; it is only the patient who can decide to whom to give information concerning his/her personal data. The doctor as recipient of that data by virtue of his/her profession, should not disclose the information except by permission from the patient, or in exceptional circumstances outlined by the law and ethics[268]; such as compulsory notification provided by law and regulation. Strict respect of this principle will go a long way to ensure greater freedom to patients. However, this principle of secrecy is one of the ethical commitments which are mostly disrespected in our health facilities by health professionals in their day-to-day activities.

3.3.1.3 Non- Advertisement of Practice

The commercialization of medical practice is forbidden in Cameroon. In fact, Section 7 of the Code of Medical Ethics stipulates that, the medical profession shall not be exercise as a trade, therefore any form of publicity or advertisement which does not have an exclusive scientific or educational purpose, is forbidden. Likewise, the doctor is also precluded from exercising his profession in fairs or markets[269], and is not allowed to give consultation in commercial premises where medicines or medical appliances are on sale, or in annexes to the said premises[270]. Today in Cameroon, physicians can be seen consulting in premises where there are pharmacies, laboratories, and some even consults in the pharmacies, thereby violating the law and undermining professional ethics.

---

267 Lee, Y K., (1967), "Professional Secrecy and the Law", *Singapore Medical Journal*, 8(20), p.87.

268 Villas, M E., (2015) "The Right and Duty of Secrecy, as a Patient Protection", *Rev. Bioet.* 23:3, at https://www.scielo.br/scielo.php?pid-S1983-80422015000300513&scripts-sci_arttext&ing-en. (accessed on the 20th day of January 2021).

269 See *supra* note 317, Section 12.

270 *Ibid.*, Section 15(2).

Commercialization has the tendency to put money first before the life of the patient. It is against the medical ethics of the profession for a medical practitioner to put his self-interest over that of his patients. This attitude has led to the proliferation of illegal hospitals in Cameroon with profit making as their main objective at the expense of patients' life. The standard of patient care is often compromised in order to inflate profit margin. The tendency of doctors forming partnerships and joint ventures with laboratories and other medical services where patients are referred to for unnecessary diagnostic test, extra x-rays, surgeries, etc., is carried out with the dubious motive of increasing medical bills.

Corruption is encouraged by commercialization of medicine. In fact, the Code forbids acceptance of a commission for any medical act whatever, and in particular, in respect of examinations, prescriptions of drugs or appliances, or consignments to a specific consulting room or clinic, a sanatorium or nursing home[271]. The same goes for any act that may enable a patient to obtain unjustified or illegal material gain. Any payment, acceptance or secret sharing of money between practitioners or sharing of fees[272]; any commission to any member of the staff is also prohibited. Any collusion between doctors and pharmacists, medical assistants and any other persons is forbidden[273].

However, what is obtained in reality is the reverse. Since consumption decision is not in the hands of the patient, when a patient visits a hospital for treatment the drugs he finally consumes and the test that he undergoes are stipulated almost entirely by the doctor. Thus, doctors use this as an opportunity to promote each other through referrals of certain brand of drugs in return for payment from the benefitting parties. The ultimate burden falls on the patient through excessive or costly medication, unnecessary and expensive diagnostic tests, prolonged and expensive hospitalization.

Charlatanism or deceitful practices[274] is also forbidden, the issuing of tendentious certificate as a favour, and the promotion of illegal practice of medicine[275] is strictly prohibited. The practice today is doctors conspire with clients and issue fake medical certificate to help clients get leave from work, get bail, or a huge financial claim in civil suits.

---

271 *Ibid*, Section 13.

272 *Ibid*, Section 33.

273 *Ibid*, Section 15(1).

274 *Ibid.*, Section 18.

275 *Ibid.*, Section 14 forbids doctors to grant any facilities to persons indulging in illegal medical practice.

3.3.1.4 Mutual Respect towards Colleagues and Professional Collaboration

As concerns relationship amongst doctors, it is expected of doctors to maintain good professional relationship with each other[276]. Maintaining good professional relationship with colleagues is an obligation as the legislator used the word "*must*"[277]. This provision strives to protect the interest of patients, by ensuring that medical practitioners do not work in a hostile environment. Good professional relation will lead to corporation amongst practitioners, at such they are obliged to support each other and collaborate in treating patients with difficult or complicated situations[278].

Unfair competition amongst doctors is forbidden by the Cameroon Medical Code of Ethics. Section 51 (1) of the Code stipulates that a doctor who, during or after his studies, has replaced a colleague for a period of more than three months, shall not, within two years after such replacement, set himself up in an establishment, where he could be in direct competition with the doctor whom he replaced, unless they have reached an agreement which shall be notified to the Council of the Association. Furthermore, no doctor shall set himself up in a building in which a colleague of the same speciality practises[279].

In furtherance of good professional relationship and mutual respect[280], a doctor must not attract the patient of his colleague[281], and he/she is forbidden to slander or disparage a colleague, or to repeat any remarks likely to harm him in the practice of his profession. Medical practitioners are expected to

---

276 *Ibid.*, Section 42, again Section 55 states that; in their relations with members of paramedical professions, particularly pharmacists and dental surgeons, doctors *must* respect the independence of such persons. They must avoid any unjustified action likely to harm them in the eyes of their clientele and they must behave courteously towards them.

277 "Doctors *must* maintain good professional relations between themselves. They owe each other moral support".

278 See *supra* note 331., Section 44-50.

279 *Ibid*, Section 52.

280 *Ibid*, Section 44 provides; A doctor called to a patient who is being tended by one of his colleagues must respect the following rules: - if the patient intends to dispense with his first doctor: the second doctor must obtain the patient's express wish and advise his colleague; - if the patient simply wanted to ask an opinion without changing his doctor; the second doctor must suggest a joint consultation and withdraw after having given only the emergency treatment necessary. In the case where, for a valid reason consultation seems impossible or inappropriate, the doctor may examine the patient, but shall reserve for his colleague his opinion on the diagnosis and treatment; - if the patient has, owing to the absence of his usual doctor, called upon him, he must give him all treatment necessary until his colleague returns and give him all necessary information.

281 *Ibid.*, Section 43.

defend fellow colleagues who are unjustly criticized, and this is deemed good professional conduct[282]. However, these provisions seem to militate against the giving of expert evidence in court. It is not clear whether evidence against the professional conduct of a colleague will amount to slander or ridicule of a colleague. This partly explains why it is difficult to secure expert evidence in cases of medical malpractice because doctors are generally reluctant to give evidence against a colleague in keeping with the ethics of the profession. The result of all these is a culture of indifference amongst doctors who indulge in malpractices.

3.3.2 Compliance with the Provisions of the Law Organizing Medical Practice in Cameroon

Medical practice in Cameroon is governed by law No. 90-36 of 10th August 1990 relating to the Organization and Practice of Medicine, and its application Decree No. 92-265-PM of 22 July 1992. This law regulates the registration procedures for practitioners in Cameroon. It sets out strict procedures to be complied with by medical doctors engaged in private practice. Given that the activities of medical practitioners' touches on the health and well-being of citizens, compliance to these registration requirements are mandatory.

3.3.2.1 Obligation to Obtain a License

By virtue of Section 2(1) of the above-mentioned law, the general practice of medicine in Cameroon is subject to a prior registration with the Cameroon Medical Association[283]. Prerequisite for membership into the Association are; Cameroonian nationality, attainment of the age of majority under civil law, possession of a State Degree or a University Doctor of Medicine Degree or their recognized equivalent. In addition, intending members must not have

282 *Ibid.*, Section 42(3).

283 The section states "persons engaged in the practice of medicine in Cameroon shall be subject to registration with the Medical Association" The second paragraph of that section states that " however, physicians of foreign nationality who fulfill the following additional conditions may engage in the practice of medicine in Cameroon: - nationals of a country with a reciprocity agreement with Cameroon - physicians who have not been struck off the roll in their countries of origin or in any other country where they had practiced medicine - physicians recruited on contract or under a co-operation agreement exclusively for the Administration, a religious body or benevolent Non-Governmental Organization (NGO) - physicians serving an approved private undertaking. The medical association is an association of all medical practitioners practicing in Cameroon.

been convicted of any ethical violation, declared bankrupt or be in a state of legal liquidation. Once registered, the doctor, within the exercise of his duties, shall be bound by the respect of law, professional secrecy, the Code of Ethics[284], and the statutory provisions of the Association[285]. The violation of these rules may result in civil, penal, and administrative liabilities of the medical professional.

This law also sets out the registration requirements for private practice of medicine in Cameroon. Where these requirements are not complied with anyone involved in private practice will be guilty of illegal practice of medicine. According to this law, an intending private practitioner must; obtain a license to practice issued by the Cameroon Medical Council, subject to the approval of the Supervisory Authority[286], which is the Ministry of Public Health. The intending private practitioner must be of Cameroonian nationality, must be registered with the Cameroon Medical Association and must be of good conduct. He/she must have effectively practiced for five years in a public or private service within Cameroon or abroad, and must take a yearly insurance policy from an approved national insurance company to cover his/her occupational hazard. Civil servants and government contract employees in active service are precluded from private practice of medicine in Cameroon[287]. Therefore, for the protection of society, the state through this law, exclude from practice those who have no license to practice, or who are found upon examination not to be fully qualified. This protects the public from charlatans and amateur medical practitioners.

However, compliance to the above provisions of the law is a far cry. There are many civil servants who are engaged in private practice of medicine, and who even prioritize their private practice over their public service responsibility. Moreover, some private practitioners actually practice without being registered with the Cameroon Medical Association. Most of them operate in private medical centres lacking the necessary equipment and human resources to function effectively. This outright violation of the law exhibits the lack of will by the government to effectively execute its own laws. Despite the efforts undertaken by the government through the Ministry of

---

284 The Minister of Public Health.

285 Law No 90/36 of 10th August 1990 Relating to the Organization and Practice of Medicine in Cameroon Section 4.

286 *Ibid.*, Section 5(1) and 8.

287 *Ibid.*, Section 13.

Public Health to crack down on these unauthorized health institutions, the number is growing on a daily basis.

Though this law prescribes sanctions for unlawful practice of medicine, it has not deterred unscrupulous practitioners from engaging in such activities. According to this law, unlawful practice of medicine include; practicing without a license, practicing under an assumed name, practicing while on suspension, practicing in a business premises where medical apparatus is sold, engaging in consultation and diagnosis and treatment without authorization, and physicians offering assistance to persons who are not authorized to practice medicine[288].

Persons guilty of unlawful practice of medicine are punished with imprisonment of from six days to six months or with fine of from two hundred thousand francs to two million francs or with both such imprisonment and fine[289]. Moreover, the Cameroon Medical Council may also order closure of the establishment irrespective of any court judgments[290]. The effective implementation of this law is yet to be achieved. There are numerous persons engaged in consultation and diagnosis unauthorized.

3.3.2.2 Obligation to take an Insurance Policy

Doctors in their services cannot completely eliminate human errors. With the development of law, such errors expose them to risk of claims from patients who have suffered loss due to perceived or real neglect, error or omission. This can pose a significant threat to the financial security of a medical practitioner. The amount they can be sued for can be very high. Doctors therefore require special insurance so as to protect themselves both financially and legally when they are sued. Professional indemnity is an insurance plan to financially safeguard medical practitioners against legal costs[291].

Hospitals can be held directly liable for their own negligence, as well as be held vicariously liable for the negligent action of an employee. Professional indemnity insurance is also essential for the technical staff and nurses in the hospital. This will assist doctors to approach their professional commitments

288 *Ibid.*, Section 16.

289 *Ibid*, Section 17.

290 *Ibid.*

291 Mathur, M C., (2020), "Professional Medical Indemnity Insurance- Protection for the Experts, by the Experts", *Indian Journal of Ophthalmology*, 68(1), Pp.3-5.

with full confidence, and enables them to take risk, thereby increasing their professional output[292].

In Cameroon, private practitioners are obligated to take out a yearly insurance policy as a prerequisite to obtain a license to practice. The law on the Organization and Practice of Medicine stipulates that;

> *Every physician or partnership of physicians shall be bound to take an insurance policy from an approved national insurance company to cover his or its occupational hazards. The receipt of the insurance policy shall be deposited with the Council of the Association at the beginning of each calendar year*[293].

In fact, failure by private practitioners to take out a yearly insurance policy shall lead to the temporary closure of the establishment by the Cameroon Medical Council[294].

However, most private medical establishments take an insurance policy at the inception or the first year of operation after which they hardly take for the other years. This goes unnoticed, mainly because; the supervision and control mechanisms of private medical establishment in Cameroon is weak.

3.4 Compliance with Standards of Regulatory Bodies

The institutional structure regulating the practice of medicine in Cameroon includes all actors involved in the regulation of medical practice both national and international. The National framework which will be considered here comprises; the Cameroon Ministry of Public Health and the Cameroon Medical Council. While at the International level, the World Health Organization, the World Medical Council, and the African Medical Association will be examined. These institutions set standards requiring compliance by medical practitioners in Cameroon. These standards oblige doctors to put up their best practices and to consider patient safety as primordial.

---

[292] Why Do Doctors Need Insurance? – Reliance General Insurance, at http//www.reliancegeneral.co. (accessed on 17th day of July 2022).

[293] Section 15(1) of Law No. 90/036 of 10th August 1990.

[294] *Ibid.*, Section 15(2) Failure to take out an insurance policy shall, on the instructions of the Council of the Association or the supervisory authority, lead to the temporary closure of the establishment. Such establishment may be re-opened only on presentation of the receipt showing payment of the insurance policy.

3.4.1 Compliance with Standards of National Regulatory Bodies

This section will analyze compliance to standards required by the Ministry of Public Health and the Cameroon Medical Council. However, due to inefficient monitoring most of these standards are hardly observed by practitioners.

3.4.1.1 Compliance with Standards Fixed by the Ministry in charge of Public Health

The Ministry in charge of Public Health in Cameroon, governed by Decree No 2013/093 of 03/04/2013, on the organization of the Ministry in charge of Public Health, is responsible for the study and implementation of health policies in Cameroon[295]. It strives to increase the performance of the health system at all levels through; standardization, regulation, accountability. It also strengthens supervision and coordination, and monitoring at all levels of the health pyramid[296]. In addition, it ensures that penalties for unethical practices are actually executed. It sets standards for the procedures of the approval and marketing of pharmaceuticals[297] to which all those involved in the domain must comply with. It also defines the terms and conditions for supplying health facilities with essential drugs and other pharmaceutical products[298]. The Ministry controls the importation of pharmaceutical products and medical devices, and in vitro diagnostic reagents[299]. It regulates the prescription of medicinal products used in the treatment of infection due to COVID-19[300]. It also controls the availability of certain drugs like tramadol[301].

The Ministry in charge of Public Health standardizes the prices of essential drugs in the public sector to make it affordable to those in remote areas where

295 Article 2 of Presidential Decree No. 2002/209 of 19 August 2002 on the Organization of the Ministry of Public Health as amended.

296 Ministry of Health, Health Sector Strategy 2016-2027

297 Decree No. 98/405/PM of October 22, 1998 Setting the Procedure for the Approval and Marketing of Pharmaceutical Products.

298 See Order No. 3827/MINSANTE of 5th December 2018 Defining the Terms and Conditions for Supplying Health Facilities with Essential Drugs and Other Pharmaceutical Products.

299 See Circular Letter of June 04 2020 Relating to the Control of Imports of Pharmaceutical Products in General and Medical Devices and in vitro Diagnostic Reagents in Particular.

300 See Circular Letter of march 23, 2020 relating to the Control of Prescription of Medicinal Products used in the treatment of infection due to the new coronavirus (COVID-19).

301 Circular Letter of December 02, 2019, relating to the Placing under Control of Tramadol.

poverty rate is high. Through Decision No. 0406/D/MINSANTE/CAB of 23 June 2014[302], it set prices and modalities for the diagnosis and treatment of malaria. It also establishes prices for malaria rapid diagnostic kits[303]. Indeed, Article 3 of the Decision No 0118/D/MINSANTE/CAB of March 13 2012, provides that rapid diagnostic test for malaria and consultation for children under the age of 5 years is free, it further provides that this test for patients above 5 years is 200 francs CFA in public health facilities.

The Ministry also develops standards for equipment in health facilities at the operational level. Unfortunately, these standards are not often respected. Indeed, a study conducted identified lack of delivery kits (25.5 per cent), dry heat sterilization system (39.5 per cent), caesarean section kits (67.5 per cent), and functional microscopes (11.6 per cent) in health facilities[304].

It establishes the form and procedure for the opening of pharmaceutical establishments and laboratories of medical biology in Cameroon, and grants approval for medical establishments and laboratories to operate[305]. The Ministry also controls the creation of medical training centres by granting authorization for the functioning of such centres and orders the closure of such where it fails to meet requirements. It is also responsible for administrative and technical supervisions of such healthcare centres. The supervision by the Ministry of Public Health is aimed at ensuring an efficient management of healthcare centres[306]. However, the control of authorization granted by the Ministry is not effective. When applying to open a health facility, most applicants use 'borrowed names' and do not respect the regulatory processing period; most of these health establishments after depositing their application to operate, go ahead and start functioning without waiting for the necessary approval.

Nonetheless, in order to bring order in the Medical Sector which has gone out of control with anybody being able to own a medical institution, in 2013, the Ministry led a campaign to crack down on illegal clinics and medical training institutions that have sprung up all over the country, most of which operate without a license, and some others operating illegally from

---

302 Decision No 0406/D/MINSANTE.CAB Of 23 June 2014 on The Pricing of Treatment for Severe Malaria in Cameroon.

303 Decision No 0118/D/MINSANTE/CAB of March 13M 2012.

304 Institute Nationale de la Statistique 2eme enquête sur le suivi de Dépense Publiques et le niveau de satisfaction des bénéficiaires dans les Secteurs de l'éducation et de la Sante au Cameroun (PETS 2) : Rapport Principal, volet Sante, 2010.

305 See *supra* note 350.

306 *Ibid.*

private homes. More than five hundred medical training centres and over six hundred private clinics were set to be closed in a four-month operation launched in December 2013[307]. Again in 2017[308], in a bid to restore sanity in Cameroon health sector, the Ministry in charge of Public Health carried out an investigation and uncovered about two thousand illegal private health care centres in Cameroon some operating without a license, while others operating in buildings originally constructed for residential purposes[309].

Despite all these, the proliferation of illegal private clinics persists in Cameroon. The campaign of the Minister did not deter perpetrators of illegal medical practice. It may be concluded that what the Minister did was just a formality with no concrete actions. From 2013 to 2017, the number of illegal private health care centres increased from over six hundred to about two thousand[310]. This is clear indication of malfunctioning of State Institutions.

Most recently[311], in a press release, the Ministry in charge of Public Health invites the general public to denounce cases of abuses in health facilities by calling a toll-free number-1506. This is a bold step by the Minister to instill standards and supervision of health personnel. It is yet to be seen what this will achieve in the long run.

As a Supervisory Authority of the Cameroon Medical Council, the Ministry in charge of Public Health acts in curtailing the privileges of self-regulation and self-policing of the Cameroon Medical Council. Though it is argued that more stringent governmental oversight of health professions impinges on their independence, government actions to restrict self-regulation is necessary where professions fail to supervise their members adequately[312]. The Ministry as the Supervisory Authority must give prior approval for an application from any physician wishing to engage in private practice in Cameroon.[313]. Indeed,

---

307 "Cameroon Clamps Down on Illicit Clinics", January 2014,Relief Web, online at http://reliefweb.int/report/cameroon/cameroon-clamps-down-illicit-clinics. (accessed on the 22nd^h day of January 2021).

308 Journal du Cameroun 10/4/2017, "2000 Illegal Hospitals Uncovered in Cameroon", at https://www.journalducameroun.com/en/2000-illegal-hospitals-uncovered-cameroon/ (accessed on the 14th day of April 2021).

309 Press statement from the Ministry of Public Health in 2017 revealed that out of 3,343 private, secular and confessional health facilities operating in Cameroon, 1,055 have at least an authorization, 2,288 are illegal and 75 were without settlement areas.

310 See *supra* note 363.

311 Press Release of 15 February 2021, Cellule De Communication No. D13-30/MINSANTE/SG/CC.

312 Ries, N M., (2014), "*Health Professionals and the Organization of Health Care*", Routeledge Handbook of Medical Law and Ethics.

313 See *supra* note 348, Section 36(3).

the Law[314] provides that the decisions of the Cameroon Medical Council must be submitted to the Supervisory Authority for prior approval, this implies that even if the Council approves an application, the Supervisory Authority, has the authority to revoke such an approval. The decision as to whether to admit any medical doctor to private practice therefore, rest wholly with the Ministry in charge of Public Health. In effect, all decisions of the Cameroon Medical Council must be submitted to the Supervisory Authority for prior approval failure of which it will be null and void[315].

3.4.1.2 Compliance with Standards of the Cameroon Medical Council

Professional Associations, as definers and guarantors of efficient medical practice, have an implied contract with society to hold their members accountable[316]. Medical Councils set out expected standards in relation to quality and accountability to which compliance is obligatory. They also highlight the duty a medical professional has to the profession, the wider community and the organization in which he/she is working. They empower patients to pursue malpractice suits as a means to hold health providers accountable by sanctioning defaulting practitioners. Overall, they serve as the institutional structure of checks and balances of medical practice. Their overriding mission is to serve the public by protecting it from incompetent, unprofessional, and improperly trained physicians. Medical boards accomplish this by striving to ensure that only qualified physicians are licensed to practice medicine and that they provide their patients with a high standard of care[317].

The Cameroon Medical Council, in its organization is geared towards achieving this goal. It sets entry-to-practice requirements, establish professional standards, investigate complaints, and exercise disciplinary powers. It ensures compliance with the principles of moral conduct and devotion essential to the practice of medicine as well as guard over the observance and strict application of the rules prescribe by the Code of Ethics[318].

---

314 *Ibid.*, Section 8(3).

315 *Ibid.*, Section 38.

316 Sylvia, R C. et al. (2000), "Professionalism: A Contract between Medicine and Society", *Canadian Medical Association Journal,162(5)*, pp.668-669.

317 Carlson, D. and Thompson, J N., (2005), "The Role of State Medical Boards", *Virtual Mentor,*7(4), pp.311-314.

318 See *supra* note 348, Section 20.

The Council is competent to rule on the application for enrolment into the Medical Association, approve application to practice medicine on a private basis, and take disciplinary measures against defaulting members of the Association. Decisions on the eligibility to practice medicine in Cameroon rest with the Medical Council subject to prior approval of the Ministry in charge of Public Health. Its decisions shall not be influenced by the political or religious acts or beliefs of its members[319]. The Council precludes any one declared to be a convict, bankrupt or insolvent from the practice of medicine in Cameroon[320].

The application to practice medicine on a private basis is governed by Decree No 92-265-Pm of July 22, 1992 setting the terms of application of Law No 90/036 of August 10, 1990 relating to the exercise and organization of the medical profession. It is addressed to the Medical Council[321]. It is subject to very strict compliance procedure[322]. Article 21 (1) of the above Decree provides that; "A license to practice in private is personal and not transferable. It indicates the location where the applicant is required to perform his art. It is granted to allow work in a private clinic, or to open a private clinic".

The Council carries out an investigation to ascertain the compliance of the institution of required standards before granting the application[323]. However,

---

319 *Ibid.*, Sections 25-32.

320 *Ibid.*, Section 35.

321 See Article 19 of Decree No 92-265-Pm of July 22, 1992 setting the terms of application of Law No. 90/036 of August 10, 1990 relating to the exercise and organization of the medical profession.

322 *Ibid*, Article 20(1) states that the authorization to practice on a private basis is subject to the production of a file, in duplicate, at the Medical Council headquarters filed against receipt and including: - A stamped request; - A certificate of nationality dated within than three (3) months; - A certified copy of the birth certificate dated within three (3) months copy; - A certified copy of the degree of Doctor of Medicine copy and, where appropriate specialty certificates and a certificate presentation said the original diploma and certificates; - An extract from criminal record dating less than three (3) months; - A certificate of professional experience of a minimum of five (5) years from the date of application to perform personally, issued by a government or employer organization; - A certificate of registration to the roll of the Order issued by the Council of the Order; - A letter of agreement in principle last release issued by the employer, if applicable; - Proof of payment of all dues to the Order issued by the Council of the Order

323 *Ibid*, Article 23 Article 23 (1) If the doctor feels he has completed his medical training to develop in accordance with the regulations, it shall inform the Council of the Order, which, in turn, took the Minister of Public Health means everywhere with written proof. (2) The Council and the Public Health Authority have, upon notification of the completion of a period of thirty (30) days to visit this training before opening to the public. If at the expiration of that period, the Council and public health Authority are not manifested, the doctor can open his clinic to the public. Article 24 (1) When the site visit reveals that the facilities do not allow to practice according to the basic rules of the art, the deficiencies shall be notified to the applicant who must fix it. (2) The opening of the facility to the public is permitted only after verification by the College Council and Public Health Authority, modifications required. Verification in the manner prescribed in Article

most often what prevails in the field is that after submitting the application, the clinic or hospital commences operation immediately and the approval or disapproval decision is of no moment. Article 26 further provides that the licensed physician in private practice should not practice in more than one clinic at a time or own more than one clinic.

The Council receives complaints about the conduct of physicians from the legal department, the supervisory authority or a physician. It also exercises jurisdiction over cases of violation of the provisions of Code of Medical Ethic[324]. It may also institute a complaint when it considers that the doctor has refused, failed or ceased to cooperate with the duty to maintain professional competence. The Disciplinary Board of the Council[325], evaluates whether a physician's professional conduct or ability to practice medicine warrants modification, suspension, or revocation of the license to practice.

The Cameroon Medical Council ensures that there is compliance to its sanction. It can reprimand a practitioner, suspend or remove his name from the register, or take such other disciplinary action against a doctor as may, in the opinion of Council be necessary or expedient[326]. The ultimate goal is to foster the professional practice of medicine and protect the public from unprofessional, improper and incompetent actions. It can conduct inquiries into facts which it deems useful for its proceedings, hold hearings and pronounce disciplinary sanctions. Section 48 of the Law organizing the practice of medicine in Cameroon[327] spells out these sanctions. They include; warning, reprimand, suspension and striking off the Roll of the Association.

Though, a physician will hardly bring a colleague before the Disciplinary Board because of their ethical obligations towards each other[328]. Moreover, the dominance of medical professionals in this Disciplinary Board has the effect of limiting the proper execution of sanctions. This runs counter to the global trend where lay representation is rising on medical regulatory boards.

Certainly, the Council has made some strides although not fruitful, at curbing illegal practice of medicine in Cameroon. In 2015, the Cameroon Medical Council called on the government to shut down about one thousand

23, paragraph (2).

324 See Section 58(1) of Decree No. 83/166 of 12 April 1983 on Code of Medical Ethics in Cameroon.

325 See *supra* note 348, Section 41.

326 *Ibid*, Section 48

327 *Ibid.*

328 See *supra* note 379, Section 42(1) stipulates that; doctors owe each other moral support and (2) provides that; It shall be forbidden to slander or disparage a colleague, or to repeat any remarks likely to harm him in the practice of his profession.

illegal and clandestine hospitals scattered all over the country[329]. The Council found out that these hospitals were operating without the necessary manpower and equipment, thereby putting the lives of millions of people in danger. The Council noted that in such hospitals unqualified doctors, nurses, laboratory technicians, midwives and others are practicing without any control thereby exposing people to early deaths. The Council said all doctors working in such hospitals and who are not members of the Council are practicing illegally, and it cannot continue to be silent while many people are suffering in the hands of charlatans[330]. Yet these illegal hospitals keep operating in flagrant violation of the requirements of this regulatory authority.

However, the Cameroon Medical Council in compelling compliance to ethical norms is limited in its function as all decisions of the Council must be subject to prior approval by the Supervisory Authority, failure of which the decision will be declared null and void[331]. This has the tendency to limit the primary function of the Council. The case of Marie 'O' Polyclinic in Douala is a vivid example. The Minister in charge of Public Health on May 13, 2020, directly ordered for the closure of Marie 'O' Polyclinic on grounds of excessive bills to patient,[332] upon receipt of a complaint by a Lebanese family of excessive bills issued by the clinic. Accordingly, it is the Disciplinary Board of the Medical Council which is supposed to take a decision to that effect and forward it to the Supervisory Authority (the Ministry of Public Health) for approval. But this was not the case. In fact, the Council was taken aback by the decision of the Minister and fumed that the Minister did not follow due process. The National Syndicate of Private Doctors (SYNAMEC) said no investigation was carried out and the doctor involved was not heard by the Disciplinary Board as provided by the Law[333]. This act of the Minister in charge

329 Kindzeka, M E., (2015),"Cameroon Medical Council Calls for Closure of Illegal Hospitals", *VOA*, at https://Www.Voanews.Com/Africa/Cameroon-Medical-Council-Calls-Closure-Illegal-Hospitals. (accessed on the 14th day of April2021).

330 *Ibid.*

331 Supra note 348, Section 38.

332 Pefok, J D., (2020), "Ministers Decision to Shut Down Douala Health Unit Sparks Controversy, Hon. Nintcheu calls on Health Minister to Resign", *Cameroon Post line*, at http//cameroonpostline.com/ministers-decision-to-shut-down-douala-health-unit-sparks-controversy-hon-nintcheu-calls-on-health-minister-to-resign/%E2%. (accessed on the 9th day of March 2021).

333 See supra note 348, section 47 provides; (1) No disciplinary sanction may be pronounced unless the physician accused has been heard or summoned to appear before the Board within a period of 30 (thirty) days following receipt of the summons with acknowledgement of receipt. (2) Where the accused physician fails to appear before the Disciplinary Board after a duty notified summons, the Board may make its rulings.

of Public Health in arbitrarily violating legislative provision[334], demonstrates vividly the ineffectiveness of the Cameroon Medical Council in fulfiling its mission of ensuring compliance to medical rules of practice.

3.4.2 Compliance with Standards of International Regulatory Bodies

Health Professional Associations facilitate best-practice sharing by serving as a key means for promoting continuous learning and the pursuit of high-quality clinical care among health professionals[335]. They play a key role in supporting national policies and high standards in health system delivery through the development of model regulatory frameworks and ethical and professional standards[336].

However, International and Regional associations may monitor the implementation of policy and practice, and raise awareness of issues, but their ability to directly enforce policies or modify national service delivery is limited. Their role as watchdogs and advocates is therefore all the more critical, as is their ability to access high-level forums and policymakers. They are also not financially sustainable. While some Regional associations collect membership fees, these are often nominal and insufficient to support the operational costs of the organization. Moreover, where multiple associations are operating in a given technical area with similar missions and objectives, it sometimes results to duplication of efforts and poor use of resources.

This section will examine the World Health Organization, World Medical Association and the African Medical Association in their role of setting standards and ensuring compliance to rules of medical practice in Cameroon.

3.4.2.1 Compliance with Standards of World Health Organization

The World Health Organization (WHO) is a specialized United Nations agency with a constitutional mandate as the "Directing and Coordinating

334 *Ibid.*

335 Rice, J., (2013), "Strong Health Professional Associations 2020: Promoting the Long-Term Viability of Health Professional Associations (Hpas) in Sub- Saharan Africa", Discussion Paper. *Management Sciences for Health* – LMG Project.

336 African Strategies for Health, (2014), "Regional Network and Associations: Results from a Landscape Analysis of Regional Health Sector Actors in Africa: Comparative Advantages, Challenges and Opportunities", *USAID*, pp.9-11.

authority on international health work"[337]. It was founded in April 7, 1948 and is made up of 194 member states[338]. The structure of WHO comprise the World Health Assembly (WHA) which is the decision-making body. WHO adheres to the United Nations values of integrity, professionalism and respect for diversity. These values reflect the principles of human rights, universality, ethical standards and equity established in WHO's Constitution. One of the three core functions of WHO[339] is its normative functions, which include international conventions and agreements, regulations and non-binding standards and recommendations[340].

The main objective of WHO is the attainment by all peoples of the highest possible level of health[341]. In this regard it works side by side with government and other partners to ensure the highest attainable level of health for all people[342]. It assists governments upon request in strengthening health policies[343], promote improved standards of teaching and training in the health, medical and related professions[344], and to standardize diagnostic procedures[345]. It set international health standards and guidelines, and gives strong advice to countries regarding rational public health measures[346]. It achieves these by providing directions, advice, and additional support when needed, provide countries with science-based recommendations for healthy policy, which includes the kind of essential medicine, and diagnostics to use in particular situations taking into account the resources of each country. It sets norms and standards and promote and monitor their implementation, articulate ethical and evidence-based policy options and oversees the implementation of the international health regulation[347].

---

337 World Health Organization, United Nations Global Market Place, at https://www.ungm.org/Shared/KnowledgeCenter/Pages/WHO. (accessed on the 9th day of March 2021)

338 Cameroon inclusive.

339 The other two core functions are the directing and coordinating functions; including its health for all, poverty and health, and essential medicine activities and its specific disease programs; research and technical cooperation functions; including disease eradication and emergencies.

340 Ruger J P. et al, (2009), "The Global Role of The World Health Organization", *Glob Health Gov.* 2(2), pp. 1-11.

341 Article 1, of the Constitution of the World Health Organization.1946.

342 World Health Organization, International Affairs online at www.linkedin.com/company/world-health-organisation, (accessed on the 9th day of march 2021)

343 Article 2(c) of WHO Constitution.

344 *Ibid.*, Article 2(o).

345 *Ibid.*, Article 2(t).

346 WHO Health Emergency Programme Director, Michael Ryan, explaining the overreaching mission of WHO in a Press Conference on April 22. 2020.

347 *Ibid.*

Actually, it has set guidelines for the care of the injured, which is a major cause of death and disability worldwide[348]. The burden of injuries can be alleviated by preventive measures and appropriate management of injury cases. In a bid to address this, WHO in collaboration with the International Association for Trauma and Intensive Care (IATSIC), developed the Essential Guidelines for Trauma care[349]. These guidelines aim at strengthening trauma care systems especially in low- and middle-income countries by providing them with reasonable low-cost trauma services.

The WHO/IATSIC Guidelines for essential trauma care have demonstrated their usefulness in assessing and promoting affordable and sustainable tools for improving trauma care capabilities[350]. Hospitals are encouraged to comply with these guidelines in taking care of injured victims. However, most hospitals in Cameroon are generally not compliant or partly compliant with the guidelines. It was discovered that hospital staff generally have received the appropriate basic training but had no additional training specifically directed towards trauma management. Skills for managing specific injuries are poor, availability and utilization of equipment is generally inadequate, and organization capabilities are non-existent[351].

WHO improves on medical training internationally in order to develop the quality and safety of medical practice, equity and equality in health care. It does this through formal training standards expressed in published guidelines. The justification for standardization of medical training is as a result of the multiplication of new medical schools worldwide, many of which are private, and of unknown quality, which appear to pose a problem to the international mobility of medical students and physician[352]. WHO in collaboration with the World Federation for Medical Education (WFME) through this standardization sought to directly influence national medical associations

---

348 Mathers, C D. *et al*, (2009), Global and Regional Causes of Death, *British Medical Bulletin*, 92(1), pp. 7-32.

349 Mock, C. *et al*, (2004), Global Strengthening of Care for the Injured, *Bull World Health Organisation*, 82(4), p.241.

350 Chichom-Mefire, A. *et al*, (2014) "Compliance of District Hospitals in the Center Region of Cameroon with WHO/IATSIC Guidelines for the Care of the Injured: A Cross-Sectional Analysis", *World Journal of Surgery*, 38(10), pp.2525-33.

351 *Ibid.*

352 Executive Council, the Education International Standards in Medical Education: Assessment and Accreditation of Medical Schools'-Educational programmes. A World Federation for Medical Education position Paper. Med Educ. at https://Doi.Org/10.1046/J.1365-2923.1998.00302. (accessed on the 20th day of July 2022).

and educational facilities[353]. It is built on the concept of community oriented medical education, that is to say, the education of health personnel should be relevant to the needs of the population being served.

In 1996 WHO outlined training requirements for doctors in its Global Strategy for Reforming Medical Training. It called on member states to support collaborative effort to define 'the desired profile of the future doctor'. This global strategy outlined five key skill sets for physicians viz; care provider, decision maker, communicator, community leader and manager. Biomedical and scientific knowledge was deemphasized in favour of communication and leadership skills that support a health promotion and community-oriented approach to medical practice[354]. Regional offices of WHO were task with offering technical support to member states as they implemented these recommendations, and also to monitor the outcome. However, it has been conceded that this recommended standard has been implemented in many but by no means the majority of medical schools.

International regulatory co-operation is at the heart of WHO's mandate. WHO strengthens regulatory systems through capacity building, and assessment. WHO aids National Regulatory Authorities fulfil their mandate[355] in an effective, efficient, predictable and transparent manner which is of critical importance in ensuring the quality, safety and efficacy of health products in an increasingly complex global environment. The Regulation and Safety priorities of WHO with regards to medical products are based on an adopted Five-Year Plan to help build effective and efficient regulatory systems entitled "Delivering Quality Assured Medical Products[356] for all 2019-2023". This plan is designed to assist national regulators to deliver regulation that protects the public while enabling timely access to quality products and encouraging innovation[357].

---

353 Weisz, G. and Nannestad, B., (2021), "The World Health Organization and the Global Standardization of Medical Training, A History", *Weisz and Nannestad Globalization and Health*, 17(96), p. 6.

354 World Health Organization, Division of Development of Human Resources for Health. Doctors For Health: A WHO Global Strategy for Changing Medical Education and Medical Practice for Health for All (WHO/HRH/96.1) GENEVA: WHO:1996, 5-8. at https://apps.who.int/iris/handle/10665/62997. (accessed on the 21st day of July 2022).

355 National Regulatory Authorities play a vital role in the health care system by providing regulatory oversight of all medical products such as medicines, vaccines, blood products, traditional or herbal medicines and medical devices.

356 Medical products included; medicines, vaccines, medical devices, including invitro diagnostics and vector control products.

357 World Health Organization, Regulation and Prequalification, available. at https://www.who.int/teams/regulation-prequalification/regulation-and-safety. (accessed on the 13th day of march

WHO facilitates the development and dissemination of drugs, vaccines and diagnostics. The WHO Secretariat has over time develop a wide range of guidelines[358] and recommendations[359] intended to assist national program managers, providers, and other stakeholders make informed decisions with respect to health care delivery[360]. The development of such guidelines follows specific internal procedures and criteria which aim at ensuring that guidelines are free from conflict of interest, meet a public health need and are consistent with the principles of a comprehensive and objective assessment of the available evidence and of transparency.

So far, the WHO has mainly exercised its normative function through the adoption of recommendations by the Health Assembly, styled as "resolutions" or sometimes as "decisions", as well the development of a diverse range of technical standards by the Secretariat[361]. Irrespective of the many names that can be assigned these recommendations (for example; codes, strategies, global plans of action, road maps or frameworks), such recommendations are not legally binding upon States. Countries are not under any legal obligations to follow these recommendations.

In addition, WHO does not have any legal authority to force countries to take its advice, no power to enforce; no power to put any form of pressure on countries to change what is their sovereign will[362]. It relies on contribution from member states and private donors for funding; this dependency puts pressure on the organization to align its goals with those of its donors. Many global health scholars have argued that WHO's reliance on voluntary and earmarked contributions creates a situation where external donors dictate the organization's priorities and action agenda[363].

Nevertheless, these recommendations represent the agreed outcome of extensive governing body consideration, and consultation processes with

---

2021).

358 That is; any document developed by the WHO containing recommendations for clinical practice or public health policy.

359 Recommendations are statements designed to help end-users make informed decisions on whether, when and how to undertake specific actions such as clinical interventions, diagnostic tests or public health measures, with the aim of achieving the best possible individual or collective health outcomes.

360 WHO Guidelines, online at https://www.who.int/publications/who-guidelines, (accessed on the 16th day of March 2021).

361 WHO Health Emergency Program Director, Micheal Ryan, explaining the overreaching mission of WHO. in a Press Conference on April 22. 2020.

362 Gostin, L O., (2015), "The future of the World Health Organization: Lessons Learned from Ebola". *The Milbank Quarterly*, 93(3), pp.475–9.

363 *Ibid.*

Member States and other stakeholders, and have been adopted by some member states, especially by national medical regulatory authorities, in framing their national standards for medical practice.

3.4.2.2 Compliance with Standards of the World Medical Association

The World Medical Association (WMA) is an International Organization representing physicians all over the world. Founded on 17 September 1947 in Paris, this organization was created to ensure the independence of physicians and to work for the highest possible standards of ethical behaviour and care by physicians at all times[364]. The purpose of the WMA is to serve humanity by endeavouring to achieve the highest international standards in medical education, medical science, medical art and medical ethics and health care for all people in the world[365]. It provides a forum for its members to communicate freely, to cooperate actively to achieve consensus on high standards of medical ethics and professional competence, and to promote the professional freedom of physicians worldwide[366]. The Cameroon Medical Association is a constituent member of WMA.

In 1948 the General Assembly of the World Medical Association modified the Hippocratic Oath with a view to aligning it with the practice and language of modern medicine. It was named the Declaration of Geneva. Not only does it address the attitude of the medical doctor vis-à-vis the patient, but it also emphasizes on the respect of dignity of the profession, medical ethics, and colleagues. Also, the standard of treatment as prescribed by the respectable body of medical opinion, and which the medical doctor must comply with is ascertained. In it the physician at the time of being admitted into the profession pledges to serve humanity, to respect human life, to practice with conscience and dignity, to prioritize the health of his/her patient, to maintain confidentiality, and not to use medical knowledge contrary to the laws of humanity[367]. The Cameroon Medical Code of Ethics is drafted along the lines of the Declaration of Geneva, as it spells out the duties of the physician, his relationship with patients, and with fellow colleagues.

---

364 World Medical Association, online at https://www.wma.net/who-we-are/about-us/ (accessed on the 6ht day of January 2021).

365 *Ibid.*

366 *Ibid.*

367 *Ibid.*

In October 1949, the 3rd General Assembly of WMA adopted the International Code of Medical Ethics known as the WMA International Code of Medical Ethics[368]. This Code was subsequently amended in 1968, 1983 and 2006 by the General Assembly of WMA. It is based on the Geneva Declaration. The Code spells out the general duties of the physician. It requires the physician to always exercise his/her independent professional judgment and maintain the highest standards of professional conduct. He/she must not be influenced in his judgment by personal profit or unfair discrimination. He/she shall be dedicated to provide competent services with compassion and respect for human dignity, respect human life, act in the patient's best interest, respect patient's right to confidentiality, and must not enter into any sexual, abusive or exploitative relationship with his/her patient. The Code encouraged physicians to report to appropriate authorities, colleagues who practice unethically or incompetently or who engage in fraud or deception. They are also expected to use health care resources in the best way to benefit patients and the community. Again, the Code compels doctors to respect National Code of Ethics[369]. The International Code of Ethics thus provides guidelines from which national medical associations can draw inspiration in drafting their national code of ethics.

The WMA provides ethical guidance to physicians through its Declarations, Resolution and Statements, which go a long way to guide National Medical Associations, Government and International Organization in the world. One of such ethical declarations is the 1975 Declaration of Tokyo, the first international statement specifically prohibiting medical complicity and participation in torture and cruel treatment even when the doctors are under threat[370]. This Declaration calls for complete clinical independence in the treatment of all patients and urges the international community to support doctors who face threat of reprisals for opposing torture. It further emphasizes the fundamental role of the doctor which is to alleviate the distress of his or her fellowman, and no motive, whether personal, collective or political shall prevail against this higher purpose[371].

---

368 World Medical Association International Code of Medical Ethics at http://www.wma.net/policies/WMA.(accessed on the 23rd day of July 2022).

369 *Ibid.*

370 British Medical Association, *The Medical Profession and Human Rights: Handbook for a Changing Agenda*, London, Zed Books Ltd, 2001, p.3.

371 *Ibid.*

Another important declaration by the WMA is the Declaration of Madrid on professionally-led regulation adopted in 2009[372]. This Declaration underscores the importance of professional self-regulation and the responsibilities that goes with it. This includes the responsibility to ensure the competence of members, enforce compliance with code of ethics, delivery of high-quality care for patience and provide transparent regulation that foster public trust and confidence[373]. National Professional Medical Associations are to comply with this responsibility in their regulatory function.

In 2019, the WMA adopted the World Medical Association Declaration on Euthanasia and Physician Assisted Suicide[374]. In this declaration the WMA reiterates its strong commitment to the principles of medical ethics, and utmost respect for human life. The WMA is firmly opposed to euthanasia and physician-assisted suicide. It defines euthanasia as a physician deliberately administering a lethal substance or carrying out an intervention to cause the death of a patient with decision-making capacity, at the patient's own voluntary request[375]. Physician-assisted suicide refers to cases in which, at the voluntary request of a patient with decision-making capacity, a physician deliberately enables a patient to end his or her own life by prescribing or providing medical substances with the intent to bring about death. In this Declaration, no physician should be forced to participate in euthanasia or assisted suicide, nor should any physician be obliged to make referral decisions to this end. However, the physician who respects the basic right of the patient to decline medical treatment does not act unethically in forgoing or withholding unwanted care, even if respecting such a wish results in the death of the patient[376]. This is echoed in the Cameroon Code of Medical ethics which uphold respect of life, by reiterate the doctor's obligation to respect life in the exercise of his profession.

The WMA Statement on Health Care Information for All[377] reiterate the need for access to relevant, reliable, unbiased, up-to-date and evidence-based

---

372 Ries, N M., (2014), "*Health Professionals and the Organization of Health Care*", Routeledge Handbook of Medical Law and Ethics.

373 *Ibid.*

374 Adopted by the 70th WMA General Assembly, Tbilisi, Georgia, October 2019.

375 The World Medical Association Declaration on Euthanasia and Physician Assisted Suicide, 2019. at https://www.wma.net/policies-post/declaration-on-euthanasia-and-physician-assisted-suicide/ (accessed on the 29th day of march 2021).

376 *Ibid.*

377 Health Care Information for All, Adopted by the 70th WMA General Assembly, Tbilisi, Georgia, October 2019.

healthcare information which is crucial for the public, patients and health personnel. Healthcare information is only useful if it is relevant, appropriate, timely, updated, understandable and accurate. In view of this the World Medical Association Promote initiatives to improve access to timely, current, evidence-based healthcare information for health professionals, patients and the public, to support appropriate decision-making, lifestyle changes, care-seeking behaviour and improved quality of care[378]. By so doing, it will be upholding the right to health, promote standards of good practice and ethics. The WMA urge governments to recognize their moral obligation to take measures to improve the availability and use of evidence-based healthcare information, to ensure that the public, patients and health workers have access to the healthcare information they need to protect their own health and the health of those for whom they are responsible. This includes; measures to increase availability of healthcare information for healthcare workers and patients at health centers[379].

The WMA Declaration of Cordoba on patient-physician relationship adopted in 2020[380] is another declaration which go a long way to ensure quality service and patient care. It emphasizes the importance of patient-physician relationship by stating that the patient-physician relationship is the fundamental core of medical practice. This relationship improves the patient health and wellbeing by knowledge sharing, common decision making, patient and physician autonomy, help, comfort and companionship in an atmosphere of trust. The relationship is also a moral activity that arises from the obligation of the physician to alleviate suffering and respect the patient's beliefs and autonomy[381]. The Cordoba Declaration reaffirms the WMA opposition to interference from governments, other agents and institutional administrations in the practice of medicine, and it reaffirms its dedication to providing competent medical service in full professional and moral independence, with respect for human dignity.

However, the WMA periodic statements have usually been sensitive but poorly publicized. The average doctor and the public at large remain ignorant of its existence and activities[382].

---

[378] *Ibid.*

[379] *Ibid.*

[380] Adopted by the 71st WMA General Assembly in Cordoba, Spain, October 2020.

[381] World Medical Association, at https://Www.Wma.Net/Policies-Post/Wma-Declaration-Of-Cordoba-On-Patient-Physician-Relationship. (accessed on the 6th day of January 2021).

[382] Richards, T., (1994), "The World Medical Association: Can Hope Triumph over Experience?", *British Medical Journal,* 308:6923, pp.262-266.

3.4.2.3 Compliance with Standards of the African Medical Association

The African Medical Association (AfMA), established in 2004 is an African structure of National Medical Associations, whose main objective is to work for the highest possible standard of ethical behavior, and care by physicians at all times. It was created out of the need of African physicians to have a representative body to act as its collective voice and to advocate for better health care for the people of Africa, and also participate actively in world health issues. It advances the art and practice of medicine and act as the representative voice for physicians. It influences policy, launches and participates in projects with the explicit goal of improving health care in Africa. It focuses amongst others in health security, patient information and communication, access to services, products, and devices, and capacity building of National Medical Associations[383].

AfMA acts as the Regional Office of the World Medical Association in Africa. It accepts and endorses the policies, statements and declarations that the WMA makes on global matters, and where appropriate it proposes additional policies or declarations that support its objectives. Through advocacy and action, it attempts to achieve the highest possible standards of health for the patients of the continent.

In its proposed statement[384] on health information to and communication with patients, it states that physicians should always act in the best interest of their patients and all efforts should be made to facilitate respectful communication within the patient-physician relationship, and ensure that patients are fully informed about their health, illnesses and the availability of treatment. In this statement it enumerated some of the principal rights of patients which physicians must support and promote. It stipulates that whenever legislation, governments and administration or institution denies patients these rights, physicians and physician organizations should pursue appropriate means to assure or to restore them. In this regard physicians should always pay specific attention to the unique needs, preferences and values of their patients[385]. This ethical imperative for physicians to always

---

383 Africa Medical Association, at http//africama.net/about-afma.htm. (accessed on the 15th day of march 2021).

384 Proposed Afma Statement of Pilanesberg on Health Information to and Communication with Patients, October 2006.

385 *Ibid.*

serve the best interest of their patients is a guiding principle in optimizing health information and communication practices in health care.

The right to information presupposes that all patients have a fundamental and legitimate right of access to accurate, relevant and comprehensive information to enable them to make informed decisions about healthcare treatment and living with their condition. The patient has the right to choose who, if anyone should be informed on his/her behalf. Information to patients should be easily accessible, timely, accurate, clear, relevant, and reliable and based on evidence or best practice. Information must be presented in an appropriate format, according to health literacy principles, considering the individual's condition, language, age, understanding, abilities and culture[386].

This right also includes communication of risk and benefits, Risks and benefits of healthcare interventions and options should be explained to patients and, where appropriate, to their families. This should specifically include awareness of the risks and benefits of prescribed medicines, and the importance of reporting and managing possible side effects. The right to confidentiality places a demand on doctors to keep private even after death, all identifiable information about a patient's health status, medical conditions, diagnosis, prognosis and treatment and all other information of a personal kind. Confidential information can only be disclosed if the patient gives explicit consent or if expressly provided for in the law.

AfMA supports the training and development of physicians and is committed to facilitate training opportunities for its members[387]. Given the tremendous health burdens of the continent, AfMA employs a rather explicit action-oriented approach, with less focus on meetings and more on projects. It firmly believes in constructively engaging with the World Health Organization (WHO) and other relevant organizations to maximize opportunities to serve the health interests and patients of Africa.

However, the effective compliance with these standards by national medical regulatory bodies and physicians is inadequate.

---

386 *Ibid.*

387 Africa Medical Association, Continuing Professional Development, at https://africama.net/con-professional-dev.htm.(accessed on the 17th day of March 2021).

3.5 Conclusion

Cameroon Code of Medical Ethics encapsulate all the basic principles of medical ethics. This is supported by the law organizing medical practice which in addition to obligations placed on medical practitioners, punishes violation of the provisions contained in the code of ethics. However, they are not enough by themselves, frequent violation of rules of ethics is rife in hospitals which has a negative impact on patients. Again, some of the international laws and standards are neither designed nor sufficiently flexible to address actual dilemmas that arise.

Unethical conduct not only weakens patient-doctor relationship, but also leads to low quality service provision and potentially high incidences of violence and abuse[388], and has the propensity to tarnish the reputation of the entire medical profession[389]. Recently, materialistic influence has produced highly selfish mentality; and while engaging in professional activities at times medical practitioners lose sight of the ethical, human, and noble values of their profession. It is uncertain whether the proliferation of standards, has the capacity to change practitioner's behaviour, when there are very weak mechanisms compelling compliance.

Accountability, standards, and supervision of health personnel and their activities is lacking in Cameroon, this explains why a medical doctor in public hospitals can afford to keep his patients waiting for long hours, and even abandon his patients in the hospital in order to pursue his private interest. Activities related to the adequate use of resources, the effectiveness of healthcare services, and compliance to required standards seems rarely done. Supervisors report at the end of supervision process either send congratulations in case of satisfactory results or guidance and orientations to those whose performances were not satisfactory; sanctions being rarely given.

Moreover, some of the standards adopted do not guarantee efficient and quality practice. Indeed, in Cameroon the approach of registration and licensing as requirement to practice is no longer a guarantee to quality standards of services expected from practitioner, the fact that a medical doctor has paid his annual contribution to the Cameroon Medical Council is no prove of competence.

---

388 Baldwin, D J. *et al*, (1998), "Unethical and Unprofessional Conduct Observed by Residents during their first year of Training", *Acad Med*, 73(11), pp.1195–1200.

389 Irvine, D., (2003), *The Doctor's Tale: Professionalism and Public Trust*, Abington, UK, Radcliffe Medical Press.

CHAPTER FOUR

Remedies for Violation of Medical Practice in Cameroon

4.1 Introduction

The practice of the medical profession is full of complexities and subtleties. Medical practitioners in the exercise of their profession are bound by law and ethics which spell out what is expected of individual physician and the profession as a whole. Violation of same may result in civil, criminal, and professional sanctions against the medical professional.

The remedies evoke the liability of the medical practitioner which is intended; to compensate patients who suffer injury as a result of doctor's malpractice, provide corrective justice by punishing physicians whose violation of medical practice causes injury to patients, thereby providing the incentives to take appropriate precautions in medical treatment[390], and to deter malpractices[391]. However, it has been observed that neither of these objectives are actually achieved. Regarding the first objective, the tort system does not provide compensation rapidly or equitably to injured patients, justice for medical malpractice claimant is subject to lengthy delays. The second objective leads to defensive medicine; avoiding needy risky treatment due to fear of being sued. Medical practitioners tend to

[390] Kessler, P D. and McClellan, B M., (1997), "The Effects of Malpractice Pressure and Liability Reforms on Physicians' Perceptions of Medical Care", *Law and Contemporary Problems*, 60(1), pp81-106.

[391] Mello, M M. *et al*, (2020), "Malpractice Liability and Health care Quality, A Review", *JAMA*, 323(4), pp. 352-366.

use treatments or diagnostic tools that do not improve the quality of care delivered to patients, but which are apt to decrease the probability of a legal claim[392].

In Cameroon remedies available to victims of malpractices are not governed by any specific legislation. Cameroon inherited its legal system from its colonial past; as such it has a bi-jural legal system with the civil law operating in the French speaking part of the country and the Common Law operating in the English-speaking regions. However, its criminal jurisdiction is harmonized. The liability of medical practitioners for wrong committed in the performance of their duties is governed by the general rules of Civil and Criminal Law. The Civil liability of a physician in Cameroon will either be established by the rules of Civil law or Common law depending on where the physician finds his/herself. Under the Common law, the doctor can be sanction for malpractices under contract, or the tort of negligence. Criminal sanction can also be imposed on medical practitioners for violation of medical practice. The doctor can also be sanctioned by the Cameroon Medical Council for serious professional misconduct.

This chapter discusses the above under two heads viz; legal remedies and extra-legal remedies. The legal remedies will examine the civil and criminal liability of medical practitioners for malpractices, while the extra-legal remedies will analyze the liability of medical practitioner for professional misconduct sanctioned by the Cameroon Medical Council.

However, it does not suffice for there to be laws and regulations providing remedies for victims of medical malpractices in Cameroon, what is paramount is the concrete and practical implementation of these written laws and regulations. Weaknesses in the practical transformation of these written instruments to reality are a major impediment in Cameroon. Violation of medical practice contributes to death, damage and injury of patients in Cameroon. It is not uncommon in Cameroon to read about multiple scandals and complaints against doctors in newspapers and magazines, yet what is obtained at the judicial setting is the reverse. Most incidence of death or injuries as a result of misdiagnosis, surgery errors, and other medical malpractice are not prosecuted because the victims do not complaint, the best they can do is grumble about it. Although the legal framework provides for redress in the form of civil and criminal sanctions, the inadequacies and ignorance of the

392 Bertoli, P. and Grembi V., (2017) "Medical Malpractice: How Legal Liability Affects Medical Decisions", *Health Econometric and Date Group*, p.2.

current legal framework, has left victims of medical malpractices with no streamlined redress

The liability of the medical practitioner is not always easy to establish. It is very difficult for a victim to prove medical malpractice against a medical professional let alone extract payment for damages. Furthermore, environmental factors are another impediment. The cultural and socio-economic condition of the country hinders its population in general and patients in particular from promoting respect of their fundamental human right. Most fatality arising out of medical malpractice is considered as fate or the 'will of God'. These tendencies make victims passive and discourage them from pursuing legal actions against doctors for malpractices. In Cameroon it is easier to accuse a grandfather/mother as the cause of a sudden sickness than to look for the scientific cause of the sickness. Poverty is another factor that has drained the possibility of pursuing a cause of action in the face of the exorbitant cost of legal procedures in Cameroon. In reality justice is more of a luxury than a necessity in Cameroon. Patients also lack the awareness that they can sue and claim damages from health care providers for malpractice.

4.2 Legal Remedies

Legal remedies evoke the liability of medical practitioners and hospital management aimed at disciplining violation of a legal obligation. These are remedies available for abuse of medical practices. They establish both the civil and criminal liability of medical practitioners for violation of medical practice.

4.2.1 Civil Remedies

In Cameroon medical malpractice law suits are relatively rare, this does not mean that there are no medical faults, but rather society's knowledge and attitude towards suing a doctor is very low, except for a few cases. The fatalistic attitude engendered by tradition plays a pivotal role. Victims of malpractices accept it as fate. In most cases, patients lack the awareness that they can sue and claim damages from health care providers.

Medical practice generally encompasses diverse activities which if not professionally handled, may give rise to legal responsibilities on the part of the medical practitioner. These liabilities may result in civil charges against the physician[393]. Civil liabilities for medical malpractice are typically tort claims under Common Law, brought against an individual physician for negligence or the tort of battery. An action may likewise be brought against the hospital management for its direct or vicarious liability towards the patient. The physician can equally be liable under contract for breach of a contractual obligation towards the patient.

However, the case of *Junior Books Ltd v. Veitchi Co Ltd*[394], highlighted the interplay between contractual obligations and tortious liability. It provided guidance on the allocation of responsibility and liability in contractual disputes. It clarifies the extent of contractual obligations and the potential for tortious liability in cases of defective workmanship[395]. In this case the House of Lords had to decide whether a duty of care in delicts exists between a contractor or subcontractor and an employer.

In this case[396] the Defendant, Veitchi Co Ltd was a specialist flooring company which was nominated as a sub-contractor to lay flooring at Plaintiff, Junior Books Ltd factory. The floor proved defective but as there was a contract only between Junior Books and the main contractor, there was no contractual relationship whereby Junior Books could sue Veitchi, the sub-contractor. Junior Books sued, alleging breach of contract and negligence in the execution of the flooring installation. It argued that Veitchi had breached its contractual obligations and failed to exercise reasonable care in the performance of the flooring installation. Junior Books sought to recover the loss from the flooring which included replacement cost. The question for the House of Lords to answer was whether the defendant, Veitchi were liable for negligence in respect of the economic loss suffered by Junior Books, and whether the relationship between the parties was enough to construct a duty of care with regards to the faulty floor[397].

The House of Lords held that Veitchi Co ltd had breached its contractual obligations and was liable for the defects in the flooring installation. Furthermore, there was sufficient degree of proximity between the parties to allow junior Books to sue in delict. The duty of care extended to avoid

---

393 Oludamilola A A. *et al*, (2020) "Legal Perspectives on Liability for Medical Negligence and Malpractices in Nigeria", *Pan African Medical Journal*, 35(44). at https:// www.panafrican-med-journal.com/content/article/35/44/full. (accessed on the 22nd day of January 2022).

394 (1983) 1AC 520

395 All Answers ltd, "Junior Books Ltd v Veitchi Co Ltd- Summary", at https://www.mylawtutor.net/cases/books-ltd-v-veitchi-co-ltd-summary. (Accessed on the 10th day of December 2024)

396 *Junior Books Ltd v. Veitchi Co. Ltd* (1983) 1 AC 520

397 See *supra* note 449

causing pure economic loss arising from the defective property. This case was described as a unique case which could not be regarded as laying down any principle of general application[398].

This section will consider the remedies under the law of contract, the tort of negligence, the tort of battery, and the liability of Hospital management. All these will be discussed hereunder.

4.2.1.1 Remedies under the Law of Contract

The practice of medicine, and its embodiment in the clinical encounter between a patient and a physician, is fundamentally a moral activity that arises from the imperative to care for patients and to alleviate suffering. The relationship between a patient and a physician is based on trust, which gives rise to physicians' ethical responsibility to place patients' welfare above the physician's own self-interest or obligations to others, to use sound medical judgment on patients' behalf, and to advocate for their patients' welfare[399]. This bring about the contractual relationship between a patient and a physician.

According to Sir Frederick pollock[400], a contract is a promise or set of promises which the law will enforce. Thus, every agreement and promise enforceable by law is a contract. To Salmond, "a contract is an agreement creating and defining obligation between two or more persons by which rights are acquired by one or more to act or forbearance on the part of others"[401]. From the foregoing, a contract consists essentially of an agreement, and a legal obligation, that is, a duty enforceable at law. An agreement is an act in the law whereby two or more persons declare their consent as to any act or thing to be done or forborne by some or one of those persons for the use of the others or other of them[402]. Such declaration may take place by the concurrence of the parties in a spoken or written form of words as expressing their common intention or offer made by some or one of them and accepted by the others or

---

398 *Ibid*

399 Oral, T., (2011), "The Definition of the Legal Relationship between a Patient and Physician", *Ankara Bar Review*, 1, p.23.

400 Pollock S. F, Bart., (1902), *Principles of Contract: A Treatise on the General Principles Concerning the Validity of Agreement in the Law of England*, 7th Edition, London, Stevens and Sons Limited, 119 &120 Chancery Lane, Law Publishers, p.1.

401 A.D. McN, (1928), "Principles of the Law of Contract, by the late Sir John Salmond and Percy H. Winfield. London. Sweet & amp; Maxwell. 1927.(30s.)". *The Cambridge Law Journal*, 3(2), pp. 310-312.

402 See supra note 455, p.2

other of them[403]. However, all agreements are not enforceable by law, therefore all agreements are not contracts[404]. The first essential element of an agreement to make it enforceable by law, is the consent of the parties, there must be the meeting of two minds in one and the same intention, and the agreement must be an act in the law, that is, capable of having legal effects, and it must determine the duties and rights of the parties. The acceptance of an agreement may be communicated by words or by conduct, or partly by the one and partly by the other. Where it is conveyed by words, it is express, where it is conveyed by conduct, it is said to be implied[405].

Where one or more of the parties to the contract dishonour terms and conditions of a contract by non-performance, failure to meet the terms of the agreement, or fails to deliver in the appropriate time frame, the contract is said to be breached which may give rise to a civil cause of action in law. The party can sue the other in order to claim damages from the breaching party.

A patient-physician contractual relationship is generally formed when a physician affirmatively acts in a patient's case by examining, diagnosing, treating, or agreeing to do so. This contractual relationship will form the basis of patients' and physicians' rights, requests and obligations[406]. In *La Fleur v. Cornelis*[407] it was held that the law will imply the existence of a contract in cases where a patient submits to treatment by a medical practitioner. This contract formed therein is legally binding, and is condition on the doctor performing his services (treatment of the patient) in return for payment from the patient for services rendered. Thus, the physician assumes the obligation of giving medical treatments, attending, caring, and giving information to the patient about his or her condition. The physician has an ethical and legal duty to continue care and not to abandon the patient. In fact, Section 22 of the Cameroon Code of Medical Ethics provides that from the moment a doctor agrees to give attention to a patient, he shall be bound to give the patient all the necessary medical care within his power, either personally or with the help of qualified third parties. Thus, at the moment the doctor accepts to treat a patient, he becomes contractually responsible towards the patient.

---

403 *Ibid* p.3

404 *Balfour v. Balfour* (1919) 2 K. B. 571 per Lord Atkin L.J. "there are agreements entered into by the parties that do not result in contracts within the meaning of this term in law. Such agreements are not contracts since the parties did not intend that they should be attended by any legal consequences".

405 See supra note 455, p.11

406 *Ibid.*

407 1979 28 NBR 2d 569.

The terms of this contract may vary depending upon the agreement, and generally may be either express or implied. Many contracts in the field between health care professionals and their patients are implied contracts. During initial examination, an implied contract is formed between the patient and the doctor. It is implied that the medical physician will act in good faith to the best of his or her abilities when forming a diagnosis and, or treatment course. It is not the implied contract of the medical physician to cure the patient, but to act in the patient's best interest to the best of his or her abilities. If the doctor does not fulfil his obligation towards his patient, the contract will be breached, and the doctor will be liable. The patient on the other hand, has an obligation to comply with physician's recommendations and treatments; otherwise, the physician will not be liable[408].

The Cameroon Code of Medical Ethics in its part two elaborate the duties of doctors towards their patients, as such where these duties are breached, it indicates that the doctor has failed to discharge his obligations toward his patient and may be liable under contract. The doctor is bound by the above Code to give the patient all the necessary medical care within his power, and to formulate his diagnosis with the greatest care, regardless of the time that his work may cost him. After having made his diagnosis and prescribed treatment, failure to ensure that the treatment is carried out, especially if the patient's life is in danger, may be considered as failure to discharge his own part of the contractual relationship towards the patients[409].

The nature of a valid contract requires that both parties enter into the contractual agreement freely and with understanding of the terms of the contract. The patient is a free moral agent. Both the patient and physician have separate responsibilities toward the identification and management of the patient's illness. Patients are free to choose their doctor and it is equally true that physicians in the private practice of medicine are free to accept or refuse to accept a person as a patient[410]. When a patient-physician relationship is mutually agreed upon, both parties retain individual rights and responsibilities. These rights and responsibilities form the terms of the contract[411]. The patient has a right to be informed. This right of the patient

---

408 See *supra* note 454 at p. 24.

409 See *supra* note 57 at p.70.

410 See *supra* note 85, Section 5 which provide that in their relations, patients are free to choose their doctors, and a doctor may refuse his services for professional or personal reasons provided in doing so he does not harm the patient.

411 Miech, R P., (1995), "The Doctor Patient Relationship: Friend or Adversary", *The Linacre Quarterly*, 62(2), p.14.

becomes the physician's responsibility. It is the informed patient that grants permission to the physician; to take a history, to examine the patient, to initiate diagnostic procedures, and to administer a specific form of therapy. The physician contractual right includes acceptance or refusal of a patient, expectation of patent's cooperation, and setting the remuneration for services rendered.

Malpractice is inextricably bound up with the idea of doctor's breach of implied contract. The physician is considered as impliedly holding himself out as possessing the degree of learning, skill and experience ordinarily possessed by the profession in similar localities. When he failed to exercise such usual knowledge and skill, in treating and diagnosing the patient, he is regarded as having breached his contractual duty to his patient[412]. It is well settled that a physician may enter into an express contract with a patient to accomplish a particular result; a subsequent breach of that contract will entitle the plaintiff to a recovery irrespective of any negligence[413]. However, the rate of success of an action under contract is not practicable.

(a) Establishing Breach of contract

A physician may be vulnerable to breach of contract action based on the provision of medical services resulting from a bad medical result if the doctor had bound himself to cure the patient or to obtain specific results. Some courts have refused to interpret a doctor's general statement about the quality of service to be performed as a guarantee or promise of a certain result. On the other hand, other courts have interpreted a doctor's statement on the conduct, outcome, or safety of a particular medical procedure as a definite guarantee, making physician potentially liable for the breach of an express warranty.

This principle is well illustrated in *Hawkins v. McGee*[414] where the New Hampshire Supreme Court held that, despite the impossibility of the promise, the court must determine whether or not the plaintiff could have possibly imputed a contract interpretation to -the words uttered. In Hawkins, the physician, although unskilled in -the art of skin grafting, had sought out the plaintiff whose hand had been severely burned in an electrical fire and had offered to make the hand "one hundred percent perfect." When the operation

---

412 Miller, A J., (1953) "The Contractual Liability of Physicians and Surgeons", *Washington University Law Quarterly*, p.413.

413 *Bishop v. Byrne*, 265 F. Supp. 460 (S.D. W. Va. 1967.

414 84 N.H. 114, 146 A. 641 (1929).

did not result in a perfect hand, the plaintiff sued the physician for breach of contract. In holding for the plaintiff, the court completely rejected the physician's contention that he had merely expressed his opinion to the plaintiff, i.e., that even if the words "one hundred percent perfect hand" were uttered, no reasonable person would interpret them to be made with the intention of making a guarantee[415]. Emphasis was placed on the physician actively recruiting the plaintiff's consent to operate on the injured hand. The court reasoned that since the solicitation surpassed all limits of normal physician-patient reassurances, the plaintiff could have relied on the statement; as a consequence, the statement was held to constitute a specific, clear, and express promise to effect a particular result.

In addition to a breach of contract action based on the provision of medical services, a patient may have a potential claim against a physician for breach of a financial contract. Whether or not a contract exists relating to the success of medical services, a financial contract exists because the relationship involves fees. The financial contract usually provide that the physician will render a specific number of services based on either time or therapeutic objectives in exchange for a certain amount of money[416].

In order to find the existence of a breach of contract, some courts require proof of a patient's payment of a separate consideration in addition to the amount paid for the physician normal duty to use reasonable care and skill, other courts have not required separate consideration if the warranty was made before the treatment and was given in order to induce the patient to consent to treatment.

In Heneberry v. Pharoan[417], the appellate court address the issue of what is required to prevail on a breach of contract claim in a medical malpractice action. The court noted that though the doctor-patient relationship is essentially contractual in nature, the doctor's obligation is to "...exercise a reasonable degree of care and medical skill, the failure to exercise that care is tortious in nature and is generally not governed by contract law". However, the Court further stated that,

> *to establish a prima facie case of breach of contract where the facts relate to a physician's performance of a medical procedure,*

---

415 *McQuaid v. Michou*, 85 N.H. 299, 157 A. 881 (1932).

416 Wilson, M., "Claims for Breach of Contract", at https:// mcwilson.com/claims-for-breach-of-contract/ (accessed on 2nd day of May 2022).

417 No. 2440, September Term 2015 (Maryland Court of Special Appeals, April 27, 2017).

> *the plaintiff must show that the physician made an additional promise or warranty separate and apart from the physician's agreement to properly perform the procedure*[418].

Therefore, generally, the courts do not recognize contract actions in medical malpractice cases unless the physician made some special promise or warranty apart from a promise to use the medical skill necessary to deliver the treatment in the manner generally accepted by other physicians in the community.

As previously stated, if a doctor makes a special contract and then fails to perform, he is liable for the breach even though he exercised the highest possible professional skill. No expert medical testimony is required; encounters with the so-called "conspiracy of silence" no longer hinder the potential plaintiffs.

For obvious reasons, physicians rarely execute written contracts with patients that purport to guarantee or otherwise ensure certain results from medical treatment. The only physician who will knowingly make a contract for a cure is one who is a fool or who thinks himself capable of miracles[419]. The argument against imposing contractual liability on the physician is that considering the unpredictability of medical results and the differences in individual patients, it is unlikely that the physician of integrity can in good faith promise a particular outcome[420].

However, damages resulting from a breach of contract based on the provision of medical services may be given to place the patient back in the financial position that he or she would have been in had the physician performed the agreement, including also compensation for any consequences which were reasonably foreseeable and within the contemplation of the parties at the time the contract was entered into.

The breach of contract may lead to injury and mental suffering. This involves failure of the defendant to perform his contract, resulting in needless pain and suffering to the plaintiff. Historically, damages for pain and suffering were not recoverable in a contract action. In *Colvin v. Smith*[421], it was stated that malpractice is predicated upon the failure to exercise requisite medical skill and is tortious in nature. The action in contract is based upon a failure

---

418 *Ibid.*

419 See *supra* note 467.

420 Jerrold, L., (2020), "Medical Malpractice or Breach of Contract", *American journal of Orthodontics and Dentofacial Orthopedics, Litigation and Legislation*, 157(2), pp. 278-279.

421 276 App. Div. 9, 92 N.Y.S.2d 794 (1949).

to perform a special agreement. Negligence, the basis of the one, is foreign to the other. The damages recoverable in malpractice are for personal injuries, including the pain and suffering which naturally flow from the tortious act. In the contract action they are restricted to the payments made and to the expenditures for nurses and medicines or other damages that flow from the breach thereof.

However, due to an increased mobility, an exception soon developed with respect to common carriers. If a breach of a duty by a common carrier caused an intentionally inflicted mental anguish to a person having a contract of carriage, damages were given for pain and suffering[422]. In *Stewart v. Rudner*[423] the Michigan Supreme Court held that damages for pain and suffering could be recovered in an action in contract. The plaintiff in Stewart had requested that her baby be delivered by Caesarian section and the doctor agreed. When the baby was due, the plaintiff's physician was not present and she was delivered through natural childbirth by a staff doctor who was unaware of the agreement. As a consequence, the infant was stillborn. The plaintiff sued the physician for breach of contract; the jury returned a verdict of $5,000 for the plaintiff. The defendant appealed, arguing that it was an error to charge the jury that damages for mental suffering were recoverable in a contract action. In upholding the award of damages for pain and suffering, the Michigan Court noted that not all contracts are commercial in nature; some contracts may involve "rights" and "emotions" which are sacred and personal in nature[424]. Using the common carrier's exception by way of analogy, the Court determined that the pain and suffering flowing from a personal contract were not remote but foreseeable and therefore affirmed the verdict for the plaintiff. The general rule of "no damages for mental suffering in a contract action" was considered inappropriate for a situation where the plaintiff's well-being is dependent on the performance of the duty undertaken.

In *Coffey v North Western Hospital Association*[425], there was a breach of contract by the defendant to provide hospital services, the court reasoned that the physical pain and mental anguish suffered might fairly be said to have been within the contemplation of the parties when the contract was made.

---

422 *Gebhardt v. Public Service Coordinated Transport*, 48 N.J. Super. 173, 137 A.2d 48 (1957); *Medlin v. Southern Ry.*, 143 S.C. 91, 141 S.E. 185 (1928).

423 349 Mich. 459, 84 N.W.2d 816 (1957).

424 *Stewart v. Rudner*, 349 Mich. 459, 469, 84 N.W.2d 816, 823 (1957).

425 96 ore.100, 183 pac.762.

In *Galveston H and S. A. Ry. Co. v Rubio*[426], the appellant having breached its agreement to provide medical care and attention, the court held that damages for both mental and physical suffering were recoverable even though the damages sought were for breach of contract since the very subject matter of the contract was the health of the employee.

An important limitation on the award of damages is the duty to mitigate[427]. The plaintiff is obliged to mitigate, or minimize, the amount of damages to a reasonable extent. Damages cannot be recoverable for losses that could have been reasonably avoided or substantially ameliorated after the breach occurred. The plaintiff failure to use reasonable diligent in mitigating the damages mean that any award of damages will be reduced by the amount that could have been reasonably avoided.

P S Atiyah[428] asserts that medical malpractice-claims for injury or misadventure arising out of medical treatment are precisely the unforeseen and accidental by-products of a contractual relationship which cannot be accommodated within contractual theory. It is worth noting that for several hundred years common lawyers have played around with the boundary between contract and tort. When the rules of contract law seemed to lead to unreasonable and unjust results, lawyers have simply bypassed traditional contract doctrine by invoking tort.

4.2.1.2 Remedies under the Tort of Negligence

Civil Liability for medical malpractice is hinged on the tortious principle of negligence as adumbrated by Lord Atkin in the 1932 case of *Donoghue V. Stevenson*[429]. In this case it is established that where a medical professional fails to give due regard to the health and welfare of their patients as governed by their oath, and deviates from the normal practice of the profession, causing injury, damage or death, it may amount to medical negligence[430].

---

426 65 s.w.1126(Tex.1901).

427 *British Westinghouse Electric Co. Ltd v. Underground Electric Railways Co, of London Ltd* (1912) A C 673.

428 Atiyah, P S., (1986), "Medical Malpractice and the Contract/Tort Boundary", *Law and Contemporary Problems*, 49(2), P. 294.

429 L Lords. *Donoghue V. Stevenson*. (1932) AC, 562.

430 Uganda Law Reform Commission, "Medical Negligence in Uganda", Issue Paper, November 2017, p.4

Medical negligence has been defined in *Blyth vs. Birmingham Water Works Co.*[431] as "the omission to do something which a reasonable man would do or doing something which a reasonable man would not do". Black's Law Dictionary[432] defines medical neglect as the failure to provide medical, dental, or psychiatric care that is necessary to prevent or to treat serious physical or emotional injury or illness. Medical malpractice is therefore professional negligence by act or omission of a health care provider in which the treatment provided falls below the accepted standard of practice in the medical community and causes injury or death of the patient[433].

However, not all acts that constitute medical malpractice may give rise to a claim in medical negligence. An act of malpractice may not give rise to any injury or damages, and thus a claim of negligence hinged solely on such an act is unlikely to succeed. Such an act may give rise to a disciplinary sanction by the medical professional body on the grounds of breach of medical ethics.

Negligence in the context of medical profession necessarily calls for a treatment with a difference. To infer negligence on the part of a medical professional, additional considerations apply. A simple lack of care, an error of judgment or an accident is not proof of negligence of a medical practitioner. So long as a doctor follows a practice acceptable to the medical profession of that day, he cannot be held liable for negligence merely because a better alternative, course or method of treatment was also available, or simple because a more skilled doctor would not have chosen to follow or resort to that practice or procedure which the accused medical doctor followed. Again, where the charge of negligence arises out of a failure to use some particular equipment, the charge will fail if the equipment was not generally available at that particular time at which it is suggested that it should have been used[434]. This is so especially in Cameroon where hospitals lack basic necessary equipment.

For a medical practitioner to be sanction under the tort of negligence, it must be established that, there is a doctor patient relationship, that the doctor owed the patient a duty to use reasonable care in treating the patient, that

---

431 *Blyth vs. Birmingham Water Works Co.* 11 Ex 784.

432 Garner, B A., (2004) *Black's Law Dictionary*, Eighth Edition, Thomson West, p. 1061.

433 Awati, A M. *et al*, (2014) "Professional Liability in Medical Practice: A 20 Years Retrospective Study at District Consumers Forum Gulbarga (1991-2011)", J *NTR Univ Health Sci*, 3(1), pp. 15-18.

434 Agarwal, A K., (2011), "Medical Negligence: Law and Interpretation", *Indian Institute of Management, Working Paper* 380 015.

the doctor was in breach of that duty and that the breach caused the injury suffered by the patient. These requirements will be treated hereunder.

(a) Doctor- Patient Relationship

Sanction under negligence stems from a doctor breaching his/her duty of care. However, doctors do not automatically have a duty to every person with whom they come into contact simply by virtue of being a doctor. It must first be established that the plaintiff was owed a duty as a patient of the doctor. The doctor-patient relationship is vital in a medical malpractice case because it shows that the doctor had a legal obligation to treat the patient. While it might seem obvious that if the injury occurred, then a doctor-patient relationship existed, that is not always the case.

Generally, doctor- patient relationship is established when the patient seeks medical treatment and the doctor consent to treat the patient. That is, where a physician affirmatively acts in a patient's case by examining, diagnosing, treating, or agreeing to do so[435]. Once the physician consensually enters into a relationship with a patient in any of these ways, a legal contract is formed in which the physician has an ethical and legal duty to that patient to continue to treat. Indeed, Section 22 of the Cameroon Code of Medical Ethics[436] admits this when it provides that; a doctor, from the moment he is called to give attention to a patient and agrees to do this, shall be bound to give the patient ail the necessary medical care within his power, either personally or with the help of qualified third parties.

In *Ricks v Budge*[437], a patient saw a doctor Dr. Budge for an injury to his hand. Upon subsequent visit several days later, his hand had become severely infected, but Dr. Budge refused to treat the hand because the patient had unpaid bills. He told the patient to go to a nearby hospital. The hospital physician immediately operated. But the hand was eventually amputated. The court decided that a patient physician relationship had been established when the patient saw Dr. Budge at the first visit because it is well settled that a doctor or surgeon, upon undertaking an operation or other case, is under the duty, in the absence of an agreement limiting the service, of continuing his attention so long as the case requires attention.

---

435 Blake, V., (2012), "When is a Patient-Physician Relationship Established?", *AMA Journal of Ethics*, 14(5), pp.403-406.

436 Decree No 83/166 of 12 April 1983 on The Code of Medical Ethics.

437 91 Utah 307, 64 P2d 208 (Utah 1937).

However, a doctor may terminate the relationship in the middle of a course of care, but must provide sufficient notice and a medical referral to a competent physician to ensure continuity of care. Only at that point does a doctor properly terminate the relationship and end his obligation to the patient[438]. Failure to provide an appropriate referral can leave the doctor open to liability even after the treatment of the patient come to an end[439]. An improper termination of the doctor-patient relationship is a form of medical malpractice known as abandonment[440]. Once the doctor patient relationship is established, it must be shown that the doctor owed a duty of care to the patient.

(b) Duty of Care

A duty of care is an obligation on one party to take care to prevent harm being suffered by another. In the relationship of medical practitioners and patients, several duties of care arise on the part of the medical practitioner towards patients. The duty of care arises where the physician embarks on the treatment and care of a patient. This was recognized by Lord Nathan who asserted that; 'the medical man's duty of care ... is based simply upon the fact that the medical man undertakes the care and treatment of the patient'[441].

The Cameroon Code of Medical Ethics acknowledges a duty of care owed by the doctor to the patient by providing for the duties of the doctor towards the patient[442]. Failure to discharge these duties towards the patience may give rise to medical negligence amongst other actions. In cases where no relationship exists between the patient and the physician, the general law on omissions applies, meaning that there is no legal obligation upon a doctor to act as the Good Samaritan.

In some cases, however, the court has imposed a duty of care in the absence of a doctor patient relationship. In *Parmanand Kataria v. Union of India*[443] it was held that every doctor, at the governmental hospital or elsewhere, has a professional obligation to extend his services with due expertise for protecting

---

438 See *Byrd v WCW*, 868 S.W.2d 767 (Tex 1994).

439 *Longmam v Jasiek*, 414 N.E.2d 520,523 (III App.Ct. 1980).

440 Indest, G F., (1996), "Patient Abandonment, Home Health Care Law Manual, the Health Law Firm", at https://www.thehealthlawfirm.com/resources/health-law-articles-and-documents/patient-abandonment.html. (accessed on the 6th day of May 2022).

441 Grubb, A., "Special Forms of Negligence: Problems of Medical law" in Markesinis, B S., and Deakin, S F., (1999), *Tort Law*, 4th edition, Oxford, Clarendon Press, p.273.

442 Part 11, Section 22-35 of Decree No 83/166 of 12 August 1983 on Code of Medical Ethics.

443 *Parmanand Kataria v. Union of India*, AIR 1989 SC 2039.

life. Thus, a doctor in a hospital owes a duty of care to patients in the ward in which he is employed to work, a doctor on duty at emergency unit in hospital owes a duty of care to any patient who present there for medical treatment. A private practitioner contracted to provide services to the employees of a company owes a duty of care to all the employees on the list.

Under a normal doctor- patient relationship, the duties of the medical practitioner include; duty to provide adequate counselling, duty to warn the patient if there is a risk of treatment or likely side effects, duty to carry out a proper diagnosis, and duty to administer proper treatment. The nature of a medical practitioner's duty of care was explained by Lord Hewart in *R. V. Bateman*[444] thus;

> *if a person holds himself out as possessing special skill and knowledge and he is consulted, as possessing such skill and knowledge, by or on behalf of a patient, he owes a duty to the patient or client to use due caution in undertaking the treatment*[445].

A patient generally approaches a doctor with expectations; that a doctor will provide medical treatment with all the knowledge and skill at his command, and that he will not do anything to harm the patient in any manner either because of his negligence, carelessness or reckless attitude. Though a doctor may not be in position to save a patient's life at all times, he is expected to use his special knowledge and skill in the most appropriate manner keeping in mind the interest of the patient who has been entrusted to him[446].

The medical practitioner's duty to provide adequate counselling and warn on the risk of treatment is geared towards helping the patient to make an informed or sensible decision on whether or not to agree to a proposed treatment[447]. In *Sideway v Bethlehem Royal Hospital Governors*[448], the plaintiff gave consent for an operation that would relieve her of pain in her neck. The surgeon did not tell her of the possibility of damage to her spinal cord, which was in any case remote. The plaintiff suffered partial paralysis in her arm after the operation, and she sued contending that her consent was nullified as

---

444 (1925) All ER 45 at 48; 19 CAR 8. *Re J* (1992) 3 WLR 507, *Barry v Henderson* (1870) LR 5 QB 295.

445 *Ibid.*

446 Pandit, M S. *et al*, (2009), "Medical Negligence: Coverage of The Profession, Duties, Ethics, Case Law and Enlightened Defence: Legal Perspective", *Indian Journal of urology*, 25(3), quoted in Uganda Law Reform Commission, "Medical Negligence in Uganda", Nov. 2017, Issue Paper, p. 19.

447 See *supra* note 446 at p. 358.

448 (1985)1 All ER 643.

all the possible risk was not disclose to her before she gave her consent. The House of Lords held: that the defendant hospital was not liable for negligence, and that in the instant case the risk of spinal injury was remote. The court said that the medical doctor satisfied the duty of prior disclosure incumbent on him. The duty does not mean a lecture on all the details of the treatment to be given. However, where a patient is inquisitive, the scope of disclosure would ostensibly increase accordingly.

A doctor has a duty to carry out a proper diagnosis of his patient, before embarking on treatment. Therefore, he has to carry out all the test or examination that the patient's symptoms require, thus where X-ray tests, blood test, stool or urine test, or other similar tests are needed to determine the ailment and treatment of the patient, they must be conducted.

(i) Standard of Care required

The doctor must exercise reasonable care and skill in treating the patient. It is immaterial that the doctor is rendering such services out of charity. The standard of care required of a medical practitioner is an objective one. It is the standard of an ordinary reasonable medical practitioner in the shoes of the defendant. Factors commonly affecting the standard of care expected of a medical practitioner include; the locality or society in question, the availability of relevant medical facilities, the specialized skill of the medical practitioner concerned, accepted medical practice, and whether there was an emergency or not . What is expected of a reasonable skilled doctor is usually contained in the Professional Code of Practice; in Cameroon it is contained in the Code of Medical Ethics. The standard of a reasonable skilled doctor was discussed by Tindall CJ in the case of *Lanphier V Phipos*[449] where he stated that every person who enters into a learned profession undertakes to bring to the exercise of it a reasonable degree of skill and care, where he is a surgeon, he does not undertake that he will perform a cure nor does he undertake to use the highest possible degree of skill. Hence if a person holds himself out as possessing special skill and knowledge, by and on behalf of a patient, he owes a duty to the patient to use due caution in undertaking the treatment.

The doctor does not have to adhere to the highest or sink to the lowest degree of care and competence in the light of the circumstance[450]. When defining reasonable care, the conduct of a physician is compared with that of

[449] (1838) 8 C&P 475 at 478.

[450] *Laxman v. Trimback*, AIR 1969 SC 128.

the *bonus medicus* or the standard of the prudent and competent physician with typical qualities and skills, and placed in the same circumstances as the defendant physician[451]. In *Bolam v Friern Management Committee*[452], McNair J stated that

> *the test is the standard of the ordinary skilled man exercising and professing to have that special skill. A man need not possesses the highest expert skill at the risk of being found negligent. It is well established law that it is sufficient if he exercises the ordinary skill of an ordinary man exercising that particular art.*

A doctor, therefore, does not have to ensure that every patient who comes to him is cured. He has only to ensure that he offers a reasonable degree of care and competence[453]. In *R v Bateman*[454] it was held that a physician is not to be judged according to the standards of the most experienced, most skillful, or most highly qualified member of the profession, but by reference to the standards of the ordinary competent practitioner in that particular field. Conversely, the doctor is not to be judged by the standards of the least qualified or least experienced practitioner.

The standard of care expected of unqualified persons and quacks is the standard of care expected of the ordinary reasonable member of the skilled group, to which he holds himself out as belonging. Thus, whenever a person holds himself out as possessing more knowledge and skill than he actually has, he will be judged by such skill that he professes to have. This was explained by Glidewell L.J in the case of *Wilsher v Essex Area Health Authority*[455] thus;

> *in my view, the law requires the trainee or learner to be judged by the same standard as his more experienced colleagues if it did not, inexperience would frequently act as a defense to an action for professional negligence*[456].

It may be necessary to note the distinction between the standard of care and the degree of care. The standard of care is a constant and remains the same

---

[451] See *supra* note 501, at p.3.
[452] (1957) 2 ALL ER 118 at 121.
[453] See *supra* note 57 at p.67.
[454] [1925] 94, LJKB 791.
[455] (1986) 3 All ER at 831 CA.
[456] *Ibid.*

in all cases. The degree of care is a variable and depends on the circumstance. It is used to refer to what actually amounts to reasonableness in a given situation[457]. Although the same standard of care is expected from a generalist and a specialist, the degree of care would be different, both are expected to take reasonable care, but the law expects the specialist to exercise the ordinary skill of his specialty and not of any ordinary doctor[458]. Thus, a medical professional having that degree of competence expected of the ordinary skillful medical professional sets the standard. He/she is a practitioner who follows the standard practice of his or her profession or at least follows practices that would not be disapproved of by responsible opinion within the profession[459].

As to the knowledge expected of a doctor, a doctor must constantly update his knowledge to meet standards expected of him. In *Bolam's case*[460], McNair J said that a health care professional cannot persistently and pigheadedly carry on with an old technique if it has been proved to be contrary to new medical practice. However, since only reasonable knowledge is required, it may not be necessary for him to be aware of all the developments that have taken place.

The Cameroon Code of Medical Ethics[461] imposes on the doctor the duty to seek patients consent before any contact or intervention in the body of the patient, for example, surgical operation and others. Also, the law governing blood transfusion[462] specifically obliges the medical personnel to seek the consent of the donor and donee before transfusion. The duty of care expected from a practitioner in this instance is the duty to properly disclose all relevant information to the patient to enable him to make an informed decision. This duty however, does not extend to disclosing all possible information, nor to warning a patient of all the normal attendant risks of an operation. The Cameroon Code of Medical Ethics provides that;

> *a serious prognosis may lawfully be concealed from the patient, and a fatal prognosis may not be divulged to him except with the greatest prudence; it must normally be divulged to*

---

457 Joga Rao S V., (2009), "Medical Negligence Liability under the Consumer Protection Act: A Review of Judicial Perspective", *Indian Journal of Urology*, 25(3), pp. 362-363.

458 Lord Scarman in *Maynard v West Midlands Regional Heath Authority* [1985] 1 All ER 635 at 638.

459 Mason &McCall Smith, *Law and Medical Ethics*, 4th Edition, (London, Butterworths, 1994) pg.199.

460 (1957) 2 ALL ER 118 at 121.

461 See *supra* note 497, Section 25(1), 26, 29.

462 Section 5 and 8 of Law No. 2003/2006 of 22 December, 2003 governing Blood Transfusion in Cameroon.

his family, unless the patient is already so aware or if he has appointed a third party to be informed[463].

Once the duty of care is established, in order to hold a doctor liable under negligence, it must be shown that the doctor breached his duty of care.

(c) Breach of Duty of Care

Failure to exercise the standard of skills and care that a reasonable medical practitioner would do in similar circumstances constitutes a breach of the duty of care. The reasonableness of the physician conduct will determine whether he has breached his duty towards his patient. Where the physician acted reasonably, liability will be excluded.

Conducts which constitute breach of professional duty include; failure to attend promptly to a patient requiring urgent attention when the practitioner was in a position to do so, making an incorrect diagnosis particularly when the clinical features were so glaring that no reasonable skillful practitioner could have failed to notice them, failure to advise, or proffering wrong advice to a patient on the risk involved in a particular operation or course of treatment, especially if such an operation or course of treatment is likely to result in serious side effects like deformity or loss of an organ, failure to obtain the consent of the patient before proceeding on any surgical procedure or course of treatment, when such consent was necessary, making a mistake in treatment, for example, prescribing the wrong drug in error for a correctly diagnosed ailment, failure to refer or transfer a patient in good time when such a referral or transfer was necessary, in short, failure to do anything that ought reasonably to have been done under any circumstance for the good of the patient.

Where a doctor holds himself out as possessing special skill and knowledge in a particular field of medicine or surgery, the doctor must exercise the same degree of care and skill as doctors who generally practice in that field[464]. This is particularly relevant in the case of doctors who run private hospitals. For example, if a doctor being a general practitioner, undertakes a complicated surgical operation when the patient could have been referred to a surgeon, the general practitioner must conform to the standard of a surgeon. If he does not, then it is negligent on his part to take the treatment knowing that he does

---

463 See *supra* note 497, Section 27(1)(2).

464 Umerah B C., (1989), *Medical Practice and the Law in Nigeria,* Longman Nigeria Limited, p.124.

not possess the special skill required of a surgeon. In *the People and 2 Others V Ndeubevam Charles Dechateau and Ministry of Public Health*[465], a dental surgeon who did not have the necessary training, performed a surgery on the claimant, which was normally done by a general practitioner. It was found that his failure to refer the patient to an expert possessed with the necessary skill amounted to negligence as the treatment he gave fell below the standard expected of a reasonable competent practitioner.

A practitioner is not liable in negligence merely because an operation is unsuccessful, or grave harm resulted from it, or because a mistake or an error of judgment occurred. This position was clearly stated by Lord Denning in his direction to the jury in *Hatcher v Black*[466] thus;

> *In a hospital when a person who is ill goes in for treatment, there is always some risk, no matter what care is used. Every surgical operation involves risks. It would be wrong. And indeed, bad law, to say that simply because a misadventure or mishap occurred, the hospital and the doctors are thereby liable. It would be disastrous to the community if it were so. It would mean that a doctor examining a patient or a surgeon operating at a table instead of getting on with his work, would be forever looking over his shoulder to see if someone was coming up with a dagger... you must not, therefore, find him negligent simply because something happens to go wrong; if, for instance, one of the risk inherent in an operation actually takes place or some complication ensues which lessens or takes away the benefits that were hoped for, or if in a matter of opinion he makes an error of judgment. You should only find him guilty of negligence when he falls short of the standard of a reasonable skillful medical man, in short, when he is deserving of censure... for negligence in a medical man is deserving of censure*[467].

In the case of Ojo V. Gharoro & Ors[468], the Appellant was told by the Respondent that she had a growth in her fallopian tube, to this effect; she needed surgical operations to remove the growth which she consented to.

---

465 *Arête No 35/CRIM of 15 June2011* (unreported).
466 [(1954) The Times, 2nd July].
467 *Ibid*
468 (2006) JELR 56140 (SC), Supreme Court, SC.251/2001, 10 Mar 2006, Nigeria.

After the operation, she complained of abdominal pain, and an x-ray was carried out. It was discovered that there was a broken needle in her abdomen. The appellant failed to adduce expert evidence to prove negligence on the part of the respondents. Relying on the statement of Lord Denning, it was held that the respondents exercised their best medical skills and so no medical negligence occurred. However, in the Cameroon case of *Agborock Lydienne v Dr Nwaobi Romanus and St John of God Hospital Nguti*, the surgeon performed an operation on the patient leaving a swap inside the patient. The court stated that had the surgeon exercise the reasonable degree of care and skill expected of a surgeon, he would not have injured the patient. Thus, the treatment was constitutive of negligence.

Again, in *Suh Mbony Beatrice V Dr. Zimmerman and Mbingo Baptist Hospital*[469], the plaintiff brought an action against the defendants for negligence and loss of earnings. The plaintiff was operated upon by Dr. Zimmerman for uterine fibroid. After the operation the plaintiff began passing out urine uncontrollably and soiling herself. She drew the attention of the first defendant who said it was normal after such an operation, and that it will soon be over. However, the situation got worse and she presented herself again to the defendants, Dr. Zimmerman recognized his fault. The plaintiff claimed 5 million francs from the defendants jointly and severally as special and general damages. After an agreement between the plaintiff and the defendants, the plaintiff applied for the matter to be settled out of court and her application was granted by the court. The plaintiff was adequately compensated out of court.

In *Ashcroft v Mersey Regional Heath Authority*[470], the judge held that in an action for negligence against a professional person in connection with his calling, the question for consideration by the Court is whether on the balance of probabilities, it has been established that the defendant failed to exercise the care required of a man possessing special skill in circumstances which requires the exercise of that special skill. If there is an added burden of prove, that burden does not rest on the person alleging negligence, on the contrary the more skilled a person is the more care which is expected from him. In this case the plaintiff submitted herself to the hospital for an operation on her left ear, Mr. Joseph Siegler, a surgeon of long experience, great skill and the highest reputation, performed it. The operation proved to be disastrous, as the

---

469 Suit No CFIF/03/06-07 (unreported).

470 QBD (1983) 2 ALL ER 245.

plaintiff was left with a partial paralysis of the left side of the face. She claimed damages alleging that the operation was performed negligently. The paralysis was caused by damages to the facial nerve. The trial judge in saying that the injury was an unforeseeable accident did not find the defendant liable.

In general negligence will be avoided if there is evidence that the physician acted in accordance with common practice of similarly placed physicians. McNair J in *Bolam v Friern Hospital Management Committee*[471], set out the test for determining the standard of care owed by medical professionals to their patients commonly known as the Bolam's test. In this case, the defendant was the body who employed a doctor who had not given a mentally ill patient (the claimant) muscle relaxant drugs nor restrained them prior to giving them electro-convulsive therapy. The claimant suffered injuries during the procedure. The claimant sued the defendant claiming the doctor was negligent for not restraining them or giving them the drug. McNair J. stated that;

> *(...) a doctor is not guilty of negligence if he has acted in accordance with a practice accepted as proper by a responsible body of medical men skilled in that art ... a doctor is not negligent, if he is acting in accordance with such a practice, merely because there is a body of opinion that takes a contrary view*[472].

Following this judgment, the courts considered compliance with an approved professional practice as conclusive evidence that the defendant was not negligent, as the methods used in this case were approved of by a responsible body of the medical profession. However, when the risks of the old procedure become known, so that it can be said that an ordinary and reasonably competent physician would have changed his practice, it will be negligent to continue to use the old procedure[473].

The recognition of an approved practice further implies that health care professionals may adhere to practices which they have never followed before or with respect to a situation they have never encountered before. In 1997, the House of Lords issued the 'new Bolam' test in *Bolitho v City and Hackney Health Authority*[474]. In the ruling, the Court emphasized the need for the body of medical opinion to be reasonable and responsible.

---

471 See *Bolam v. Friern Hospital Management Committee* (1957) 2 ALLER118 at 121.

472 *Ibid.*

473 *Ibid.*

474 [1996] ALL ER 771.

In most cases the fact that distinguished experts in the field are of a particular opinion, will demonstrate the reasonableness of that opinion. A reasonable view necessarily presupposes that the relative risks and benefits have been weighted by the experts in forming their opinions. But if, in a rare case, it can be demonstrated that the professional opinion is not capable of withstanding logical analysis, the judge is entitled to hold that the body of opinion is not reasonable or responsible[475].

(d) Causation

For a medical practitioner to be sanction under the law of negligence, the plaintiff must establish, not merely that the defendant owed and breached a duty of care to the plaintiff, but also that such breach caused, materially contributed to, or increased the risk of, the injury of which the plaintiff complains[476]. Thus, a causal connection must be established between the tortious act of the defendant and damage which the plaintiff suffers[477]. It must be established that the patients could not have suffered the damage, injury or loss if the doctor had provided the correct standard of care based on the skills of that profession[478].

It will do the patient no good to establish negligence on the part of a doctor unless he is able to prove that the damage, injury or loss he or she has suffered was caused by that negligence[479]. In *Wilshire Vs. Essex Area Health*

---

475 Herman, NYS., (2005), "Report on Medical Liability on Council of Europe Member States: A Comparative Study of the Legal and Factual Situation in Member States of the Council of Europe", *European Committee on Legal Cooperation*, 3(1), p.9.

476 In *Barnett v Chelsea and Kensington Hospital Management Committee [*1969] 1 QB 428, the court examined whether the plaintiff's death was a result of the negligence of the defendant. The court held that the plaintiff has failed to establish, on the balance of probabilities, that the defendants' negligence caused the death of the deceased.

477 McMahon & Binchy, (2013), *Law of Torts*, 4th ed, Bloomsbury Professional Ltd, at para 2.03, state: "First there is the problem of causation. It is said that the defendant cannot be liable to the plaintiff unless he has caused the damage in question. This means at the outset that the act of the defendant must be linked in a factual or scientific way to the injury of the plaintiff if the defendant is to be considered as being potentially liable. This involves a factual investigation. If there is no connection between the defendant's conduct and the plaintiff's injury then the defendant cannot be liable to the plaintiff. But just because the defendant caused in a factual sense the plaintiff's injury does not necessarily mean that he will be liable in law to the plaintiff. Before the courts will hold the defendant liable in law they must also be satisfied on policy grounds, that the defendant legally caused the damage to the plaintiff. ..." It should be noted that a causal connection may be insufficient in certain situations to impose liability, particularly if there is a new intervening act between the defendant's tortious act and damage.

478 "Medical Negligence in Uganda", (2017), Uganda Law Reform Commission, Issues Paper, p.21.

479 See *Bolam Vs. Friern Hospital Management Committee* [1957] 1 WLR.

Authority[480], it was held that to establish causal link, the plaintiff is required to establish on a balance of probabilities that the defendants act was a necessary cause of his or her damage, injuries or loss and that the onus of proof lies on the plaintiff or one who claims to be injured.

The *'but for test'* principle[481] has been consistently reaffirmed by the courts as the general test for causation. A breach will be regarded a cause of the injury if it satisfies the 'but for test', that is to say; would the patient have sustained such injuries 'but for' the defendant's breach of duty? Thus, if the injuries would have occurred in any event, then the breach of duty will not be considered the cause of the injuries. A classic example of this can be gleaned from the case of *Barnett v. Chelsea and Kensington Hospital Management Committee*[482]. In this case, the plaintiff was the widow of a man who died of arsenic poisoning from contaminated sandwiches after he had attended the defendant hospital and negligently been sent home without treatment. The deceased was a night watch-man working over New Year's Eve. The nurse on duty informed the casualty officer of the man's condition, but the casualty officer, who suspected that the man had simply overindulged on New Year's Eve, instructed the nurse to inform the plaintiff to return home and come back on another occasion. The man was admitted to hospital later that morning, after considerable delay but died sometime later. The question examined by the court was whether had deceased would have died had the defendant acted without negligence and admitted him earlier.

The court was of the opinion on the basis of evidence that, even if the defendant had acted with due care and admitted the deceased, he would still have died of arsenic poisoning as the poison had already irretrievably and fatally taken its hold. Nield J, in deciding causation, stated:

> *But that, since he must have died of the poisoning even if he had been admitted to the wards five hours before his death, and treated with all care, the plaintiff had failed to establish*

---

480 (1988) 2 WLR 557.

481 In *Cork v Kirby Maclean Ltd* [1952] 2 All ER 402 (CA), the Court of Appeal approached the question of causal requirement. Denning LJ (at 407) stated: "Subject to the question of remoteness, causation is I think, a question of fact. If you can say that the damage would not have happened but for a particular fault, then that fault is in fact a cause of the damage; but if you can say that the damage would have happened just the same, fault or no fault, then the fault is not a cause of the damage. It often happens that each of the parties at fault can truly say to the other: 'But for your fault, it would not have happened.' In such a case both faults are in fact causes of the damage."

482 [1969] 1 Q B 428.

on the balance of probabilities that the defendants' negligence had caused the death.

Although the defendants were held negligent in failing to treat him[483], it was held that the refusal to treat him was not a cause of the deceased's death because the nature of the arsenic introduced into his tea was such that he would have died regardless. Consequently, when a physician has made an error in diagnosis but a correct diagnosis would not have led to a different treatment, it cannot be said that the error caused damage for which the physician was responsible.

In general, the '*but for test*' can be seen as a filter to exclude actions that did not affect the outcome. The Court in the case of *McGhee v National Coal Board*[484] stated that liability will be imposed if it can be established that the negligence of the defendant materially increased the risk of the plaintiff being damaged in the way in question.

However, the House of Lords in *Fairchild v Glenhaven Funeral Services Ltd*[485] modified the traditional *"but for" test* of causal connection. In adopting its new approach, their Lordships placed great emphasis on considerations of fairness and reasonableness and on policy. In Fairchild, the plaintiff had worked at different times under different employers and, during the course of his employment with them, had inhaled substantial quantities of asbestos dust containing asbestos fibre which caused him to suffer mesothelioma, a fatal disease. He was unable to prove on the balance of probabilities that his injury resulted during his employment with any one employer. There was no dispute but that all the employers had been negligent in exposing him to the asbestos dust; but the defendant contended that the plaintiff had not established by evidence that it had been its breach of duty that was a cause of the injury.

In finding liability against the defendants, the House of Lords considered the approach of the Supreme Court of California in the famous hunting expedition case of *Summers v Tice*[486]. There, each of two defendants at or about the same time had shot at a quail and in doing so fired negligently in the direction of the plaintiff, who was struck by shot from one of the defendants.

---

483 The Court found the defendants liable for breach of duty of care. Nield J (at 434), stated: "[T]he defendants' casualty officer was negligent in failing to see and examined the deceased, and that, had he done so, his duty would have been to admit the deceased to the ward and to have treated him or caused him to be treated."

484 (1972) 3 ALL ER 1008 At 1011.

485 6 [2003] AC 32.

486 (1948) 33 Cal.2d 80.

The Supreme Court of California held that both were jointly and severally liable even though it could not be identified which of them had actually injured the plaintiff[487]. The House of Lords, on the basis that medical science could not establish on a balance of probabilities the source of the fibre or fibres which caused the plaintiff's mesothelioma, based its decision on policy considerations similar to those which the courts have been applying over the years to extend or restrict the duty of care[488].

In many cases, it is possible to have more than one cause that satisfies the '*but for test*'. It is then up to the court to choose which of these has to be treated as the cause in law[489]. The court is not obliged to establish one action as the sole legal cause. In case there are two unrelated potential causes which can both have caused the injury; causality will depend on the nature of the events and the order in which they occurred. It is also possible that an act of another person, without which the damage would not have occurred, occurs between the physician's negligence and the patient's injury. In these situations, the court must decide whether the defendant is accountable or whether there was a so-called *novus actus interveniens* in which case the causal connection has been broken.

(e) Burden of Proof

As is the case for negligence claims generally, the burden of proof rests on the plaintiff to prove all aspects of his or her case to the required standard on the balance of probabilities[490] or preponderance of evidence, that a duty was owed by the defendant; that this duty was breached; and that the breach was the proximate cause of the injury or damage. The plaintiff, in seeking to prove his/ her case, may resort to both direct and circumstantial evidence.

---

487 *Summers v Tice* (1948) 33 Cal.2d 80, at paras 6 and 10, Carter J, stated: "When we consider the relative position of the parties and the results that would flow if plaintiff was required to pin the injury on one of the defendants only, a requirement that the burden of proof on that subject be shifted to defendants becomes manifest. They are both wrongdoers – both negligent toward plaintiff. They brought about a situation where the negligence of one of them injured the plaintiff, hence it should rest within them each to absolve himself if he can. ... We have seen that for the reasons of policy discussed herein, the case is based upon the legal proposition that, under the circumstances here presented, each defendant is liable for the whole damage whether they are deemed to be acting in concert or independently."

488 In *Dorset Yacht Co Ltd v Home Office* [1969] 2 All ER 564, at 567, Lord Denning stated: "It is, I think, at bottom a matter of public policy which we, as judges, must resolve. This task of 'duty' or 'no duty' is simply a way of limiting the range of liability for negligence."

489 Decision of the House of Lords in *Bonnington Castings v. Wardlaw*, 1956] A.C. 613.

490 See *Pickford v. Imperial Chem. Indus. Plc.*, [1998] 3 All E.R. 362, [1998] 1 W.L.R. 1189 (H.L.).

Direct evidence is a proof of fact arising from the testimony of what a witness personally saw, or heard or did establishing such a fact without inference or presumption, while circumstantial evidence[491] is evidence that does not expressly prove the fact asserted but generates a reasonable inference that it is so.

Since the burden of proof is a heavy one on the plaintiff, the Courts have adopted the maxim *res ipsa loquitor*, a Latin phrase which means "the facts speak for itself", to ease the burden on the plaintiff. The fundamental requirements of *res ipsa loquitur* applies if it is proved by the plaintiff: (i) that the thing causing the injury was under the management or control of the defendant or his servants, and (ii) that the accident in the ordinary course of things does not happen if those who have the management or control use proper care[492]. Thus, where an accident occurs in circumstances in which it would not ordinarily happen if proper care is used, and the defendant is in control of the state of affairs which caused the harm, the Court may infer negligence on the part of the defendant without calling on the plaintiff to show the respect in which the defendant has been negligent[493]. This will establish a case against the physician and holds him liable unless the physician can offer an explanation of how the injuries might have occurred without any form of negligence on his part.

Thus, *res ipsa loquitor* applies only in the absence of explanation. Therefore, if the plaintiff can show how the damage occurred then there is no room for inference, and the maxim does not apply. Essentially, then, *res ipsa loquitur* is just an elaborate way of saying that there will occasionally be circumstances in which a judge would be entitled to find that the defendant had been negligent without the need for expert witnesses to establish that the defendant's actions fell below the appropriate standard of care. However, it does not reverse the burden of proof, such that it is for the defendant to prove that she was not negligent, rather it applies in simple and unusual cases where negligence can be inferred by a lay person, from the facts themselves[494].

---

491 *Vogreg v Shepard Ambulance Service* (1955) 47 Wn.2d 659, at 662; 289 P.2d 350, the Supreme Court of Washington stated: "A case in which the doctrine of *res ipsa loquitur* is applicable is a circumstantial-evidence case. In it, the jury is permitted to infer negligence from an accident which ordinarily would not have occurred unless someone was negligent. The jury may make the inference of negligence or it may refuse to do so."

492 See *Scott v London & St. Katherine Docks Co* (1865) 3 H & C 596; 159 ER 665, at 601; 159 ER 665, at 667.

493 See *supra* note 519 at p 127.

494 *Ibid* at p.143.

In *Ratcliffe v Plymouth & Torbay Health Authority & Anor*[495], the Court of Appeal offered a detailed analysis on the applicability of *res ipsa loquitur* to medical negligence cases. The Court noted that the maxim can apply in simple situations in the medical negligence field, such as where a surgeon cuts off the right foot instead of the left foot or a swab is left in the operation site. In more complex fact situations, the plaintiff's evidence is likely to be buttressed by expert evidence, contradicted by expert evidence adduced on behalf of the defendant. Thus, any initial reference based on *res ipsa loquitur* will have been overtaken by a clash of competing expert evidence, to be resolved by the court on conventional principles of the respective weight of each party's evidence. Hobhouse LJ stated:

> *Res ipsa loquitur is not a principle of law: it does not relate to or raise any presumption. It is merely a guide to help to identify when a prima facie case is being made out. Where experts and factual evidence has been called on both sides at a trial its usefulness will normally have long since been exhausted.*

In *Plateau State Health Services Management Board & Anor v Philip Fitoka*[496], the plaintiff, an Inspector of Police, was taken ill and went to the second defendant's hospital for treatment for pneumonia. After the administration of drugs on him, he became completely deaf. He brought a claim in negligence and successfully pleaded *res ipsa loquitur* against the defendants. Alagao JSC concluded:

> *[T]he evidence led by the plaintiff and lack of same by the defendants having chickened out of an opportunity to state their own position ... and the sheer force of the other exhibits ...having been rejected, the defendants were properly found liable in negligence and res ipsa loquitur applied*[497].

The failure of the defendants to have availed themselves of the opportunity to provide some plausible explanation of the plaintiff's injury consistent with the absence of negligence on their part was fatal to their defence.

Conversely in *Ojo* V. Gharoro & Ors[498], the plaintiff had been unable to get pregnant and went to hospital where it was medically ascertained that

495 [1998] Lloyd's Rep Med 162.
496 [2013] 2 NWLR 383.
497 *Ibid.*
498 [2006] 10 NWLR 173.

the removal of a growth might make it possible for her to have a pregnancy. The surgical procedure was done by the first defendant who was assisted by the third defendant. The defendants negligently left in the plaintiff's womb a broken needle as a result of which she experienced great pains. The plaintiff brought action and pleaded *res ipsa loquitur*. The Supreme Court held that the plaintiff's failure to call an expert witness was fatal to her case. The Court found on the basis of the evidence that the defendants had rebutted the presumption of negligence. Tobi JSC concluded: "From the totality of the case before the trial court, I believe the evidence of the defendants that 'the needle in this case got broken accidentally and proper care was taken to locate the pieces"[499].

The Learned Supreme Court Judge finding the defendant doctor not liable, said that negligence is a negative tort, the law therefore places a burden on the plaintiff to prove that the defendant was negligent, and in the circumstances of this case the act of leaving the piece or pieces of needle in the abdomen of the appellant (which qualifies as the happening event) says it all. In prove of the act, the plaintiff must satisfy the twin but alternative standard of prove; balance of probability, and preponderance of evidence. In either of these standards, the plaintiff must come out clearly with cogent evidence as to the specific act or acts of the defendant, which resulted in negligence, and not merely an agglomeration of act or acts lacking specificity[500]. For *res ipsa loquitor* to apply the event which gave rise to the negligence must tell its own story and it must invariably be a clear and unambiguous story of lack of duty of care.

In the Ghanian case of *Asantekramo alias Kumah v Attorney-General*[501], the plaintiff was referred by her private medical practitioner to the defendants' hospital, having been diagnosed as suffering from a ruptured ectopic pregnancy. The plaintiff was examined there and an urgent operation was recommended. The operation was successful, but her right arm became swollen and gangrenous, resulting in its eventual amputation, following a blood transfusion administered on her by the nursing staff, through a vein in that arm. The High Court held that the onus of proof shifted on the defendants to show that the gas gangrene which developed had occurred through no fault of the doctors and nurses or those persons who took charge of the plaintiff. Imposing liability, Taylor J stated: "[N]o evidence of any sort was led by the

---

499 *Ibid.*, at 216.

500 *Ibid.*

501 [1975] 1 GLR 319.

defendant as to whether the needle used and the apparatus were sterilized. Evidence was not led that the dextrose drip and the blood given were not contaminated"[502].

From the foregoing, medical expert evidence is necessary to show that an act or omission of the doctor is negligent, given the complex and indeterminate nature of medical science. Unless the defendant admits negligence, it is only a doctor who can show that the treatment given by another doctor falls below the required standard. The patient has the burden of proof but the physician must adduce evidence to rebut the inference of negligence, in order to avoid a finding of liability. This is where patients find difficulties; adducing medical expert evidence is not easy because doctors are usually reluctant to testify against their colleagues. The fact that the culpability of a medical practitioner is largely dependent on the expert evidence of a colleague has been largely criticized on the grounds that the approach seems to be in favour of the medical profession over and above the patient and hence, support from colleagues arguably makes it easy to escape liability for negligence[503].

Indeed, the Cameroon Code of Medical ethics reinforced this by stating that doctors owe each other moral support, and that; "it shall be forbidden to slander or disparage a colleague, or to repeat any remarks likely to harm him in the practice of his profession. It goes further to state that "defence of a colleague unjustly criticized shall be deemed good professional conduct"[504]. Thus, to testify that a procedure adopted or a treatment administered by a colleague is negligent is tantamount to disparaging or slandering a colleague. Moreover, a violation of the provision of the Code of Medical Ethics is liable to professional sanctions by the Disciplinary Board of the Medical Council, this tend to act as a shield to medical professionals, and is a hurdle that hinder the prosecution of negligent doctors.

(f) Consequential Damages

It is not sufficient that a health care professional violated the standard of care, the patient must also prove that he/she sustained physical or emotional injury or suffered some harm that would not have occurred in the absence of negligence, such as; disability, loss of income, unusual pain, suffering and

---

502 *Ibid.*

503 See *supra* note 485.

504 Section 42(1)(2)(3) of Decree No 83/166 of 12 August 1983 on Code of Medical Ethics in Cameroon.

hardship, or significant past and future medical bills. If there is an injury without negligence or negligence that did not cause an injury, there is no case.

In addition, to establishing that the injury was caused by the defendant's negligence, the injury must be a direct and not a remote consequence of the defendant's action. In *R V Akerelele*[505], it was noted that causation cannot be based on assumptions especially in cases of medical negligence and hence, must be proved or at the minimum, show that the claimant's injury was caused substantially by the defendant's actions. The law does not hold a person responsible for all the direct consequences of that person's negligent act. Thus, the doctor is liable only for such consequences as a reasonable man will foresee as the natural and probable consequence of the act. The medical practitioner's ability to reasonably foresee damage or injury as a direct result of his action is thus crucial. Consequences which are not foreseeable are regarded by the law as "too remote"[506].

(g) Defences available to the Medical Practitioner under the tort of Negligence

There are a number of possible defences to a negligence action, which a medical practitioner could plead in order to exculpate himself from sanction, these include; contributory negligence, voluntary assumption of the risk, foreseeability, statute of limitation.

i. Contributory Negligence of the Patient

It is possible for a patient who has been the victim of medical negligence not to be entitled to full compensation for the injury suffered on account of his/ her contributory negligence in failing to have taken proper care of himself/ herself. The doctrine of contributory negligence reduces the compensation which the victim of a wrong receives where the victim was partly to blame for his or her own damage[507]. Courts have found the defence of contributory negligence to be available in medical negligence litigation in a wide range of circumstances[508]. Some of these instances will be discuss here.

---

505 (1941) 8 WACA 56.

506 See *supra* note 519.

507 J.Goudkamp and D,Nolan, ,(2016), "Contributory Negligence In The Twenty-First Century: Empirical Study Of First Instance Decisions", *The Modern Law Review,* Vol.79, Issue 4, pp. 575-622.

508 Binchy & Komolafe, .(2011), "Patients, Contributory Negligence and Medical Negligence Litigation" *Quarterly Review of Tort Law,* Vol. 4, Issue 2, p.21.

ii. Failure of the patient to disclose pertinent information

Where a patient fails to disclose pertinent information to the doctor, the doctor's conduct, based on insufficient or misleading information, simply may not fall below the professional standard of care[509], because doctors depend to a considerable degree on patients to give them a good medical history and a clear account of their symptoms. In determining the issue of contributory negligence, courts have acknowledged the need to have regard to the patient's particular circumstances. To require that a patient with learning difficulties, for example, should act according to more demanding standards than those of which he /she is capable would be so obviously unjust. In the Kenyan case of *Jimmy Paul Semenye v Aga Khan Health Services*[510], a baby boy suffered Erbs palsy or brachial injury under the care of the defendants, the defendants alleged that the mother had withheld vital information arising from complications she had had in previous deliveries. During the trial, records of the defendant were produced which showed that the mother had in fact disclosed two earlier miscarriages. The Kenya High Court imposed liability and made no finding of contributory negligence against the mother, Angawa J stated:

> "*I find no contributory negligence against the [mother] who provided all the relevant information ... If the defendants [had been] computerized they would have reconfirmed that the [mother] was their patient in one of the earlier pregnancies and would have been more diligent*"[511].

iii. Failure to comply with medical instructions

A patient sometimes fails to comply with the instructions given him or her by the doctor and other health professionals. For example, when told to take a course of antibiotics until the tablets are all gone, some patients, feeling better after a couple of days, stop taking the tablets prematurely. Other

---

509 In *Harmse No obo Jacobus v MEC for Health*: Gauteng Province [2010] ZAGPJHC 110, at para 31, the South Gauteng High Court, Johannesburg found the defendant's conduct fell below the professional standard for his failure to heed the plaintiff's previous medical history or to notice the surgical scars on the plaintiff's right femoral leg. Mathopo J stated: "[T]he fact that the doctors were unaware of the [plaintiff's] previous history and surgical scars is indicative of their failure to properly and physically examine him. In my view members of the society expects that once they are admitted at the hospital the doctors would treat them with the necessary skill and care that is required of a reasonable practitioner."

510 8 [2006] eKLR.

511 *Ibid.*, para 83.

patients fail to keep appointments or to advise doctors of deterioration in their health. Still other patients fail to adhere to lifestyle prescriptions designed to protect them from the risk of heart attack or stroke. All of these types of case can involve a finding of contributory negligence against the patient but, in many instances, doctors will find that, in pointing the finger at the patient, they may excite the attention of the court to the prior question of whether they communicated clear instructions to the patient[512]. Most patients find it difficult to comprehend complex information, especially when conveyed orally. Moreover, many patients find it very hard to understand directions as to when to take medicines and the amounts to be taken at particular times.

In Cameroon poor literacy, limited education and poor communication makes it difficult for patients to absorb complex directives especially when communicated orally, such as directives as to when to take medication and the amount to be taken at a time. Moreover, many patients suffer from a serious lack of financial resources. After the first dose of medicine provided by the hospital, patients often find themselves unable to pay for any further dose. Again, given the context in Cameroon, there may be reasons why a patient fails to comply with the treatment regime prescribed by the doctor which do not necessarily indicate contributory negligence on the patient's part: low level of education, unstable living condition, unemployment, high transportation cost, long distance from treatment centre, cultural beliefs associated with illness, and forgetfulness. These are considerations to be taken by the Courts before making a finding of contributory negligence.

Where children are patients, they are inevitably dependent on their parents (or other care givers) to look after their healthcare. In *Kgosiemang v MEC for the Department of Health, North-West Province*[513], where a nine-year old plaintiff claimed damages for negligent treatment at a hospital, the defence of contributory negligence was made, based on her alleged failure to return to the hospital or go to an ophthalmology clinic and her alleged failure to heed the instructions on the medication she was taking. *Landman J* rejected this evidence. Referring to the plaintiff's age, *Landman J* observed that she would have been "entirely dependent on her mother for guidance, and the means to seek medical attention, and as regards the intake of medicine and application of ointment"[514].

---

512 Obafemi K A R., (2017), "Medical Negligence Litigation in Nigeria: Identifying the Challenges and Proposing a Model Law Reform Act", (Ph.D. Thesis), School of Law, Trinity College, Dublin.

513 [2013] ZANWHC 14.

514 *Ibid.*

iv. Dangerous lifestyle

Generally speaking, it is not open to a doctor to argue that, because the patient whom he consulted was, for example, an alcoholic, or drug addict, that some reduction in compensation should on that account alone be made. This is not saying that the court should ignore these facts. Indeed, the effect of patient's lifestyle choices may impact on issues of causation or damages, So, a doctor who operated negligently on a patient's liver is perfectly entitled to point to the ravages already inflicted on the liver by the patient's overindulgence in alcohol to the extent that this element may affect the court's determination of the issues of causation and damages, but not contributory negligence. If the same patient persisted in drinking excessively after the operation, contrary to clear medical advice, the court would rightly reduce compensation to take account of that contributory negligence (as well as factoring this conduct into the issues of causation and quantum of damages)[515].

In many instances[516], the courts have reduced the compensation awarded to patients on account of their contributory negligence in smoking. The courts in Cameroon should be well disposed to adopt same since the dangers of smoking is well appreciated by all the segments of the society, due to its destructive effect on health.

It seems only just that there should be some reduction in the compensation awarded to a patient who is the victim of medical negligence in cases where the patient has been guilty in taking care of his or her own welfare. The challenge for the court is to apply this principle in a way that is practical to the circumstances of the particular patient, for example, his/ her financial viability, level of education and literacy, cultural background, age, and mental development.

v. Voluntary Assumption of Risk

Volenti non fit injuria ('no injury is done to one who voluntarily consents') is a complete defence to an action in negligence[517]. For this defence to prevail; the risk must be known to the plaintiff. When the plaintiff has the knowledge

[515] Pandit, M S. and Pandit, S., (2009), "Medical Negligence Coverage of the Profession, Duties, Ethics, Case Law, and Enlightened Defence. A Legal Perspective", Indian *Journal of Urology*, 25(3), pp.372-378.

[516] In *Badger v Ministry of Defence* [2006] 3 All ER 173, [2005] EWHC 2941 (QB); *Horseley v Cascade Insulation Services Ltd* [2007] EWHC 2945, *Shortell v Bical Construction* Ltd (16 May 2008), English HC, Mackay J.

[517] *Rootes v Shelton* (1967) 116 CLR 383.

that the act is going to cause harm or loss and in spite of that accept to do it, agreeing to suffer the injury, then the defendant will not be liable for such act. But merely having the knowledge of such a risk is not enough for the application of this maxim, mere knowledge only constitutes a partial defence and does not amount to consenting to the risk.

If a plaintiff, with full knowledge, voluntarily accepts the risk of injury, he or she will not recover any damages. The defendant needs to prove not only that the plaintiff accepted the risk of injury but also accepted that if injury should happen, the plaintiff would accept the legal risk[518]. The plaintiff has to prove, on the balance of probabilities, that he or she was not aware of an obvious risk. This reverses the onus of proof and makes *volenti non fit injuria* easier to use. The effect of these provisions is that a plaintiff is rebuttably presumed to be aware of a risk where the risk would have been obvious to a reasonable person in the position of the plaintiff. A plaintiff cannot rebut the presumption by claiming that even though he or she was aware of the general risk of harm, he or she was not aware of all its possible manifestations, including the one that eventuated[519].

Where a doctor explains all the risk to the patient, and the patient agrees to assume these risks, the doctor is not responsible if those risks resulted in an injury. The doctor will claim that the patient's particular injury was a recognized risk of the procedure and the risk was properly explained to the patient, and the patient gave informed consent to undergo the risks of the procedure. There is no liability for the materialization of an inherent risk (a risk of something occurring that cannot be avoided by the exercise of reasonable care and skill) For example; there would be no liability for the inherent risks involved in a medical procedure. But this does not affect the duty to warn of the risks[520]. However, in relation to health professionals, the defence of *volenti non fit injuria* does not really apply because consent to medical treatment does not amount to an assumption of the risk. Even in the situation where a patient is told by a doctor that they are inexperienced, the appropriate argument would be about the relevant standard of care and not about the defence of *volenti*.

518 *Smith v Charles Baker & Sons* [1891] AC 325; *Canterbury Municipal Council v Taylor* [2002] NSWCA 24.

519 *Carey v Lake Macquarie City Council* [2007] NSWCA 4, [90] (McClellan CJ).

520 Yule J., (2011) "Defences in Medical Negligence: To What Extent Has Tort Law Reform in Australia Limited the Liability of Health Professionals?" *Journal of the Australian Law Teachers Association*, 4(1&2), pp.53-63.

In *Lakshmir Rajan* v *Malar Hosdpital Ltd*[521], a 40-year-old woman, noticed the development of a painful lump in her breast, however, it had no effect on her uterus but during the operation, her uterus was removed without providing due justification. The court held that the hospital was liable for deficiency in service and that the patient's consent for the operation did not extend as consent for the removal of her uterus, thus they could not claim that the patient voluntarily accepted the risk by giving consent.

There are exceptions to the defence of *volenti non fit injuria*, and this include where the consent is obtained under compulsion, or by fraud where the act of the defendant is done negligently, as where a doctor obtain consent to perform surgery and he perform it negligently, he cannot benefit from this defence. Although it seems like a good defence, in actual practice this defence is often unsuccessful where owing to the different facts and circumstances the action of the defendant often manifest into negligence.

vi. Foreseeability

A doctor is responsible for protecting patients from risks that they can see or know about beforehand, which is; foreseeable risks or dangers. In order to establish a defence, the doctor can claim that the injury was an unforeseeable consequence of the medical treatment. As such, where a patient suffered injury as a result of side effects from medication given to him by his doctor, the doctor can argue that the side effects were so rare that they were not foreseeable.

vii. Statute of limitation

Where a negligent action has been successfully proven by a plaintiff, the courts may award compensatory damages. The purpose of compensatory damages is to put the plaintiff back in the position they would have been but for the negligence of the defendant. The assessment of damages is governed by common law principles with the court exercising its discretion in determining the quantum of the damages The purpose of statutory limits is to limit the amount and extent of liability and to thereby make it less attractive for plaintiffs to commence proceedings.

---

521 (III (1998)) CPJ 586 (Tamil Hadu SCDRC).

Generally, limitation period for cause of action for tort in Cameroon is six years[522], except for actions in tort for personal injuries, where the period tends to be shorter, which is three years. The reason for this disparity in limitation periods has been identified as resting on the fact that victims of personal injury need to be compensated within a reasonable time, however this limitation period tends to curtail the right of action of victims of personal injuries. Thus, an action for medical negligence is barred after six years and after three years where the claim is for personal injuries,

Common law Courts have held four different views on the construction of the statute to determine the time when a cause of action accrues in the context of negligence. The first is that a cause of action accrues when damage caused by wrongful act occurs[523]. The second view is that a cause of action accrues when plaintiff could first reasonably have become aware of the damage[524]. The third view holds that a cause of action accrues when plaintiff could first reasonably have become aware of the damage and the fact that the damage was caused by the defendant[525]. The last view is that a cause of action accrues when plaintiff could first reasonably have become aware of the damage and the fact that the damage was caused by the defendant and also that the defendant was legally to blame[526].

---

522 The applicable law in Anglophone Cameroon is bases on Section 11 of the Southern Cameroon High Court Law (SCHCL) 1958 which provide for the application of English common law, the doctrine of equity, and statute of general application which were in force in England on January 1 1900. On the basis of this a number of English statutes apply in Cameroon. England's Limitation Act 1623 applied as a "statute of general application" to common law jurisdictions. The Limitation Act 1623 remained in force in England without substantial amendment until 1939. Section 2(1) provided: that an action founded on tort should not be brought after the expiration of six years from the date on which the cause of action accrued.

523 *Pirelli General Cable Works Ltd v Oscar Faber & Partners [1983] 2 AC 1.*

524 *Cartledge v E. Jopling & Sons Ltd [1963] AC 758.*

525 Purchas LJ in *Nash v Eli Lilly & Co* [1993] 1 WLR 782, at 792, stated: "... we shall proceed on the basis that knowledge is a condition of mind which imports a degree of certainty and that the degree of certainty which is appropriate for this purpose is that which, for the particular plaintiff, may reasonably be regarded as sufficient to justify embarking upon the preliminaries to the making of a claim for compensation such as the taking of legal or other advice."

526 The English Court of Appeal in *Spargo v North Essex District Health Authority* [1997] 37 BMLR 99; [1997] PIQR P235, at P242, developed what the law required in order to establish actual knowledge. Brooke LJ stated: "A plaintiff has the requisite knowledge when she knows enough to make it reasonably for her to begin to investigate whether or not she has a case against the defendant. Another way of putting this is to say that she will have such knowledge if she so firmly believes that her condition is capable of being attributed to an act or omission which she can identify (in broad terms) that she goes to a solicitor to seek advice about making a claim for compensation."

All in all, action under negligence is less likely to yield any positive result. It is a long, tedious, cumbersome and expensive litigation in which a plaintiff may not succeed to receive any compensation for his injury because the burden of prove on the plaintiff/ patient is a difficult one to discharge. However, where this burden is sufficiently discharged, the court may award damages.

Damages awarded by the court are the monetary compensation available to a person who suffers injury, harm, or even death as a result of the malpractice of a medical practitioner or institution. Requiring the tortfeasor to compensate the victim forces him/her to internalize the costs of him/her risky behaviour and deters him/her from engaging in inappropriately risky activities[527]. The higher the expected compensatory damages he is to pay, the greater the cost of engaging in the risky activity, and the more he will be deterred from engaging in the activity without proper precautions.

The plaintiff's damages include compensatory and punitive damages. Compensatory damages are both economic and non-economic. Damages for economic loss (Special Damages) include; past and future medical costs, out-of-pocket expenses related to the injury, and lost wages; non-economic damages (General Damages) include; physical and psychological harm, such as loss of vision, loss of a limb or organ, disability or loss of a loved one, severe pain and emotional distress or pain and suffering. Punitive damages are awarded in the event of want-on and reckless conduct, and are designed to punish the offending doctor and dissuade other doctors from making similar mistakes.

The fundamental goal of damage awards is to return the plaintiff as closely as possible to his or her condition before the accident. This was reiterated in *Victoria Laundry (Windsor), Ltd., v. Newman Indus. Ltd*[528] that "It is well settled that the governing purpose of damages is to put the party whose rights have been violated in the same position, so far as money can do so, as if his rights had been observed." This general principle is derived from the words of Lord Blackburn in *Livingstone v. Rawyards Coal Co*[529] thus; "that the sum of money which will put the party who has been injured or who has suffered in the same position as he would have been in if he had not sustained the wrong for which he is now getting his compensation or reparation".

527 Shepherd, J. (2014), "Uncovering the Silent Victims of the American Medical Liability Systems", *Vanderbilt Law Review*, 67(12), p.158.

528 [1949] 2 K.B. 528, 539.

529 (1880) 5 App. CAS 25,39.

A patient can only recover compensation in respect of negligent medical treatment if he has actually suffered damage. Damages will be determined by comparing the current situation with the situation the patient would be in, if the fault had not occurred.

About the quantum of compensation payable to an injured patient, it was observed in the case of *IMA* v. *V.P. Shanta and Ors*[530]. as follows:

> *A patient who has been injured by an act of medical negligence has suffered in a way which is recognized by the law, and by the public at large as deserving compensation. This loss may be continuing and what may seem like an unduly large award may be little more than that sum which is required to compensate him for such matters as loss of future earnings and the future cost of medical or nursing care. To deny a legitimate claim or to restrict arbitrarily the size of an award would amount to substantial injustice. After all, there is no difference in legal theory between the plaintiff injured through medical negligence and the plaintiff injured in an industrial or motor accident*[531].

The general rule is that, damages must be assessed once and for all at the trial as "it is a well settled rule of law that damages resulting from one and the same cause of action must be assessed and recovered once and for all"[532]. The rule that, damages must be assessed once and for all was illustrated in the case of *Derrick v. Williams*[533] where a child was killed by the negligence of the defendant; an action was brought for damages in respect of the death but not for loss of expectation of life. It was held that, the acceptance of the sum paid into the court in satisfaction of the claim barred a second action for damages for loss of expectation of life.

Special damages are compensation to cover the financial losses and expenses incurred as a result of negligent medical treatment. Special damages are out-of-pocket expenses that can be determined by adding together all the plaintiff's quantifiable financial losses. Special damages must be specifically pleaded and proved. They must be explicitly claimed on the pleadings and at the trial, it must be proved by compelling and accurate evidence both that

---

530 III (1995) CPJ I (SC).

531 *Ibid.*

532 Per Browen L.J in *Brunsden v Humphrey* (1884) 14 QBD 191, at p.147.

533 (1939) 2 All ER 559.

the loss incurred and that it was the direct result of the defendant's conduct. Special damages include amongst others; short-term medical expenses, the cost of travelling to and from the hospital, loss of earning or earning capacity, expenses for nursing care and assistance. Special damages seek to affect a "restitution in interregnum", that is to put the plaintiff in the position that he would have been, had the injury not been inflicted on him. The plaintiff is entitled to recover such expenses which he has reasonably incurred up to the time of trial.

General damages refer to the patient's cost of suffering that, although real, cannot by its nature have a definite price. The most common examples are: loss of enjoyment of life or lower quality of life, physical and mental pain and suffering, loss of future earning capacity, loss of companionship for wrongful death cases. The monetary amount of the loss or injury does not have to be specifically proven. General damages are awarded on the notion that there is no medium exchange of happiness and no market for expectation of life.

In *Felker v. Bangor Railway*[534], it was held that there is no standard by which the damage for such injuries as are shown in the case can be measured. In the end the question must be left to the sound sense and good judgment of the jury, to award such damages as seem to them to be fairly compensatory[535]. The sheer fact is that there is no objective yardstick for translating non pecuniary losses such as pain and suffering and loss of amenities into monetary terms[536]. Money cannot provide true restitution; however, it can provide for proper care and this is the paramount concern of the courts while awarding damages for personal injury as there must be adequate future care.

Generally, the compensation that is awarded for general damages depends on the type and severity of the injury and its long-term impact on the victim. Therefore, general damages are implied by the law and awarded at the discretion of the court. As such the guiding principle can be expressed only in such vague terms as awarding what is "fair" and "proper"[537]. General damages include amongst others; pain and suffering, permanent impairment or loss of function, disfigurement, loss of ability to enjoy life's pleasures, loss of consortium.

The uncertainty in general damage awards produces a potential problem of individual unfairness. Equally situated individuals may experience

534 91 A. 980 (Me. 1914).
535 *Ibid.*, at 981.
536 See *supra* note 485 at p.24.
537 Per Harman L.J in *Warren V. King* (1964)1 WLR 10.

substantially different outcomes. If fairness and justice require that we treat like cases alike and different cases differently, such variability in general damages undermines these values[538]. When two similar people suffer the same physical injury and are awarded very different amounts in general damages, there are no commonly agreed upon criteria by which we could say that one amount is correct and the other amount is incorrect[539]. the combination of incommensurability, incalculability due to the absence of a market against which to judge appropriateness, and the absence of any meaningful guidance to courts when they are asked to decide cases, results in unprincipled differences in outcome[540].

Damages for death can be awarded to the executors or administrators of the deceased estate. It is the sum that would have compensated the deceased so far as money could do for the destruction of his capacity to carry on life's activities, as he would have done had he not been killed, including the destruction of his earning capacity. A claim for bereavement can also be initiated by a husband or wife or parents. The measure of damages here is the amount of pecuniary advantage or benefit which is reasonably probable the dependents would have got if the deceased had not died[541].

4.2.1.3 Tort of Battery

The relationship between a physician and his patient is a consensual one wherein the patient knowingly seeks the assistance of the physician and the physician knowingly accepts him as a patient. A physician, therefore, cannot treat a patient unless he has first obtained his/her consent to do so. A doctor is therefore liable when he carries out any medical procedure which requires bodily contact with the patient and it is done without the patient's consent or without lawful justification. The law views the need for consent as essential to the lawful touching by a doctor, of a competent adult, in the absence of which the doctor will be liable for battery. In the Ontario case of *Allan v. New Mount Sinai Hospital*[542], Linden J., said; "While the courts resist advising the medical profession about how to conduct their practice, our law is clear that consent

---

538 Sanders, J., (2008), 'Reforming General Damages: A Good Tort Reform", *Roger Williams University Law Review*, 13(115), p.128.

539 *Ibid.*

540 King, J H., (2004), "Pain and Suffering, Noneconomic Damages, and the Goals of Tort Law", *S.M.U. L. Rev*, 57(163), p.175.

541 *Ibid.*

542 [1980] 28 Ont. 2d 356, 364.

of a patient must be obtained before any surgical procedure can be conducted. Without a consent. . . no surgery may be performed". The need for consent in the medical context is derived from the individual's right to decide what should be done with his or her body.

Failure to inform a patient of inherent risks in an operation, and receive his consent may also give rise to an action in battery (unconsented touching)[543]. Battery is the intentional infliction of harmful bodily contact on the person of the plaintiff. The typical situation in which it arises is where an operation or treatment is performed on a patient who has not consented to it[544]. For example, should a surgeon receive authorization to perform a given operation and then performs an additional or alternative procedure without the patient's consent, such conduct can give rise to a battery claim. In *Mohr v Williams*[545], the physician obtained his patient's consent to an operation on her right ear, then performed an operation on her left ear. In *Pratt v. Davis*[546] the patient consented to an operation on her womb. The operation went far beyond her expectations and her ovaries and uterus were entirely removed. In all two cases, the defendants were held liable.

It is not necessary to show actual physical injury to recover damages in battery cases. Any treatment which is unauthorized has invaded the patient's right to be free from unwanted contact, and the invasion of this interest is compensable. The principal item of damages is "bodily harm." Pain or any impairment or alteration of the physical condition of the body constitutes bodily harm[547]. In *Rogers v. Lumbermens Mutual Casualty Company*[548], the surgeon extended his appendectomy operation and performed a hysterectomy. Apparently good surgery and medical ethics both dictated that the operation be extended, but the lack of an emergency made the extension tortious. Even though the results were beneficial, damages were awarded. The special circumstances that justified the award were the patient's background. After having one child, she remarried, and desperately wanted to have more children. She had been consulting doctors for six years in a fruitless quest to become capable of having children, and convincing testimony was elicited to the effect that she attached great importance to

543 See *Halushka v. University of Saskatchewan*, [1965] 53 D.L.R. 2d 436.
544 Smith, D S., (1967) "Battery in Medical Torts", *Clev. Marshall Law Review*, 16,(22), p.22.
545 95 Minn. 261, 104 N. W. 12, 1 L. R. A. (n. s.) 439 (1905).
546 224 Ill. 300, 79 N. E. 562, 7 L. R. A. (n. s.) 609 (1906).
547 See *Corpman v. Boyer*, 171 Ohio St. 233, 169 N. E. 2d 14 (1960).
548 119 So. 2d 649 (La. App. 2d Cir. 1960),

this and would never have consented to an operation that would remove her reproductive organs[549].

The tort of battery is useful enough when the medical treatment is wholly without consent, when the operation extends to parts of the body not within the immediate area the treatment was scheduled for, and when the physician has deceived the patient.

The physician has a duty to make a reasonable disclosure of available choices with respect to a proposed treatment option and of the significant or common dangers potentially involved with each choice. Failing to provide such disclosure creates a basis for a claim of lack of informed consent[550]. In order to prevail in such a case, the patient must show; that the physician failed to provide the patient with adequate information to enable him or her to make an intelligent choice regarding the course of treatment; and that a reasonable patient would not have consented to a given course of treatment or procedure, had the appropriate and pertinent information been disclosed[551].

The nature of the information is generally not the subject of expert testimony. The judge is to determine whether or not a reasonable patient would have consented to or refused a given treatment or procedure if the omitted information had, in fact, been provided. In *Ediger v Johnston*[552], The plaintiff, Cassidy Ediger, suffered from persistent bradycardia (slow heartrate) during birth resulting in severe brain damage. During the delivery procedure, the doctor attempted a mid-level forceps procedure as plaintiff's mother's labour was not progressing. Dr. Johnston did not inform plaintiff's mother of the risks involved in the procedure including bradycardia and hence did not receive her consent. The trial judge found Dr. Johnston in breached of his standard of care by failing to inform Cassidy's mother of the risks involved in the forceps procedure and not receiving her consent for the same.

Such information may be transmitted in writing or verbally, or it may even be implied in limited circumstances. Once a patient had shown a touching by the doctor as a result of the treatment or operation, the burden would then pass to the doctor to prove consent[553]. In emergency situations,

---

549 *Ibid.*

550 Gittler, G J. and Goldstein, J C., (1996), "The Elements of Medical Malpractices: An Overview", *Medicolegal Case Reviews*, 23, p.1153.

551 *Ibid.*, p.1154.

552 2013 SCC 18.

553 *Kelley v. Hazlett*, 75 D.L.R.3d 536 (1976); *Reibl v. Hughes*, 114 D.L.R. 3d 1 (1980),

consent to treatment is usually presumed by law. Here, practitioners are to proceed in a manner that is likely to have the best outcome and chance for survival. Full disclosure is not demanded where an explanation of every risk may result in alarming a patient who is already apprehensive and where such disclosure would tend to increase the risk itself by subjecting the patient to emotional upset[554]. The Cameroon Code of Medical Ethics[555] provides that a serious prognosis may not be divulge to the patient.

4.2.1.4 Liabilities of Hospital Management for Violation of Medical Practice

Apart from the liability of medical practitioners in their individual capacities, a hospital may also be sanction for medical malpractices. This is especially because hospitals are no longer being regarded solely as 'venues for treatment' but as 'providers of treatment'[556]. This development has given rise to the liability of hospitals either directly or vicariously for acts of negligence of its employees. It is considered that the hospital owes some duties to the patient and that is why it will be held directly liable for failure to discharge these duties.

(a) Direct Liabilities of Hospital Management

Direct liability for negligence will arise where a hospital has failed to provide an environment and facilities that will facilitate safe treatment of patients. Examples include; unavailability of required equipment, non-functional equipment, unhygienic conditions, hiring of incompetence employees, mishandling of patients record, non-functional ambulance and transmission of infections amongst others[557]. In *Wilsher v Essex AHA*[558], the Court of Appeal was of the view that the health authority owed patients a duty of care to provide properly skilled medical staff, and an adequately equipped hospital. In this case, Sir Nicolas Browne-Wilkinson V-C said; "In my judgment, a health authority which so conducts its hospital that it fails to provide doctors of sufficient skill and experience to give the

---

554 *Salgo v. Leland,* 154 Cal. App. 2d 560, 317 P. 2d 170 (1957).
555 Section 27(1) of the Cameroon Code of Medical Ethics.
556 Agarwal, S S., (2009), "Medical Negligence. Hospital's Responsibility". *J Indian Acad Forensic Med.* 31, pp.164–170.
557 *Kent V. Griffiths* (2002) 2 All ER, 474.
558 [1987] QB 730.

treatment offered at the hospital may be directly liable in negligence to the patient"[559].

Traditionally, the hospital owed a direct duty to the patient to furnish equipment that is not defective, improper, or inadequate[560]. Thus, if the harm is caused by a defect in the hospital's apparatus, as opposed to the negligent use of the apparatus by an employee, the hospital can be held directly liable under the theory of corporate negligence. Where it does not have the proper equipment and facilities to treat adequately a patient's condition, a hospital might have a duty to transfer the patient to another hospital that does have such facilities. In the 1963 California case of *Carrasco v. Bankoff*[561], the Court held the hospital liable when a patient with third-degree burns was retained in the hospital for 53 days and the institution did not have facilities for skin grafting or for the "open" method treatment of burns. Since it was established that these facilities were required for proper treatment of third-degree burns, the hospital was under a duty to transfer the patient to another hospital.

In Cameroon patients injured as a result of the negligent operation of government hospitals are not likely to receive any compensation because the problem of resource allocation by the Government or the Ministry of Public Health, has such a political component as to place it out of the remit of the duty of care. For example, in the Report of the Commission set up by the Medical Council to investigate the death of *Dr Ngo Kana* it was found out that the ambulance of the L'hopital Gyneco-Obstetrique et Pediatrique de Douala was not available(the driver of the ambulance was nowhere to be found and was not picking his call) to transport the deceased (Dr, Ngo Kana), to L'hopital General de Douala given her critical condition, to the extent that they had to transport her with a private car which lack the necessary apparatus, more to that the hospital did not have a functional re-animation unit, situations which partly contributed to her death. The recommendations of the commission did not inculpate medical staffs of the hospital nor the hospital itself.

Generally, the hospital authority has the duty of exercising reasonable care in making the premises safe for the patient and their visitors, and in warning them of dangerous conditions which are known to the hospital[562]. This duty requires the hospital authority to guard against any danger arising

---

559 *Ibid.*

560 Hanson, L R. and Stromberg, E R., (1969), "Hospital Liability for Negligence", *Hasting Law Journal*, 21(1), p.11.

561 220 Cal. App. 2d 230, 33 Cal. Rptr. 673.

562 See *supra* note 615 at p.12.

from any state of disrepair of the premises, against danger arising from works of construction and repair, to provide adequate lighting at night for the safety of visitors. In *Slade v Battersea* and *Putney Gourp Hospital Management Commiteee*[563] the plaintiff, a 67-year-old lady, was granted permission to visit her husband who was a patient at a hospital. As she was leaving the hospital, she slipped and fell on a part of the floor of the ward where polish had just been spread. The floor was slippery and dangerous because the polish had not been polished off at the time of the accident. The plaintiff did not know that polish was spread on the floor and no warning of this was given. Her action against the hospital authority for damages for the injury she sustained succeeded.

In *Dickson Igbokwe v University College Hospital Board of Management*[564], the deceased was admitted into a fourth-floor maternity ward of the defendant Hospital Board where she gave birth to a baby on the 23rd of December 1958. After the birth she was suspected of being mentally deranged and was put on sedative drugs. A nurse was instructed to keep an eye on her. On two sides of the ward where she was admitted there was an open veranda about seventy feet from the ground protected by railings. In the morning of the 29th of December 1958, the deceased was missing from her bed and was found dead from injuries she received when she fell from the fourth floor. Her dependents claimed damages for her death contending that the circumstances pointed to negligence on the part of the hospital authority and they relied on *res ipsa loquitor*. The court awarded the sum of £250 as damages and shared it amongst the six children of the deceased. Her husband who was also a claimant was left out because he failed to prove satisfactorily that he was married to the deceased under native law and custom.

(b) Vicarious Liabilities of Hospital Management

Vicarious liability on the other hand will arise where the hospital is being held liable for acts, omissions and failure of its employees, in the discharge of their responsibilities in the hospital. In *Gold v Essex County Council*[565], Lord Greene first proposed the duty to impose liability on a hospital for the negligence of a radiographer. He stated that the question in determining the

---

563 1 All ER. 429 (1955).
564 (1961) W.N.L.R.173.
565 [1942] 2 KB 293.

defendant's duty to patients was to ask what obligation he had assumed[566]. The hospital was in breach of its duty to treat the patient and was found vicariously liable for the negligent conduct of the radiographer. In *Cassidy V. Minister of Health*[567] the Court of Appeal considers the primary duty which a hospital authority owes to its patients generally, Lord Denning stated;

> *"Who employs the doctor or surgeon – is it the patient or the hospital authorities? If the patient himself selects and employs the doctor or surgeon, ... the hospital authorities are of course not liable for his negligence, because he is not employed by them. But where the doctor or surgeon, be he a consultant or not, is employed and paid, not by the patient but by the hospital authorities, I am of opinion that the hospital* authorities are liable for his negligence in treating *the patient. It does not depend on whether the contract under which he was employed was a contract of service or a contract for service. That is a fine distinction which is sometimes of importance; but not in cases ..., where the hospital authorities are themselves under a duty to use care in treating the patient. I take it to be clear law, as well as good sense, that, where a person is himself under a duty to use care, he cannot get rid of his responsibility by delegating the performance of it to someone else, no matter whether the delegation be to a servant under a contract of service or to an independent contractor under a contract for service*[568].

566 *Ibid*, at 301-304, "... but in each case the first task is to discover the extent of the obligation assumed by the person whom it is ought to make liable. Once this is discovered, it follows of necessity that the person accused of a breach of the obligation cannot escape liability because he has employed another person, whether a servant or agent, to discharge it on his behalf, and this is equally true whether or not the obligation involves the use of skill. It is also true that, if the obligation is undertaken by a corporation, or a body of trustees or governors, they cannot escape liability for its breach, any more than can an individual, and it is no answer to say that the obligation is one which on the face of it they could never perform themselves. Nor can it make any difference that the obligation is assumed gratuitously by a person, body or corporation which does not act for profit. ... It is clear, therefore, that the powers of the defendants include the power of treating patients, and that they are entitled, and, indeed, bound in a proper case, to recover the just expense of doing so. If they exercise that power, the obligation which they undertake is an obligation to treat, and they are liable if the persons employed by them to perform the obligation on their behalf act without due care."

567 *Cassidy V. Minister of Health (1951) 2KB 343.*

568 *Ibid.*, at 362-363.

This was reiterated by Kelly J in *Byrne v Ryan*[569] where in his judgment holding the hospital vicariously liable, he remarked;

> *The plaintiff was referred not to a particular surgeon but to the [defendant's hospital]. She had no say in the choice of who would carry out her sterilization. It was done by ... He was part of the 'organization' or permanent staff of the hospital. The performance of the operation was part of a service provided by the hospital to the plaintiff. [Defendant] was the person in the hospital's organization via whom that service was provided*[570].

A senior medical practitioner may also be held vicariously liable for the actions or omissions of a junior or any member of the medical team that he leads or who is under his supervision and control[571]. This is the *captain- of- the-ship doctrine*. It is a principle of medical malpractice law, holding a surgeon liable for the action of assistants who are under the surgeon's control but who are employees of the hospital, not the surgeon. The surgeon as the "captain of the ship", is directly responsible for errors or acts of alleged negligence because he/she controls and directs the actions of those in assistance. This common law doctrine is often applied in operating room situations[572].

While many health care providers who work in hospitals are independent contractors (i.e., not direct employees of the hospital), some are full- or part-time hospital employees. Because the hospital is liable for the negligence of its employees, a patient harmed by the medical malpractice of an employee doctor or other health care professional would be entitled to sue both the hospital and the individual doctor jointly or either of them. The hospital is joint as the defendant because the hospital is considered financially more viable than the individual doctor. It is immaterial that the hospital has done no wrong. In the case of *Agborok Lydienne V Dr. Nwaobi Romanus and St John of God Hospital Nguti*, the hospital was jointly sued with the doctor, since the hospital was the employer of the doctor and more viable financially than the individual doctor. In *Lushaba v MEC for Health, Gauteng*[573], liability was imposed on a

---

569 7 [2009] 4 IR 542.

570 *Byrne v Ryan* [2009] 4 IR 542, at 573.

571 Emiri, F O., (2012), *Medical Law and Ethics in Nigeria,* 1st Edition, Nigeria. Malthouse Press Limited.

572 Shaikh A., (2015) "Doctor-Patient Relationships: The Distinction between Contractual and Tortious Liability", *Academike,* online at https://www.loctopus.com. (accessed on 10th day of April 2022).

573 2 [2015] ZAGPJHC 13.

hospital for the failure of its medical staff to respond appropriately and with due expedition when a woman, 36 weeks pregnant, presented herself at the maternity obstetrician unit with constant pain in her abdomen, demonstrating symptoms indicative of abruptio placentae. This condition placed her unborn child in danger of being deprived of oxygen. Delivery by caesarean section was thus essential but was delayed for two hours, resulting in the baby's suffering cerebral palsy.

In *Herman Nyangala Tsuma v Kenya Hospital Association & Ors*[574], there was a clear endorsement of the principles of imposing vicarious liability based on a hospital's duty of care. The plaintiff was admitted into the first defendant hospital and was attended by the second defendant, a locum, who diagnosed pneumonia and referred the plaintiff to the third defendant who was the consultant on duty that day, since the plaintiff's condition required immediate attention. The plaintiff suffered injury as a result of the negligence of the second and third defendants. Odunga J had no hesitation in finding the hospital vicariously liable for the acts of the second defendant, stating

> *That he was a locum or was in temporary employment is neither here nor there. He was an employee of the first defendant and was carrying out his duties pursuant to the instructions of the first defendant. He, for example had no admission rights and was reporting to the first defendant. I therefore have no difficulty in finding that the first defendant is vicariously liable for the acts and omission of the second defendant*[575].

He went further to assert that it is clear law and good sense that where a person is under a duty of care, he cannot get rid of his responsibility by delegating the performance of it to someone else no matter whether the delegation of it be to a servant under a contract of service or an independent contractor under a contract for service. The law therefore applies the principle of respondent superior in the case of a hospital just as it does in any other sphere of activity, and it does not matter if the servant does work of a skillful character for which he is specially qualified, the hospital is responsible for all those who are in charge of a patient in its establishment.

---

574 [2012] eKLR.

575 *Ibid.*, at para 50.

Again, in In *Igbokwe v University College Hospital Board of Management*[576], the High Court of Nigeria imposed vicarious liability on a hospital for the negligence of the hospital staff in failing to monitor the condition of a woman who had recently given birth and was suffering from a suspected condition of post-partum psychosis. The woman died when she fell from the fourth floor of the hospital. A doctor had instructed a staff nurse to "keep an eye" on the deceased. Irwin J considered it to be "well settled that a hospital authority is responsible for the acts or omissions of the whole of its staff whether they are surgeons, physicians, nurses or other employees ..."[577].

Under the tort of negligence, the issue of causation and proof leaves victims of medical negligence helpless, another avenue for redress is the criminal law.

4.2.1.5 Criminal Offences for violation of Medical Practice

Society entrusts the sacred duty of preserving the virtues of life and good health to the medical professionals. Hence, only the most qualified individuals should engage in this profession[578]. A medical practitioner in the exercise of his profession brings into play all his knowledge and skill, and use all available resources at his disposal to treat his patient. However, failure to observe prescribe norms of his profession might turn out to be fatal to his patient. When this happens, he may be held criminally liable.

The criminal sanction of a doctor for the negligent treatment of a patient rests on a breach of duty which the doctor owes to the patient. This duty is imposed by law irrespective of any contractual relationship between a doctor and the patient[579]. Injury to patients may occur during medical intervention, during follow-up after intervention or during diagnosis. Liability of the doctor may also result from negligent omission, for example, failure to prescribe treatment, or failure to follow-up a patient after operation, or failure to assist. In all these situations criminal proceeding may be instituted against the medical practitioner by the injured patient or by the State. Section 385(1) of the Cameroon Criminal Procedure Code provides that anyone who alleges that he suffered injury as a result of the

576 [1961] WNLR 173 (HC, Nigeria).

577 *Ibid.*, at 175 (HC. Nigeria).

578 Darwin, P A., (2011) "A Framework of Philippine Medical Malpractice Law", *Phil L. J.*, 85, p.1

579 Okonkwo, C O., "Medical Negligence and the Legal Implications", In Umerah, B C., et al, (1989), *Medical Practice and the Law in Nigeria*, Longman Nigeria Limited, p.122.

commission of an offence may make an oral or written application for damages in court.

However, due to the technicality of medicine, to establish the criminal responsibility of the medical practitioner is not easy. The Criminal Procedure Code[580] provides that the burden of proof always lies with the prosecution or the party who institutes a criminal action: they must prove beyond all reasonable doubt that the defendant, herein the doctor, committed the offence he is accused of. Indeed, the constituent element of a crime must be proven, which are; the *Actus Reus*[581] and *Mens Rea*[582]. It must be established that the practitioner committed the act, and that he intended the act to result in injury to the patient. it must also be clear that he failed to observe a norm or standard, or he acted without prudence, negligently or recklessly.

The level of negligence that the doctor must have manifested to be criminally liable, is considerably above that on which civil liability may be incurred. Traditionally it has been defined as 'gross' or 'extreme' negligence. The facts must be such that the negligence of the accused went beyond a mere matter of compensation between subjects and showed such disregard for the life and safety of others as to amount to a crime against the State and conduct deserving punishment[583]. This was reiterated in *R v. Akerele*[584] where the Court held that the degree of negligence required in criminal cases must go beyond that of civil liability and it must be shown that there has been such a disregard for life and safety of others to amount to manslaughter. This is in tandem with the rule of evidence relating to standard of proof beyond reasonable doubt for criminal cases.

It has been said that doctors should not be held criminally responsible unless there is prime facie evidence before the court in the form of a credible opinion from another competent doctor, preferably a government doctor in the same field of medicine supporting the charges of a rash and negligent act[585]. Therefore, the burden of prove that rest on the patient/plaintiff requires expert evidence to successfully discharge same. Indeed, section 203 (1) of the Cameroon Criminal Procedure Code provides that "where a technical problem

580 Section 307 of the Cameroon Criminal Procedure Code.

581 Latinism for wrongful act.

582 *Ibid* for guilty mind.

583 Lord Hewart in *R v Batemen*, (1925) 94 LJ KB 791.

584 (1941) 8 WACA 56, Privy Council Appeal No 17, 1942.

585 Awati, A M. et al, (2014), "Professional Liability in Medical Practice: A 20 Years Retrospective Study at District Consumers Forum Gulbarga (1991-2011)", *J NTR Univ Health Sci*, 3(1), pp. 15-18.

arises in the course of the preliminary inquiry, the Examining Magistrate may, of his own motion or on the application of any of the parties... make an order for expert opinion and appoint one or more experts". The chosen expert shall, subject to his report being declared null and void, take oath to perform his duties on his honour and in keeping with his conscience[586].

Where the patient cannot adduce expert evidence, the likelihood is the doctor being discharged and acquitted. Given the duties that doctors owe their colleagues under the Code of Medical Ethics[587], it is unlikely for a doctor to give expert evidence against another doctor. In *State Counsel and Kana Irene v. Madam Mbarga née Ndzie Manga*[588], the Court of First Instance of Kribi released the accused person because the chosen expert did not show up and the judge did not have any medical expertise to base his decision on. This confirms how hard it is to adduce expert evidence against a medical practitioner who at the same time is protected by the law and has the moral and unfailing support of his colleagues, unless his fault is obvious.

The court is called upon to exercise his discretion and punish the accused on behalf of society. The sanction should be rational and objective and the Court should not allow emotions to cloud their judgment as to what is a suitable sentence. The principle of legality expresses in latin as nullum crimen, nulla poena, sine lege, requires that for an offence to be punishable, it must be prescribed by law. In fact, this principle is upheld by the Cameroonian legislation[589]. Once the offence is prescribed it becomes general and applies to everyone without discrimination, the medical practitioner inclusive, and that is why Section 1(1) of the Cameroon Penal Code reiterate equality of all before the criminal law.

To be effective, criminal sanctions must be appropriate to the severity of the crime committed and must fulfil its aim taking into consideration the financial, social, cultural and health circumstances of the offender[590].

---

586 Section 204 of the Criminal Procedure Code.

587 Section 42 of the Cameroon Code of Medical Ethics provides that doctors must maintain good professional relations between themselves. They also owe each other moral support. They are further forbidden to slander or disparage a colleague, or from repeating any remark likely to harm a colleague in the practice of his profession. Subsection 3 states; *"defence of a colleague unjustly criticized shall be deemed good professional conduct"*.

588 Court of First Instance Kribi, jgt. N° 713/Cor du 11 Avril 1995.

589 The Preamble of the revised 1996 Constitution of Cameroon and section 17 of the Cameroon Penal Code. It states that, no penalty or measure may be imposed except in respect of an offence lawfully defined.

590 The aim of the criminal sanction may be to punish the offender, deter the offender, deter others, compensate the victim, rehabilitate the offender, and protect the public or a combination of all.

According to Bentham[591], where the social cost of imposing punishment is too high relative to the benefit that would be obtained by the punishment, punishment ought not to be inflicted. Even when, on balance, harm has been caused by the conduct, punishment should still not be imposed when the cost of its imposition both to the offender and the society at large are too great. Likewise, punishment ought not to be imposed where punishment would be ineffective since the offender would not be deterred. Essentially, for Bentham, the standard against which a proposed criminal offence is measured is the effect on the aggregate welfare of the society such that the harm that the criminal law seeks to prevent is weighed against the harm that the punishment imposes[592]. Thus, the needs of the individual and the interests of society should be balanced with care and understanding when sentencing.

The criminal Courts in imposing sanctions takes into account a number of factors; the gravity of the offence, the prescription period of the offence, the possibility of execution of the sanction, the past criminal record of the offender is considered to determine whether the offender is a recidivist[593]. In deciding the length of the sentence, the court considers the maximum penalty prescribed for the offence, the degree of blame on the offender, whether the offender pleaded guilty, and at what stage of the proceedings, the presence of any aggravating circumstances or mitigating factors, and the impact of the crime on the victim and society.

In Cameroon, the Criminal Procedure Code in its Section 157 gives the possibility of an aggrieved victim to lodge a criminal complaint with a civil claim attached therein. This section states that any person who alleges that he/she has suffered injury resulting from a felony or misdemeanour may when lodging a complaint with the competent Examining Magistrate, file a claim for damages[594], and the complaint in which the victim claims damages will set the criminal action in motion.

Generally, the courts are quite often too reluctant to pronounce an imprisonment term for medical malpractice given the place a medical doctor occupies in the society and the effect of an imprisonment term on his career, except the evidence are so overwhelming and the seriousness of the offence is such that imprisonment is the only sentence warranted.

---

591 Bentham, J., (1948) *Principles of Morals and Legislation*, New York: Hafner Press, p 171-77.

592 *Ibid.*

593 A recidivist is a person who repeatedly commits crimes despite being punished for them.

594 Section 157 of Law No 2005/007 of 27th July 2005 on the Criminal Procedure Code in Cameroon

This section will examine some criminal offences which medical practitioners may be charged with for violation of medical practice in Cameroon.

(a) Capital Murder, Murder, Euthanasia

When medical malpractices result in death, the practitioner may be charged with murder. Section 275 of the Cameroon Penal Code punishes *'whoever'* causes another's death. Thus, a medical practitioner who causes the death of a patient may be charged for murder. To hold a medical practitioner liable for murder it has to be shown that he intentionally caused the death of the patient or that the act by which death was caused was likely to endangered human life and was done in the prosecution of an unlawful purpose[595]. It has to be shown that the doctor intended to cause death or that the doctor knew or had reasons to know that death would be the probable consequences of such an act. Where a doctor, out of pity, wilfully terminate the life of a patient suffering from agonizing and incurable terminal disease(euthanasia), it is considered as murder in Cameroon even though it is legalized in some countries[596]. It is usually done with the patient's consent. Passively doing nothing to prolong life or withdrawing life-support measures will also result in criminal charges being brought against physicians.

Again Section 276 of same Penal Code punishes capital murder and defines it as the commission of murder after premeditation, or by poisoning or with a view of trafficking the organs of the victim or in the preparation or facilitation or commission of a felony or misdemeanour.

(b) Unintentional Killing

What frequently occurs is that in the course of medical intervention the doctor through his recklessness may cause the death of a patient. Also, a doctor can wilfully neglect to prescribe treatment for a seriously sick patient admitted under his care, maybe because the patient failed to conduct a test required by the doctor in a particular laboratory, or the patient did not meet up with financial requirements, or did not bribe the doctor, and the patient dies.

---

595 See *supra* note 634 at p.119.

596 For example, Netherland and Korea.

Thus, where a medical practitioner by lack of due skill or disregard of the rules and regulation of his profession or by carelessness or rashness, causes death to the patient, he will be held liable for unintentional killing punishable under Section 289(1) of the Penal Code. In *The People of Cameroon v. Ebesoh Dieudonne Nchapbanu and 2 Ors*[597], the first accused, a medical doctor together with two other nurses, were charged with unintentionally causing death of one Etongwe Racheal, a pregnant woman and her baby who both died after being operated upon by the first accused. Both accused pleaded guilty. The doctor explained that the baby suffered in the womb for about five days and died in asphyxia. He conceded that he was negligent as he failed to refer the deceased to another hospital for proper medical attention. Both accused were sentenced to eight months imprisonment and cost of 163,000 FCFA was awarded.

However, in *The People of Cameroon v. Doctor Jeremiah Esua*[598], the accused, Dr. Jerry Etabong Esua who owns a private hospital in kumba, “Hope Parma Hospital” was detained and charged with manslaughter by the State Counsel of Kumba after a complaint from the parents of a deceased baby[599]. A premature baby was born in his health facility and unfortunately died after 4 days of care. He was charged for involuntary manslaughter, as a result of carelessness and negligence. A pregnant woman at 24 weeks visiting Cameroon from Germany arrived at the Hope Parma hospital at 1:05 am on 06/04/2016. She gave birth to a male foetus weighing 1000g shortly after arriving the hospital. The premature new born was kept alive for four days until about 4:30pm on 10/04/2016 when the infant died. According to the parents of the baby, the death was as a result of negligence of the doctor, and lack of facilities in the hospital to take care of premature babies. The doctor said the baby died from premature complications. He was arrested and detained at the Central Police Station[600]. The complainant did not adduce any expert evidence to proof the negligence of the doctor, who on his part was able to provide an investigative report from the Cameroon Medical Council stating that the accused’s hospital has all the necessary facilities to take care of a premature baby. He was accordingly discharge and acquitted.

597 CFIK/FD/018C/2021, Court of First Instance Kumba (unreported).

598 CFIK/59c/2016, Kumba Court of First Instance (unreported).

599 MedCamer, “Doctor illegal Arrest in Kumba: A Few minutes with Dr, Jerry Esua in Detention”, 12/4/2016, at https://www.medcamer.org/en/doctor-illegal-arrest-in-kumba/. (accessed on 11th day of April 2021).

600 *Ibid.*

The President of Medcamer (Cameroon Medical Doctors), Dr. Etienne Ndzie Atangana had this to say in the wake of Dr. Jerry's arrest for unintentional killing; "the stake of this trial henceforth is that of the safety of the doctors at work, the seriousness and sincerity of the caregivers who continue to do everything to save lives, and the working conditions of the doctors in Cameroon". He called on the entire medical community to affirm their solidarity for Jerry in the fight which he carries out on their behalf. He went further to state; "Either the story will retain from us a magnificent solidarity movement credited once again to the good faith and honor of the doctors in Cameroon, or this trial will pave the way for a series of abuses and wacky lawsuits against the medical staff"[601]. What can be deciphered from this assertion is that to successfully hold a medical practitioner criminally liable in Cameroon is not an easy task. With this solidarity attitude amongst doctors, adducing expert evidence is even more difficult.

(c) Assault Occasioning Death

The Cameroon Penal Code punishes anyone who by force or interference unintentionally causes death to another[602]. Thus, a medical practitioner who by force or illegal interference causes death to a patient is guilty of assault occasioning death, which is punishable with imprisonment for from six to twenty years[603]. In *The People of Cameroon v. Yilareng Elias Afoni*[604], the accused a private medical practitioner, was charged with causing death of a pregnant lady who arrived the accused clinic in severe pains. The accused claimed she came to the hospital with a lifeless foetus. The Court held that the evidence adduced by the prosecution was grossly insufficient to buttress the charge of assault occasioning death. The accused doctor was therefore discharge and acquitted.

(d) Grievous Harm, Simple Harm and Slight Harm

Where the gross negligence of the medical practitioner does not amount to death but result in the deprivation of the use of the whole or any part of any member organ or sense, he will be criminally liable for causing grievous

601 Message by the President of MedCamer, Dr..Etienne Ndzie Atangana, Yaoundé, April 17, 2016, MedCamer to the Cameroon Medical Community.

602 Section 278 of the Cameroon Penal Code.

603 *Ibid.*

604 Suit No HCK/15c/2020, High Court Meme (Unreported).

harm which constitutes an offence under Section 277 of the Cameroon Penal Code and punishable with imprisonment for from ten to twenty years. Indeed, the Law on blood transfusion[605] in Cameroon holds a medical practitioner liable, who in the course of collecting blood; inflict injury to the donor that results to deprivation of the use of the whole or any part of any member, organ or sense. The Penal Code[606] also holds a doctor criminally liable where he intentionally or unintentionally causes to another any sickness or inability to work lasting more than 30 days by force or interference. In the same vein, where the interference causes sickness or inability to work lasting for more than 8 days, the doctor will equally be criminally liable[607]. However, the doctor is exonerated from liability where such interference was for reasons of medical treatment and interest of the victim[608].

(e) Abortion

The Cameroon constitution[609] protect and encourage the family, which is the base of human society, that is why the legislator has taken measures to protect the child and the family by prohibiting abortion in Section 337 of the Penal Code. In fact, any medical practitioner involved in abortion will receive double punishment for this act. Indeed, section 337(2) of the Penal Code states that whoever procures the abortion of a woman notwithstanding her consent shall be punished with imprisonment of from one to five years, and with fine of from one hundred thousand to two million francs. This punishment is doubled where the offender practices the profession of medicine[610]. In addition, the court may order closure of his professional premises and a ban on his occupation[611].

This is reinforced by Section 29 of the Code of Medical Ethics which provides that all acts of abortion are forbidden. However, since respect for life is the paramount duty of the practitioner, saving the life of a mother in

605 Section 15(2) Of Law No 2002/2006 of 22 December 2003 on Blood Transfusion in Cameroon.

606 See *supra* note, 657, Section 280.

607 *Ibid.*, Section 281.

608 *Ibid.*, Section 286, provides that sections 277 to 281 inclusive shall not apply to the professional services of any person duly authorized to render them, where performed with the consent either of the patient or of such person that may have custody of him while 287 of penal code. Section 287 states that the infliction of harm and the use of force shall not constitute an offence where it is proved to be justified by the immediate necessity of avoiding greater harm to the victim.

609 See the Preamble to the 1996 Revise Constitution.

610 See supra note 657, Section 337(3)(B).

611 *Ibid.* Section 337(4).

serious circumstances will permit the doctor to indulge in abortion. In this case section 339 of the Penal Code also permit abortion where the pregnancy is as a result from rape, after an attestation from state prosecutor. In the same light the Maputo Protocol[612] of July 2003, Section 14 recognizes the right of the woman to health and control of her reproductive organ, and sub section 2 further enjoins all states to take measures to protect the reproductive right of the woman, particularly to legalize medical abortion in case of aggression.

However, even though therapeutic abortion is permitted in the Code of Medical Ethics, it must follow strict procedure[613] failure of which it becomes punishable. The doctor must first obtain the opinions of two colleagues, one of whom shall be chosen from the civil court list of experts and the other a member of the council of the Association, who will give a written attestation that the life of the mother can only be preserved by such therapy. However, where the opinion of two colleagues cannot easily be obtained, the decision to induce therapeutic abortion shall be at the discretion of the doctor in charge, who must forthwith send a circumstantial report to the Minister of Public Health and to the President of the National Council of the Medical Association[614]. During difficult or prolonged labour, the doctor must consider himself as the sole judge of the respective interests of the mother and child, without letting himself be influenced by considerations of a family nature. Doctors in Cameroon frequently violate this provision.

(f) False Medical Certificate

A certificate is a formal document that maybe used to prove that the contents or facts it testifies to are true[615]. It's quite common in Cameroon's public hospitals to see doctor receive money to deliver fake medical certificate. Thus, the Penal code[616] sanctions any medical personnel who, to help or harm someone, issues a certificate which falsely certifies, or conceals the existence of a disease or the result of a vaccination, or provides deceitful information

---

612 Maputo Protocol (11 July 2003) acknowledges to the women the right to health including sexual and reproductive health. This includes the rights to control their fertility, to decide whether to have children, the number of children and the spacing of children, to choose any method of contraception, to self-protection and to be protected against sexually transmitted infections, including HIV/AIDS. Hence, States Parties to the Protocol shall authorize medical abortion.

613 Section 29(2((3)(4) of Decree No 83/166 of 12 April 1983 on Code of Medical Ethics in Cameroon.

614 *Ibid.*, Section 29 (3).

615 Ayangwe, C., (2011), *Criminal Law in Cameroon: Specific Offences*, Bamenda, Langaa Research and Publishing CIG, p. 498.

616 See *supra* note 657, Section 259.

about the origin of a disease, the length of a disability, or the cause of a death. The punishment is from two months to three years and with fine of from five thousand francs to one hundred thousand. In addition, the medical personnel may be excluded from public service, and prohibited from being an expert referee or sworn expert[617]. In *Metongo Bohamba Annette v. Edima Marie Thérèse*[618], and *State Counsel and Tetsoulack Andre v. Kamga Elie*[619], the plaintiffs tendered a doubtful medical certificate whereupon the judge released all the accused persons. However, there was no further investigation as to the origin of the doubtful medical certificate.

Indeed, Section 21 of the Code of Medical Ethics stipulates that it is a serious offence to issue a tendentious certificate or to issue a certificate as a favour. Again, the Penal Code[620] punishes anyone who forges or issues a false certificate. A false certificate is a certificate which is not genuine but is made to look real to deceive people.

(g) Failure to assist

The Penal Code[621] punishes whoever fails to render assistance to a person in danger of death or grievous harm if it is in his power to do so or to call for help where he incurs no risk in so doing. The punishment is imprisonment of from one month to three years, or a fine of twenty thousand to one million francs, or with both such imprisonment and fine[622]. Failure to assist is rife in medical practice in Cameroon especially during emergencies, and where hospitals insist on payment before treatment and patients die as a result.

(h) Breach of confidentiality

The medical practitioner has the obligation to respect the life of the patient at every level. In treating his patient, he observes the norm of his profession. He is enjoined to respect the private life of his patient and the personal information he acquired while treating the patient. He is bound by professional secrecy not to divulge this information except provided by the law. Section 310 of the Penal Code punishes anyone who reveals confidential

617 *Ibid.*, Section 259(3) as read together with Section 30.
618 T.P.I., Kribi, Jugement N°976/Cor. Du 25/06/96.
619 T.P.I.,Kribi, Jugement N°481/Cor. Du 13 Février 1996.
620 See *supra* note 671.
621 *Ibid*, Section 283.
622 *Ibid.*

fact that has come to his knowledge or which has been confided to him solely by reason of his profession or duty. The medical doctor is liable only when such revelation is done without the consent of the patient, and the patient has to prove that the fact divulged was indeed a confidential fact, and it was indeed revealed, even if only partially. How and where and to whom it was disclosed is immaterial. However, the doctor is discharged from this obligation within the scope of a commission from the prosecution or of his reference as an expert referee. The sanction for breach of confidentiality is both imprisonment and fine.[623]

(i) False Arrest

A medical practitioner who detains patients in hospital for failure to pay hospital bills can be charge with false arrest. Section 291 of the Cameroon Penal Code provides; whoever in any manner deprives another of his liberty shall be punished with imprisonment from five to ten years and with fine of from twenty thousand francs to one million francs. This punishment is doubled where the deprivation of liberty last for more than a month, or where it is accompanied with physical or mental torture[624].

Such false arrest is common with patients suffering from mental illness. These patients are usually chained to their beds at psychiatric hospitals, however, this practice is accepted and considered normal especially by their relatives who do not seem to see anything wrong with it.

In addition to criminal sanctions imposed for violating medical practice, the Cameroon Medical Council also punishes violation of the ethics of the profession through its Disciplinary Board. This will be considered hereunder.

4.3 Extra Legal Remedies

The Disciplinary Board of the Cameroon Medical Council[625] also has jurisdiction to sanction medical practitioners for violation of medical practice. Extra-legal sanctions here will examine sanctions for professional misconduct

---

623 *Ibid.*, Section 310 provides... shall be punished with imprisonment for from three months to three years and with fine of from twenty thousand to one hundred thousand francs.

624 *Ibid* Section 291(2)(a)(b).

625 Section 58(1) of Decree No 83/166 of 12 April 1983 on the Code of Medical Ethics in Cameroon provides that "any infringement of the provisions of the present Code shall fall within the jurisdiction of the Council of the Association sitting as the Disciplinary Board in conformity with the law".

by the Cameroon Medical Council. This section will also examine amicable settlement or out of court settlement as a form of sanction for medical malpractices.

4.3.1 Remedies by the Cameroon Medical Council

Incompetence and impaired medical practice may do serious harm to patience. A competent physician who is doing something for which he or she has not been adequately trained and who therefore performs ineptly is also a source of pain to the patient. The professional liability of medical personnel has its recognizable causes both in the scientific/technical component of the medical practice as well as in the ethical component[626]. Before commencement of practice the medical doctor swears to the Hippocratic oath. The Hippocratic Oath poses multiple ethical obligations to the practitioner[627]. These obligations can be summarized as the obligation to safe life, and the obligation to treat. These obligations are encapsulated in the Cameroon Code of Medical Ethics[628] and the Law organizing the practice of medicine in Cameroon[629]. These instruments impose ethical duties and responsibilities on the practitioner, breach of which may attracts disciplinary sanctions.

Disciplinary sanctions enable the profession to enforce its standards and to underscore to its members the value and ethos which undergird its work. Broader public interest considerations are paramount and will commonly be at the forefront when determining the appropriate sentence that should be imposed in each case[630]. Vital public interest considerations include the need to uphold the standing and reputation of the profession, as well as to prevent an erosion of public confidence in the trustworthiness and competence of its members. This is undoubtedly true for medical practitioners, in whom the public and, in particular, patients repose utmost trust and reliance in matters relating to personal hygiene, including matters of life and death[631].

---

626 Pituru, S. *et al*, (2015), "Malpractice and Professional Liabilities of Medical Personnel", *Farmacia*, 63(2), p.318.

627 These include the obligation to be faithful to his master, to advice the patient, not to have self-interest, not to use poison, to keep patient's information confidential, etc.

628 Decree No 83/166 of 12 April 1983 on Code of Medical Ethics in Cameroon.

629 Law No 90/036 of 10August 1990 on the organization and practice of Medicine in Cameroon.

630 *Wong Meng Hang v. Singapore Medical Council and other matters* [2018] SGHC 253, para 23.

631 *Ibid.*

The law organizing the practice of medicine in Cameroon[632] provides that the Medical Council shall exercise disciplinary jurisdiction at first instance within the medical association. In this capacity it shall appoint a Disciplinary Board amongst its members which shall comprise four members and be presided over by the President of the Council. The Disciplinary Board can be seized by the Supervisory Authority, the Legal Department and any physician who has an interest at stake[633]. The Disciplinary Board has material jurisdiction over any conviction for any offence of a nature to discredit or jeopardize the reputation of the profession committed within or outside the national territory, and any conviction for professional misconduct[634]. It also has jurisdiction over offences committed which are in violation of the provisions of the Code of Medical Ethics[635].

Accordingly, the Medical Council has the responsibility to investigate any complaint of medical negligence, professional misconduct, malpractice or any breach of the Code of Practice against a registered medical practitioner. Thus, upon receipt of a complaint the Disciplinary Board may order investigations into the fact[636]. Section 47(1) of the Law relating to the Organization and Practice of Medicine prescribes that no disciplinary sanction may be pronounce unless the physician accused has been heard or summoned to appear before the Board within a period of 30 (thirty) days following receipt of the summons with acknowledgement of receipt. The physician accused of an offence has the right to be assisted by Counsel of his choice, and he may exercise the right of exclusion and objection in accordance with ordinary law procedure[637]. Where the accused physician fails to appear before the Disciplinary Board after a duly notified summons, the Board may make its rulings. However, the Disciplinary Board can only sanction medical officers who are public servants after obtaining an authorization from the Ministry of Public health[638]. The sanctions imposed by the Disciplinary Board include;

---

632 See *Supra* note 684, Section 41.

633 *Ibid.*, Section 42(1).

634 *Ibid.*, Section 43.

635 See *supra* note 684, Section 58 (1) provide; Any infringement of the provisions of the present Code shall fall within the jurisdiction of the Council of the Association sitting as the Disciplinary Board in conformity with the law. (2) The initiative to refer a matter to this Board shall be jointly taken by the Association and the Minister in charge of Public Health.

636 *Ibid*, Section 44 which stipulates; The Disciplinary Board may, at the request of the parties or on its own initiative, order an inquiry into any facts the findings of which it deems useful for its proceedings.

637 *Ibid.*, Section 45.

638 *Ibid*, Section 42(2) stipulates that only the authority responsible for Public Health or the Council

warning, reprimand, suspension, and striking off the Roll of the Association. In imposing disciplinary sanctions, the Board considers the initial record of the doctor, the gravity of the offence, the recurrence of the offence, and the interests affected[639].

Some instances of violation of rules of medical practice for which disciplinary sanctions are imposed on practitioners will be discussed hereunder.

4.3.1.1 Breach of Professional Secrecy

A secret acquired by the doctor is the secret of the patient and not that of the doctor. The patient has prima facie right in law to require that the secret shall not be divulge to any third party, and to seek redress if it is so divulged, unless the doctor can show that there is some paramount reason which overrides the patient's prima facie right. Indeed, section 4 of the law organizing the practice of medicine in Cameroon provides; "*A physician in service in the Administration or in the private sector shall be bound by Professional secrecy*". This is reinforced by the Cameroon Code of Medical Ethics[640] which stipulates that professional secrecy shall be binding on the doctor except provided by law, provided it is not harmful to the interest of the patient.

Professional secrecy is based on the obligation to be discrete and to respect others. It also has a contractual basis; thus, the doctor is under a contractual obligation to be silent and not to divulge the patient's information except provided by law, failure of which will invoke his liability. Indeed, in 2010, the Cameroon Medical Council, in a press release dated May 4th, flared at the then Minister of Communication, Issa Tchiroma, for announcing that a journalist who died in prison on April 22 was HIV positive. The Council scorned the announcement which the Minister made on April 29 on CRTV as a stark violation of medical confidentiality and ethics. The CMC holds that the secrecy of a patient's medical status is the absolute right of the patient and is not meant for public consumption. The CMC held that Issa Tchiroma violated

---

of the Association after consultation with the Supervisory Authority may bring a physician serving the State before the Disciplinary Board for acts committed in the performance of his duties. The Supervisory Authority shall take a decision within 30 (thirty) days from the date a matter is referred to it. After this time-limit, if the supervisory authority does not reply it shall be considered as upheld.

639 Dr Akwa of the Clinique Medico-Chirugical SOS Ouest Sante, in Bafoussam, in an unstructured interview with the researcher.

640 See *supra* note 683, Section 4.

Section 4 of the Code of Medical Ethics, and it considered slamming sanctions on the doctor who released the journalist's medical record to the Minister[641].

In April 2019, the Minister of Public Health Manaouda Malachie suspended three nurses at the Deido District Hospital for unprofessionalism. The nurses were suspended for three months for demonstrating unprofessionalism in handling the case of a stabbed student of the Government Bilingual High School Deido, who was brought to the hospital and later died. The nurses, *Ndonda epse Mbella Fidèle Marie, Ntogni Celestine epse Kouamo*, and *Nlontchi Ndeko* were all found guilty of filming the dying student and later sharing the images on social media[642]. Likewise, two nurses at the Obala District Hospital *Mvondo Essomba Antoine* and *Ngoumela Fosso* were also suspended for posting pictures of patients on social media. They were suspended for three months renewable during which period they will not be entitled to any salary[643].

4.3.1.2 Breach of Duty to Disclose Information to Patient

A patient has the right to be informed by his physician. The right to receive information and the duty to obtain consent from the patient are laid down by the law[644]. Failure to inform and receive consent will attract not only professional liability but may also attract liability under tort, contract, human right and criminal law. In the present era of medical practice, it is inappropriate for a physician to neglect to attempt to educate a patient. The current status of modern man has invalidated the assumption that all patients are totally incapable of understanding the physician's explanation of the medical assessment of an illness and its therapy[645].

In general, the information which needs to be given should include diagnosis, choice of treatment, risks, pain, alternatives, effects of treatment

641 Nsom, K Y., (2010), "Medical Council Flays Tchiroma", *Cameroon Post line*, at https://cameroonpostline.com/medical-council-flays-tchiroma. (accessed on 1st day of June 2021).

642 Cameroon: Minister Suspends Three Nurses for Filming Dying Student in Douala Hospital, *Journal du Cameroun*, published on 02/04/2019. online at http://www.journalducameroun.com/en/cameroon-minister-suspends-three-nurses-for-filming-dying-student-in-douala-hospital/ (accessed on 16th day of June 2021).

643 Cameroon: Two Nurses Suspended for Posting Pictures of Patient on social media, *Journal du Cameroun*, Published on 20/01/2020, Online at https://Www.Journalducameroun.Com/En/Cameroon-Two-Nurses-Suspended-For-Posting-Pictures-Of-Patient-On-Social-Media/. (accessed on the 1st day of June 2021).

644 For instance, Sections 5 and 8 of the Law Regulating Blood Transfusion requires the practitioner to obtain the consent of both the donor and the done before transfusing.

645 Miech, R P., (1995), "Doctor Patient Relationship: Friend or Adversary", *Linacre Quarterly*, p.17.

and non-treatment and more. Additionally, a physician needs to inform his patient in due time so that he is able to evaluate all aspects of the treatment before consenting to it. Where this duty is breached, the physician may be professionally liable and will incur disciplinary sanction from the Disciplinary board. Moreover, a patient injured as a result of failure to properly informed, may bring an action under the tort of negligence or breach of fundamental right of the patient. In all the cases, it has to be proven that the physician fails in his obligation to inform the patient, or did not respect the right of the patient to be informed, or that he improperly informed the patient, and in addition, it has to be shown that, if the patient had been properly informed, he would not have consented to the treatment which has resulted to injury.

The duty of the practitioner to inform may be limited in emergency situations, in which case he is not obliged to give all required information to the patient at the moment of treating him. In addition, when the physician has good reason to withhold information in the best interest of the patient, he may withhold information. Indeed, section 27(1) of the Code of Medical Ethics stipulates that a serious prognosis may lawfully be concealed from the patient.

4.3.1.3 Breach of Duty to Obtain Consent

Once properly informed, the patient has to consent to the treatment. The prerequisite of consent before treatment is built on self-determination and respect for physical integrity. The requirement of a valid consent as a condition precedent to medical treatment can be met in several ways. First, the physician can obtain the express consent of the patient either orally or in writing, Secondly, if there is no express affirmation, consent may be implied in fact from the actions of the patient who knowingly accepts the treatment recommended by his physician[646]. Lastly, consent may be implied in law when the patient, by his age or condition, is unable to give the required consent[647]. Again, if delay in treatment would threaten the life or health of the patient in an emergency situation, the patient's consent is implied or dispensed with as a matter of law on the theory that the patient would not have withheld his consent if he had been given a choice[648]. The consent of a patient needs to be given freely, and is only valid for the treatment consented to. The consent

646 See *McGuire v. Rix*, 118 Neb. 434, 225 N.W. 120 (1929).

647 *Luke v. Lowrie* 171 ,Mich.122,136 N.W.1106B(1912).

648 *Bennan v. Parsonnet*, 83 N.J.L., 20,83 A. 948.

should be real, voluntary and not reached as a result of undue influence. Failure to obtain consent is a breach of ethical obligation which attracts sanction by the Disciplinary Board of the CMC[649].

Since the physician cannot anticipate a patient's reaction to the disclosure of certain facts, the doctor is justified in taking a conservative approach to the problem. It is generally accepted, however, that excessive disclosure may amount to bad medical practice[650]. The Cameroon Code of Medical Ethics[651] specifically states that a serious prognosis may lawfully be concealed from the patient, and a fatal prognosis may not be divulged to him except with the greatest prudence; it must normally be divulged to his family, unless the patient is already so aware or if he has appointed a third party to be informed.

However, most Cameroonian patients are not provided with sufficient information to enable them to make a fully informed decision as to their treatment. The process is regarded generally as one that involves obtaining signatures without providing full disclosure of risks. For the less educated patients, disclosure of several risks to treatment implies a confession of incompetence on the part of the doctor, leading to a loss of confidence in his or her abilities. A second challenge to the notion of individualistic informed consent in Cameroon is one deriving from an aspect of Cameroon socio-cultural belief that the medical practitioner is all knowing and as such whatever he decides is best for the patient.

4.3.1.4 Charlatan Practices and Incompetence

Given the importance of his profession to the society and his primary goal which is lifesaving, competence, honesty and moral integrity must characterize the conduct of a medical practitioner. Fake medical practitioners are all over the place in Cameroon. A person who is not trained as a medical doctor parades himself as a doctor and indulges in all kind of practices to the detriment of the helpless patient. Some of these fake doctors are owners of private clinics. The code of medical practice states that a doctor must not indulge in practices that will bring disgrace to the profession. That is why the Code of Medical Ethics condemns and forbid any deceitful practice, in particular charlatanism[652]. He must exhibit competence at all time. In *Affaire*

[649] See *supra* note 683, Section 58.
[650] See *Williams v. Menehan*, 191 Kan. 6, 379 P.2d 292 (1963).
[651] Section 27(1)(2) of the Cameroon Code of Medical Ethics.
[652] *Ibid.*, Section 18.

Ministère Public and Nkouamo Charles Séraphin v. Ndeumeni Noubevan Charles Dechateau[653], the Wouri High Court in finding a dentist surgeon guilty of malpractice, held him liable for amongst other things, the violation of the provisions of section 18 of the Code of Medical Ethics which forbids any deceitful practices likely to discredit the profession and in particular charlatanism. The Cameroon Medical Council was a civil party in this criminal suit, and claimed that Ndeumeni has tarnished the image of the profession by involving in charlatan practice.

Doctors who fail to give their patient all the necessary medical care and attention within his power either personally or with the help of a qualified third parties, and who fail to use care in formulating his diagnosis, and prescribe wrong treatment to patients, fail to follow-up the treatment of his patient, is liable for exhibiting incompetence. In fact, the Code of Medical Ethics forbids such conduct of medical practitioners[654].

In May 10, 2019, five medical personnel of the Garoua Regional hospital were suspended by the Minister of Public Health for a period of three months, following the dead of an 8-month-old baby[655]. Four of these medical personnel who were present during the unfortunate intervention that led to the death of the baby were suspended for serious breach of ethics and professional conduct.

Closure of establishment may be ordered by the Council of the Association where a physician is found guilty of unlawful practice of medicine[656]. Indeed, section 17(3) of the law regulating the practice of medicine in Cameroon provides that; "any person who violates the provisions of this law shall cease

---

653 *Affaire Ministère Public et Nkouamo Charles Séraphin vs. Ndeumeni Noubevan Charles Dechateau*, jugement N° 223/Crim. Du 23 Décembre 2004 rendu par le Tribunal de Grande Instance (TGI) du Wouri. In this case, Ndeumeni, a dentist surgeon, operated upon one of his patient suffering from hemorrhoid. The outcome was tragic, since he was not trained to carry out such an operation, he gravely mutilated the lower organs of the patient to the extent that he had to be using a catheter to excrete. Nkouamo and the council of the CMA were the civil party in the criminal action.

654 See *supra* note 707, Section 22 and 23.

655 Cameroon: 5 Medical Personnel Of Garoua Regional Hospital Suspended, *Journal du Cameroun*, published on 13/05/2019, at http://www.journalducameroun.com/en/cameroon-5-medical-personnel-of-garoua-regional-hospital-suspended/ (accessed on the 16th day of May 2021).

656 According to section 16(1)-(4) of the Law relating to the Organization and Practice of Medicine in Cameroon, unlawful practice of medicine includes; any physician who practices under an assumed physician name or who grants consultations in business premises where some of the apparatus he prescribes or uses are sold; any unauthorized person who, even in the presence of a physician, habitually or under supervision, provides diagnosis or treatment for diseases on a personal basis by consultation or by any other procedure;) any physician who exercises his profession in violation of the provisions under section al above or who offers his assistance to persons who are not authorized to practice; any physician who exercises his profession while on temporary or permanent suspension.

his activity with immediate effect. Furthermore, the closure of his surgery or clinic may be ordered by the Council of the Association, irrespective of any court judgment".

Closure of establishment will also be ordered where a medical practitioner does not to take out an insurance policy. The insurance policy covers occupational risk whose nature is specified by the rules of the profession. The receipt of the payment of insurance is presented to the Council of the Association each Calendar Year[657]. Indeed, the law regulating the practice of medicine in Cameroon[658] stipulates that failure to take out an insurance policy shall, on the instructions of the Council of the Association or the Supervisory Authority, lead to the temporary closure of the establishment. Such establishment may be re-opened only on presentation of the receipt showing payment of the insurance policy.

Likewise, where a medical institution is operating without the required license and authorization, or operating illegally from home or lack trained and appropriate staff, equipment and infrastructure to operate, it will also be closed down. The unauthorized practice of medicine includes advertising your services as a physician, or holding yourself out to the public as a physician, doctor, surgeon, or someone licensed to practice medicine whereas you are not.

4.3.1.5 Collusion

In Cameroon it is very common to find medical doctors colluding with pharmacists, laboratories and hospitals to profit at the expense of the patient. Unnecessary prescriptions, treatments and referrals tuned to maximization of revenues rather than enhancement of patient's wellbeing is rampant among practitioners[659]. This act is forbidden by Section 15(1) of the Code of Medical Ethics. Again Section 13 of same Code forbids any payment, acceptance and sharing of money between practitioners in respect of examination, prescription of drugs or appliances, or consignment to a specific consulting room or clinic or nursing home. This practice is common in hospitals and the perpetrators

---

657 Section 22(2) of Decree No. 92-265-Pm July 22, 1992 Fixing the Application of Law No. 90/ 036 of 10 August 1990 on the Organization and Practice of the Medical Profession.

658 See *supra* note 690, Section 15(2).

659 (2008),"Collusion among Health Service Providers in India: Need for Effective Regulatory Enforcement", *CUTS International, Briefing Paper 10,* p.1, at http//Briefing_Paper10-Collusion_among_Health_Service_Providers_in_India.pdf (accessed on 11th day of May 2021).

are not held liable because the victim/patient is not in a position to decide which medical test to undergo, or which drug should be prescribed by the doctor, at such the patient does not see any misconduct in the practitioner sending him/her to a particular clinic, or laboratory for a particular test, or pharmacy.

Indeed, the Code[660] further forbids any sharing of fees between a doctor and a consultant or surgeon or specialist at the time of consultation or operation. It further states that such act shall be a serious professional offence. This is reinforced by section 24 of the same Code which obliges a doctor not to prescribe costly treatment, and to always prescribe treatment within the limits of the condition of the patient. Costly treatment can only be prescribed after informing the patient, and where the benefit to be derived therefrom is worth the sacrifice. In Cameroon it is no uncommon to find medical doctors with astonished behaviour.

4.3.1.6 Commercialization of Medical Practice

Dr. Jordan J. Cohen[661] declared that medicine can survive and flourish only if physicians exercise constant vigilance to ensure that medical science is used only for service to humanity. This vigilance must include resistance to the temptations of wealth, prestige, and power. He went further to say that physicians should question themselves on whether it is the principle of morality or the marketplace that governs their relationship with the patient. The term "morality" refers to the basic human concept of right and wrong. For physicians, morality means doing what is right for the patients and speaking or acting out against what is wrong. No such moral absolute can be found in the marketplace[662].

The market is driven by revenue, profit margins, and market share. No patients exist in a market-driven practice of medicine, only consumers for whom the watchword is caveat emptor[663]. A great danger to the practice of medicine is the transformation of physicians to businessmen, cold and without compassion, and patients to the status of commodities. In the

660 See *supra* note 683,, Section 13.

661 Cohen, J I., (1996), "An Awesome Responsibility for Medical Educators", *Acad Physician Sci.*, Cohen Discussion in a Conference entitled "Hippocrates Betrayed: Medicine in the Third Reich", held on the 50th anniversary of the Nuremberg Doctor's Trial.

662 James, T C., (1996), "The Patient -Physician Relationship: Covenant or Contract?", *Mayo Clin Proc*, 71, p.918.

663 *Ibid*.

Hippocratic model of medicine, the patient represents a vulnerable person in need; the first and only priority of the physician. In the commercial model of medicine, the patient is at best a consumer; at worst, a source of revenue to the physician. In this system, physicians make economic (not clinical) decisions and provide medical explanations for those decisions. Patients are left to fend for themselves and to face the consequences alone. The Cameroon Code of Medical Ethics forbids the commercialization of medical practice by stating that the profession of medicine shall not be exercise like a trade[664]. Thus, any form of direct or indirect advertisement to attract patients/clients, or spectacular occasion not having a scientific or educational purpose is forbidden. The exercise of medicine in fairs or markets is also forbidden[665].

In addition to the above liabilities of medical practitioners violating the ethics of the profession, the Code of Medical Ethics further forbids doctors from issuing tendentious certificate or report as a favour[666]. In addition to the criminal responsibility that such an act may give rise to, the doctor will also face the disciplinary board of the council of the Association. Moreover, doctors who slander or disparage a colleague, or make any remark that is likely to hurt a colleague in the exercise of his profession is in breach of the ethics of the profession and is liable to sanction from the council of the Association. Soliciting the patient of another colleague is a professional misconduct that warrants sanctions from the council[667]. Medical practitioners who promote the illegal practice of medicine are liable and in breach of the provision of the Code of Medical ethics[668].

Professional discipline seeks to protect public welfare by sanctioning deviant or dangerous physicians. Access to the Disciplinary Board of the Cameroon Medical Council is limited[669], thus, an aggrieved patient cannot directly seize the Disciplinary Board of the Council. Moreover, the composition of the Disciplinary Board gives one the impression that they will tend to protect the physician rather than the public. It is made up exclusively of doctors, members are appointed amongst the members of the Council of the Association. It is made up of five members, the president of the Council

---

664 See *supra* note 683. Section 7.

665 *Ibid.*, Section 12.

666 *Ibid.*, Section 20 and 21.

667 *Ibid.*, Section43.

668 *Ibid.*, Section 14.

669 According to section 42 of Law No 90/036 of 10 August 1990 organizing the practice of medicine only the supervisory authority, the legal department, and a practitioner who has an interest at stake have access to the Disciplinary Board.

presides over the Disciplinary Board, with four other members elected from within the council[670].

However, it has been posited that in relying on disciplinary boards dominated by physicians for the implementation and enforcement discipline laws, the system implicitly recognizes that professional members are better situated to evaluate the unique question of competence and of fitness to practice ; a board composed of laypeople would have much greater difficulty evaluating, for example, whether a licensed physician's practice is consistent with the standard of care in his medical community[671].

The most common criticism that has been traditionally levied against medical boards is that they simply do not discipline physicians often enough to have a substantial impact on patient safety and public health. Indeed, in 2016, the Cameroon Medical Council set up a Commission[672] to investigate the death of one *Dr. Ngo Kana*, whose death was blamed on negligence on the part of medical practitioners in the different hospitals she visited (Clinique Gros Chene, l'Hôpital Général de Douala and l'Hôpital Gynéco-Obstétrique et Pédiatrique de Douala). The Commission, set up by the president of the Cameroon Medical Council, was made up of five members, all medical practitioners. In the report of their investigation, the Commission found out that when the patient visited these hospitals, her critical condition was not taken into account; there was complete absence of qualified personnel to take immediate care of the patient and enormous internal malfunctioning of the private clinic. The report of the Commission further revealed that in these hospitals, there was absence of empathy, no ambulance to transport patients in emergency situations, and non-respect of the rules and regulation pertaining to on calls medical services. All of these, the Commission noted, contributed to the death of *Dr. Ngo Kana*. One would have expected the commission to recommend sanctions but rather they come up with proposals for reform. This partly explains why nonchalant attitude of practitioners persist in Cameroon.

---

670 *Ibid*, Section 41(1)(2).

671 Sawicki, N N., (2010), "Character, Competence, and the Principles of Medical Discipline", *Journal of Heath Care Law and Policy*, 13(2), p.296.

672 Commission d'enquête, chargée d'élucider les circonstances de la mort du Dr NGO KANA survenue le 10 janvier 2016 à 4h55 à l'HGD.

4.3.2 Amicable Settlement

Settlement is a process of accommodation between two parties who have a conflict. The conflict is resolved by negotiating an agreement which sets forth the terms and conditions by which the complaining party agrees to waive his legal right to bring a lawsuit and proceed to trial. The claimant usually agrees to release the defendant from liability upon receipt of a specific amount of money[673].

Medical malpractice suits can cause a great amount of stress on the doctors, nurses, and other medical professionals in the medical field. As a result, many hospitals and doctors aim for a resolution through a settlement instead of getting into a trial proceeding that can potentially leave them liable for a much larger amount. Most cases of medical malpractice claim end in a settlement before or during trial proceedings. Furthermore, many patients are eager to settle in order to obtain compensation faster and to avoid a difficult and extended legal process which can stretch over several years[674]. Moreover, material inaccessibility of the courts (the cost of initiating a matter in court, the cost of hiring a lawyer etc.) may cause the patient to easily agree to settle out of court.

Out of court settlement or amicable settlement offers the parties a quick and private means of resolving their dispute. This may be particularly attractive to medical practitioners for whom the publicity of Court proceedings is likely to destroy their reputation, even if (months or years later) the Court holds in their favour[675]. It also gives some advantages to patients, who, under present conditions in Cameroon, simply do not have the resources or skill to present convincing expert evidence to the court. Moreover, often injured patients are seeking explanations as well as apologies in some cases. They are by no means invariably looking for a high award of damages. Out of court settlement might be a better way to obtain such explanations. However, one should not lose sight of the fact that this settlement reflects the balance of power between the parties. In the context of healthcare, doctors, not patients, hold most of the power. Doctors are thus likely to drive hard bargains through the out of court settlement process.

---

673 National Research Council, (1978), *Beyond Malpractice: Compensation for Medical Injuries*, Washington DC: The National Academies Press, p.13.

674 Susila, M E., (2021), "The Use of Amicable Settlement for Resolving Medical Malpractice Disputes in Indonesia", *Medicine, Law and Society*, 14(1), Pp. 119-134.

675 *Ibid.at* p.132.

Patients who have suffered from medical malpractice deserve compensation to aid them with their injuries. The amount of damage the victim is seeking, and the overall strength of his/her case may influence whether it is more advantageous to seek an out-of-court settlement or go to trial. Two major benefits of settling out of court are security and speed. If there are medical bills and other expenses pilling up, a lengthy trial can be too long to wait to recover the needed compensation. An out-of-court settlement provides more security than relying on the decision made by a judge. With an out-of-court settlement at least some form of compensation is secured. Medical malpractice cases lend themselves to settlement if all sides are realistic and understand the uncertainty inherent in taking these cases to trial.

The principle forming the cornerstone of compromise agreement was adumbrated in the English case of *Holsworthy Urban District Council v Holsworthy Rural Council*[676] in which it was stated that, the parties in the case may settle their disputes, the subject matter of the litigation without any adjudication from the court. This settlement then is by way of compromise between them and takes effect as a contract. The dispute is thereby disposed of and may not be re-opened in another subsequent action. If the parties want the compromise or settlement of their dispute to have the force of a formal judgement, they may request the court to enter a judgement in the action embodying the terms of the compromise.

In the Cameroonian case of *Ngwa George Mobanjoh v Jan Ndima Joseph and 2 Others*[677], Evande LJ pointed out that, "This settlement is by way of compromise and takes effect as a contract. The dispute is thereby disposed of and may not be re-opened in another subsequent action. The defendant in this suit shall pay to the plaintiff herein Ngwa George Mobanjoh the sum of 5 000 000 Frs. in total fulfilment of his claim of 20 000 000 Frs. This payment shall discharge the 1st, 2nd and 3rd defendants from any further claim by the plaintiff on the same cause of action."

In *Suh Mbony Beatrice V Dr. Zimmerman and Mbingo Baptist Hospital*[678], the plaintiff brought an action against the defendants for negligence and loss of earnings. The plaintiff was operated upon by Dr. Zimmerman for uterine fibroid. After the operation the plaintiff began passing out urine

---

676 (1907) 2 CH62.

677 Suit No HCK/3/2009 (unreported).

678 Suit No CFIF/03/06-07(unreported).

uncontrollably and soiling herself. She drew the attention of the first defendant who said it was normal after such an operation, and that it will soon be over. However, the situation got worse and she was unable to go to work. She presented herself again to the defendants, Dr. Zimmerman recognized his fault but refused to admit same and instead direct the plaintiff to a different hospital at her own expense. She was later operated again at the Douala General Hospital and the Limbe general hospital where the situation was corrected at her own cost. The plaintiff claimed 5 million thousand francs from the defendants jointly and severally as special and general damages. After an agreement between the plaintiff and the defendants, the plaintiff applied for the matter to be settled out of court and her application was granted by the court. The plaintiff was adequately compensated out of court.

Settlement process affords both parties control over the process, reduce cost of litigation and expedite resolution of dispute for both parties[679]. Trials can be unpredictable and volatile for both sides. This is because medical malpractice trials are so "testimony-dependent," such that weak medical malpractice cases can become strong and strong cases can become weak, as the trial progresses. The unpredictability of the result in medical malpractice trials encourages the case to settle. Agreeing to an appropriate settlement without going through an ulcer-producing trial is a wonderful outcome for all concerned.

Most at times simple apologies from the practitioner may decrease feelings of frustration and anger that drive some plaintiffs to file lawsuits[680]. An apology is a statement given by one who has injured another that includes recognition of the error that has occurred, admits fault and takes responsibility, and it should communicate a sincere sense of regret or remorse for having caused harm[681]. At their most complete, apologies may also include promises to refrain from engaging in similar conduct in the future and compensation

679 National Arbitration and Mediation, Resolving Medical Malpractice Matters- Positive Outcomes through Mediation, March 2020, at https://www.jdsupra.com/legalnews/resolving-medical-malpractice-matters-44779/ (accessed on 13th day of June 2021).

680 Ackerman, B G., (2018), "The Impact of Physicians' Apologies Medical Malpractice Litigation", *The National Law Review,* 8(310), at https://www.natlawreview.com/article/you-had-me-i-m-sorry-impact-physicians-apologies-medical-malpractice-litigation. (accessed on the 25th day of May 2921).

681 Tavuchis, N., (1991), *Mea Culpa: A Sociology of Apology and Reconciliation*, Stanford CA: Stanford University Press; p.15-44.

for the harm that has been done[682]. It can decrease blame, decrease anger, increase trust, and improve relationships. Importantly, apologies also have the potential to decrease the risk of a medical malpractice lawsuit and can play a role in the effective resolution of disputes related to medical error.

In line with the duty of candour, medical practitioners have a duty to be open and honest with patients when something goes wrong with their treatment or care and causes, harm or distress. The medical practitioner must inform the patient or, where appropriate, the patient's family, and apologize to the patient. He/she can offer an appropriate remedy or support to put matters right (if possible), explain fully to the patient or, where appropriate, the patient's family, the short- and long-term effects of what has happened. Indeed, physicians can avoid litigation through prompt error disclosure, apology and compensation.

The relationship between the physician and patient is one that involves considerable intimacy, vulnerability, and trust. When a patient is injured by a medical error, this relationship may be injured. Incorporating apology into conversations between physicians and patients can address the needs of both patients and physicians. Patients desire and expect to be informed promptly about a medical error; to be given information about what occurred, why and how it occurred, how their health will be affected, and what steps will be taken to prevent future harm; and to receive an apology that signals a sense of regret and a desire to do better.[683]

However, health care providers are reluctant to make any offers of compensation for medical errors unless and until a lawsuit is filed[684]. Some doctors explicitly referred to the error as an 'error' or a 'mistake' while others either described the event as a 'complication' or 'problem'. The inclination to offer an apology is even smaller when the error is one that would be less apparent to the patient. The norms, values, and practices that constitute the culture of medicine may play a greater role in encouraging or inhibiting disclosure and apologies than does the risk of liability[685]. Moreover, self-regulation and expectation of perfection from self, peers and patients may

---

682 Scher, S J. and Darley, J M., (1997), "How Effective are the Things People Say to Apologize? Effects of the Realization of the Apology Speech Act", J *Psycholinguistic Res*. 26, pp.127–140.

683 Gallagher, T H. *et al*, (2003), "Patients' and Physicians' Attitudes Regarding the Disclosure of Medical Errors", *JAMA*. 289, pp.1001–1007.

684 Berlinger, N., (2005), "After Harm: Medical Error and the Ethics of Forgiveness", *Johns Hopkins University Press*, 31, pp.61–62.

685 *Ibid*.

make it difficult for the doctor to apologize for errors[686]. Acknowledging an error conflicts with a striving for perfection and can result in a sense of vulnerability[687].

Moreover, apologies are considered a statement against interest because taking the blame for something bad that happened would not be in the best interest of the doctor or hospital. As statements against interest, these apologies can be introduced at trial as evidence of liability, in fact, it implies fault or liability. Thus, there is a resistance to apologies when there is a pending legal battle[688].

Besides, apology may not be an appropriate remedy unless it is followed by a desire to compensate the victim. *Berlinger*[689] has argued, "If a physician apologizes to an injured patient, if a physician genuinely fells remorse for having injured the patient, if a physician acknowledges that the mistake was his/her fault, but there are no provisions for fairly compensating the patient for the cost of medical care and lost wages resulting from the injury and no provisions for helping this physician to avoid injuring other patients, nothing has happened[690].

It is difficult to imagine a medical practitioner or health care facility apologizing to an injured patient in Cameroon. With their paternalistic tendencies, they tend to justify their action or bully the victim. The case of the little 5-year-old girl who died in *Polyclinique Achange* in Douala, as a result of an overdose of anaesthesia is a typical example of this. When the father of the child started protesting, the hospital called the police and he was arrested. As if that was not enough, the hospital declined all responsibilities and instead threatened to sue the father for destruction of its equipment.

4.4 Conclusion

The relationship between the patient and the physician is based on the expectation that the physician will put the needs of the patient first, over and beyond the interests of the physician or any third party. This relationship

686 Wei, M., (2007), "Doctors, Apologies, and the Law: An Analysis and Critique of Apology Laws", *J Health Law*. 40, pp.107–159.
687 Kaldjian, L C. *et al*, (2006), "An Empirically Derived Taxonomy of Factors Affecting Physicians' Willingness to Disclose Medical Errors". *J Gen Intern Med*. 21, pp.942–948.
688 O'Hara, E A. & Douglas, Y D., (2002), "Note & Comment, On Apology and Consilience", *Wash. L. Rev*., 77, pp.1121, 1122.
689 See *supra* note 737.
690 *Ibid*.

is the foundation on which the practice of medicine is built and dates to the era of Hippocrates. However, physicians have not always upheld their responsibility to put the needs of the patient first. Greed, prestige, and power have all succeeded at some time in displacing patients as the top priority of physicians[691]. Hence, the physician's interests are at odds with the patient's interests, this partly account for malpractices.

The medical practitioner cannot always guarantee the efficiency or success of a medical intervention. It is a known fact that with the best skill in the world, things sometimes go wrong in medical treatment or surgical operation. A doctor is not to be held negligent simply because something went wrong. Nevertheless, when it is proven that the doctor has fallen short of the standard of reasonable medical care, he should be held liable. However, the twin objectives of medical malpractice liability[692] are hardly attained.

The real difficulty lies in proving the negligence of the medical practitioner, particularly when loyalty and solidarity among medical professionals is considered. Quite often the expert and second opinion that are required are not provided, since it is the medical profession, and not the legal profession, that has the responsibility to determine whether therapeutic failures are the result of mal-occurrence, malpractice, or patient noncompliance. More so, it is not in all cases that a person may be able to prove that he suffered actual damages even though some wrong had been done to him in the course of receiving treatment. The reasonable man's test appears to be unduly protective of the medical practitioner and this may be to the detriment of the patient.

The main considerations of sanctions are; public interest, upholding public trust in the medical profession, and achieving effective deterrence. Generally, deterrence should discourage doctors from similar mistakes that led the doctor to be found guilty of professional misconduct and uphold the standing of the medical profession in society. However, instead of achieving the desired deterrent effects, at times these sanctions may instead lead to defensive medicine. Defensive medicine occurs when the doctor-patient relationship is supplanted by a doctor-potential plaintiff relationship. The doctor's decisions are no longer primarily driven by his desire to do good (benevolence) but by his perceived need to avoid being sued by a potential plaintiff. Indeed, it

---

691 See *supra* note 716.

692 These are; compensation of patients injured as a result of the negligence of medical practitioner, and to deter medical practitioners from practicing the profession negligently.

occurs when doctors order tests, procedures, primarily (but not necessarily solely) to reduce their exposure to malpractice liability[693].

Thus, in meting out sanctions the court must strike a balance between the public interest and the medical doctors' ability to exercise their profession without the feeling that laws are so overwhelming as to represent a sword of Damocles permanently hanging over their head[694]. Nevertheless, in providing sanctions for malpractices, it is hoped that the fields of the medical profession will be protected against incompetent individuals, and the victims is appeased.

Generally, the remedies available to an injured patient for malpractices of a medical doctor are clear and well stipulated, but very few victims avail themselves of these remedies. This can be explained by the fact that doctors are more likely to win medical malpractice lawsuits than patients, even when patients have strong evidence supporting their claims. Traditionally, the Courts usually provide the benefit of the doubt to physicians, at such doctors' benefit from an extra layer of protection in the Court's presumptions about them[695], unless a clear mistake is made, most Courts are highly sceptical of their guilt. Nevertheless, recently there have been a host of medical malpractice 'scandals' that have raised doubts about the wisdom of assuming that all medical practitioners in Cameroon are of good conscience.

However, the sanctions imposed on medical practitioners for violation of medical practice are far from achieving the desired objective; that of dissuading doctors from indulging in practices that injure patients physically, emotionally and financially. What obtain in practice are continuous malpractices by medical practitioner to the detriment of the helpless patients. The inability of the legislature to obtained the desired deterrent effect through imposition of sanctions for malpractices, imposes a restraint on the regulation of medical practice in Cameroon.

---

693 Definition of defensive medicine by the United States Congress' Office of Technology Assessment in its 1994 report titled 'Defensive Medicine and Medical Malpractice':

694 See *supra* note 64, p.105.

695 See *supra* note 62, p. 227.

CHAPTER FIVE

Constraints to the Regulation of Medical Practice in Cameroon

5.1 Introduction

The ethical standard of medical practice in Cameroon keeps declining in spite of the existence of legislation and regulatory authorities to ensure safe practice. In fact, the professional practice of health personnel all over the country is so deplorable such that there are doubts as to the effectiveness of these regulatory mechanisms. The Cameroon medical services are characterized by poor reception; double payments, corruption, and diversion of patients, parallel sale of drugs, and the illegal practice of medicine[696]. Absenteeism, quackery, favouritism, and commoditization of services[697] are the order of the day. As the government turns a blind eye or is powerless to contain the expansion of these unethical anti-values in public health institutions, these institutions have been transformed into vast market where medical practitioners and patients are engaged in several types of transactions[698], all at the detriment of the patient.

---

696 Pittsburgh courier, (2020),"Quadruplets Die in Government-Run Hospital", at https://newspittsburghcourier.com/020/07/08/quadruplets-die-in-government-run-hospital. (accessed on the 2nd day of November 2020).

697 Shu, C A., (2010), "Public and Private Hospitals in Cameroon: Service Quality and Patients' Choice of Hospitals", (unpublished Masters Thesis), Institute of Graduate Studies and Research, Eastern Mediterranean University, North Cyprus.

698 Djoko, C., (2010), "Comprendre la Corruption au Cameroun", *Le Grand Soir,* at http://www.legrandsoir.info/comrendre-la-crruption-au-cameroon.html. (accessed on 5th day of November 2020).

The legal aspect of the regulatory machinery which penalizes these malpractices of doctors is not being fully exploited by victims of medical malpractices. This is because the people have lost faith and confidence in the legal machinery, due to its numerous substantive and procedural obstacles, which make it almost impossible for victims to resort to. Where medical practitioners are aware that they can commit a wrong and get away with it, they become indifferent and less cautious in the performance of their duties. This accounts for the repeated cases of carelessness exhibited by medical personnel, causing harm and injuries on an everyday basis. The persistence of these malpractices and inability of the victims to seek redress through legal recourse are a constraint to the effective regulation of malpractices in Cameroon.

This chapter analyses the legal and extra-legal constraint to the regulation of malpractices in Cameroon.

5.2 Legal Constraints to the Regulation of Medical practice in Cameroon

Access to justice refers to the substantive and procedural mechanisms existing in any particular society designed to ensure that citizens have the opportunity of seeking redress for violation of their legal right within the system[699]. It includes the time it takes for delivering justice, the moral quality of the dispenser of justice, the affordability of the cost of seeking justice in terms of time and money, and the quality of the legal system[700]. Where the courts are not sufficiently manned, or are manned by men and women who are morally depraved, such a court can hardly guarantee justice to its litigant. Moreover, where procedural delays and high cost are endemic in a judicial system, judicial redress becomes a far cry. These are the characteristics typical of the Cameroon judicial system[701]. There is therefore a general apathy in reporting cases of medical malpractice and miscreant doctors persist in their deviant behaviour.

---

699 Zzouedja, T A., (2021), "Access to Justice and Human Rights Protection in the Common Law Jurisdiction in Cameroon: Problems and Prospects", *Zien Journal of Social Sciences and Humanities*, 1(1), p.201.

700 Gwangudi, M I., (2002), "Problems Militating Against Women's Access to Justice in Nigeria", *University of Maiduguri Law Journal*, No. 5, pp.13-14.

701 Asanga, I N., (2020), "Access to Justice and Legal Aid in Cameroon: A Critical Analysis", *Journal of Legal Studies and Research*, 6(1), p. 242.

5.2.1 Inefficient Enforcement of Existing Laws

There exist several pieces of legislation regulating medical practice in Cameroon. Prominent amongst these legislations are; Law No 80/7 of 14 July 1980 amended and supplemented by Law No 90/036 of 10th August 1990 relating to the Organization and Practice of Medicine in Cameroon, and Decree No 83/166 of 12th April 1983 of the Code of Medical Ethics. These Law and Decree regulate the entry into the profession of medicine, the adherence to the code of practice and disciplinary measures for violators of the law. However, it is exasperating that these pieces of legislation are not fully implemented.

The explosion of illegal clinics in the country points to this. In fact, in 2017, 2000 illegal private health care centres were uncovered in Cameroon[702]. Health care providers (nurses, laboratory technicians, midwifes etc.) with no qualification and license, are engaged in operating clinics and health centres here and there without the necessary infrastructure, equipment and human resources. It is surprising that some of them employed doctors to work with them, and have authorization numbers from Ministry in charge of Public Health, how they got the authorization is beyond comprehension. The operation of these illegal health centres is particularly rampant in metropolitan cities like Douala, Yaoundé, Bafoussam, where they can be found in almost every street or neighbourhood. Even qualified medical practitioners are also engaged in the unlawful practice of medicine, The Law relating to the organization and practice of medicine specifically prohibit the illegal practice of medicine. This law defines unlawful practice to include; practicing without a license, practicing under an assume name, practicing while on suspension, practicing in a business premises where medical apparatus is sold, engaging in consultation and diagnosis and treatment without authorization, and physicians offering assistance to persons who are not authorized to practice medicine are also guilty of unlawful practice[703].

Unlawful medical practices can attract severe administrative, civil and penal sanctions. According to the Law Organizing the Practice of Medicine in Cameroon, persons guilty of unlawful practice of medicine are punished with imprisonment of from six days to six months or with fine of from two hundred

702 2000 Illegal Hospitals Uncovered in Cameroon, *Journal du Cameroun*. 10th April 2017, at https://www.journalducameroun.com. (accessed on 3oth day of May 2022).

703 Section 16 of Law No 90/ 038 of 10th December 1990 relating to the Organization and Practice of Medicine in Cameroon.

thousand francs to two million francs or with both such imprisonment and fine[704]. Moreover, the Council of the Cameroon Medical Association may also order closure of the establishment irrespective of any court judgments[705]. The effective implementation of this law is yet to be achieved, as there are outright violations of these provisions. The failure to effectively implement the law and curtailed the proliferation of these unauthorized clinics and practice, constitute a restraint to effective regulation of malpractices

5.2.2 Ignorance of the law

Literacy level is still very low in Cameroon[706] despite government efforts at virtually all levels to ensure that the citizens acquire education. Majority of Cameroonians even the literate is ignorant of their rights due to low public enlightenment, consequently, they do not know when their rights have been violated, or when a breach has occurred, and neither do they know the measures to take to seek redress. They often adopt the mentality of leaving everything in God's hand. Laws are promulgated and published in both French and English in the official gazette in Cameroon. Not everyone has access to these gazettes. They are also published in newspapers and announced over the national radio, however, these newspapers and radio station do not cover the entire territory, and citizens continue to live in ignorance. As a result, many health practitioners and authorities have been escaping liability where their actions or omissions have been called to question.

It is quite obvious that Cameroonians are not litigious as those in the western world. Litigation is not their method of dispute resolution especially when the cases are against renowned individuals or against a person who is seen literarily as working or doing everything to save life (medical practitioners). The society seems to frown at or discourage such litigants who want to redress the injury they have suffered. Most Cameroonians may look for causes of their poorly handled medical cases to their relationship with the social, natural and spiritual environments and may not want to put the blame on the doorstep of the attending clinician who is perceived as all-knowing in medical care. This default position often projects clinicians to paternalistic

---

704 *Ibid.* Section 17.

705 *Ibid.*

706 Cameroon literacy Rate stands at 77.07 per cent, World Bank, at http//www.macrotrends. net/ countries/ CMR/Cameroon/literacy-rate>Cameroon Literacy Rate 1976-2022. (accessed on 16th day of July 2022).

tendencies which often lead to increasing occurrence of medical malpractices. This has made health care providers in Cameroon indifferent in the presence of gross medical errors and negligence.

Lack of formal complaints and law suits for medical malpractices in Cameroon, has led to a silence in which malpractice thrives. It does not suffice to know there is malpractice, what is important is having the courage to stand up to it. This is the problem in Cameroon, people do not know how, and also do not want to take legal action against. The victims can tell their story, but none is prepared to take legal action. Most are not aware that they can actually initiate a civil or criminal action in court against a medical practitioner.

In theory, patients should be protected from some aspect of poor health care by the litigation relating to medical malpractice. Such litigation encourages medical practitioners to maintain at least a basic standard of health care. Even though to err is human most errors in the provision of health care could be avoided if patients are encouraged to report cases of medical malpractices[707]. There is the need to create awareness amongst patient on their rights to report cases whenever they are not satisfied with the treatment receive in hospitals. However, most of the time accessibility to justice hinders them from doing so.

5.2.3 Access to Legal Redress

There are a number of substantive and procedural obstacles or impediments that preclude the masses in general from having access to judicial redress in Cameroon. Relative to the economic situation in Cameroon, the cost of litigation is so high that the ordinary Cameroonian can hardly afford adequate legal representation when he/she has a legal matter to pursue before the ordinary courts. A medical malpractice victim intending to contest his/her claim in Court has a lot of things to consider; firstly, the cost of hiring a lawyer. Lawyers are few in number[708], located in urban areas and command high fees, which the poorest and most marginalized in rural communities can neither physically access nor afford. Legal practitioners in Cameroon have devised the method of collecting not only their professional fees but also transportation fees each time they go to court, thus invariably adding to the financial burden of the litigant. However, when this is considered against the background that a

[707] Zhan, W, *et al*, (2017), "Records of Medical Malpractice Litigation: A Potential Indicator of Health Care Quality in China", *Bulletin of The World Health Organization*, 95(6), pp. 430-435.

[708] According to the Cameroon Bar Roll 2022, Cameroon has a total of about 3500 lawyers.

particular case may last for more than three years in court, then the enormity of the financial burden on litigants can better be appreciated[709].

Secondly, the litigant must consider the cost of filing a claim in court. Filing a suit in court involves a lot of expenditure. The plaintiff is expected to pay the filing fee plus the cost of stamp duty. This requirement by the courts for litigants in a civil suit to deposit 5 per cent of the quantum of claim before the suit is filed[710] regardless of the chances of success of the action is a great hindrance to access to justice because litigants who cannot afford this 5 per cent cannot get legal redress. In *Ejupu Paulette Efila v ENEO Cameroon*[711], the plaintiff prepared a suit for filing in 2009 wherein she was claiming 92.450.000 FCFA as Special and General Damages for negligence and murder. The suit was rejected by the Court Registrar for want of 5per cent pre-tax fee on the amount claimed. The plaintiff was able to raise part of the pre-tax fee and filing fee after two years, and the action was filed in 2011. Even though the action was filed upon the payment of less than 1per cent of compulsory 5per cent pre-tax fee, the action was thrown out of court in 2015 by a newly appointed registrar in chief, who requested for a receipt from the plaintiff evidencing the 5per cent pre-tax fee which stood at 4.622.500 FCFA. The plaintiff could not furnish the receipt, she was therefore denied access to court. This is more disturbing when one considers that the law on Judicial Organization in Cameroon provides that justice shall be administered free of charge[712], subject only to the fiscal provisions concerning stamp duty and registration.

All these serve as a hindrance to access to judicial remedy. This explains why most at times the victims or their relatives assault medical practitioners for malpractices immediately it occurs because they know that they do not stand a chance before the law courts. Poverty[713] therefore prevents most people from contemplating litigation in the courts even if aware of their entitlement to one, and serves as an obstacle to access legal redress in Cameroon. *Sir Jack I. H. Jacob* had this to say on the implication of poverty and high cost of litigation;

---

709 See *supra* note 754, p.203.

710 This is in conformity with the Minister of Justice and Keeper of the Seals CIRCULAR NO 001/ MG/SG/DAG of 13 March 1996 which demands that 5 per cent of the claim in civil suits be deposited in the court as stamp duty.

711 HCK/41/2011(unreported).

712 Section 8(1) of Law No 2006/015 of 29 December 2006 on Judicial Organization in Cameroon as amended.

713 The National Health Development Plan 2016-2020 reports that 40 per cent of Cameroon population is still living below the poverty threshold, Published by the Ministry of Public Health in 2016.

> *the most serious blemish in the system of costs was and still is the excessive and prohibitive amount of the costs of resorting to the courts for determination or resolution of civil disputes or questions. The effect is to put justice out of reach of people who may be classed as poor or even those with moderate means. Grave injustice may thereby be occasioned and many meritorious claims go unaddressed*"[714].

There is however the possibility of the victim to get legal aid. Legal aid has increasingly been recognized to play a significant role in improving access to justice for impoverished, marginalized and excluded groups, and in providing them with access to legal entitlements, resolution of disputes, and justice processes[715]. Legal aid is generally understood as free or subsidized services to eligible individuals or groups, mainly poor and vulnerable people, provided as a means to strengthen their access to justice[716]. It includes legal advice, assistance and representation" in statutory justice systems, as well as concepts of legal education, access to legal information, and other services provided for persons through alternative dispute resolution mechanisms.

Legal Aid service providers, whether lawyers or paralegals, can help correct some of the power imbalances by supporting people in navigating the justice system, as well as by advising and/or representing them to claim their rights and entitlements. Strengthen legal aid and enhance access to justice is to foster a culture of accountability in state institutions, which stimulates responsiveness and effectiveness in service delivery[717].

In Cameroon, there is no developed system of legal aid. The Law of Legal Aid[718] is fraught with many delays and a lot of procedural obstacles in its application such that it is not effective in assisting poor citizens to access justice[719]. Not only are many citizens unaware of the existence of Legal Aid Commission but they scarcely meet the requirements. In Cameroon, Legal Aid Commissions are set up in the Court of First Instance, Military Tribunal, Court

---

714 Peter, C M., (2008), "Access to Justice: Creating a Role for Paralegal in the Administration of Justice in Africa", *Recht in Afrika*, 11(1), pp.101-129.

715 Legal Aid Service Provision A Guide on Programming in Africa, United Nations Development Programme, May 2016.

716 See *supra* note 756, p. 242.

717 *Ibid.*

718 Law No 2009/004 of 14 April 2009 to organize Legal Aid in Cameroon.

719 Sama, N J., (2017), "Providing Legal Aid in Criminal Justice in Cameroon: The Role of Lawyers", in Access to Justice in Africa and Beyond, Making the Rule of Law a Reality. Penal Reform International and Bluhum Legal Clinic of the North western University School of law. Pp.153-227.

of Appeal and Supreme Court. An application for legal aid is addressed orally or in writing to the secretary of the legal aid commission, who is the registrar of the competent court. The application made must include the following; document of proof of impecuniosity, a copy of the tax roll or certificate from the head of the administrative unit specifying where appropriate if the applicant is liable to discharge tax, a certificate of lack of means by the mayor following inquiries by the appropriate social service. Failure on the part of the applicant to furnish these documents thirty (30) days after having been summoned to do so shall render the application inadmissible[720]. The secretary of the commission then forwards the application to the chairperson of the legal aid commission, who is the president of the competent court, who, in consultation with the counsel, makes a decision on whether the applicant qualifies for aid. The legal aid commission has the right to gather independently all information necessary to determine the inadequacy of the resources of the applicant[721].

The decision on whether to grant legal aid rests entirely with members of the Legal Aid commission. They have the pretext to disregard the law as voting power rest with them to decide whether or not to grant legal aid, In *Mme Bate Nkongho Regina Manyo v. Bate Oscar*[722], the plaintiff Mme Bate Nee Nkongho Regina Manyoh had on the 23rd day of march, 2011, applied for legal aid as she lacked the means to hire a lawyer and pay the cost of proceedings, but for over eight years has not gotten any reply form the commission. Quite apart from the fact that the composition of commission gives its members the perfect opportunity to discriminatory disregard applications, in this particular case, the application was motivated in view of pursuing a claim for which an advocate and magistrate who could influence the decision of the commission were involved.

Moreover, many lawyers are discouraged from taking on legally aided cases because the procedure for obtaining the funds are cumbersome and in addition the payments are very minimal and very few lawyers are prepared to work for free. Moreover, there is fear among lawyers that giving too much legal advice for free may give Cameroonian a wrong impression[723].

---

720 *Ibid.*

721 See *supra* note 773, Section 20(1).

722 Suit No HCK/AB/40/2011.

723 Eta Besong Junior, former President of the Cameroon Bar Association said "we are in a country where people do not understand the usefulness of advocates, so if you try to push pro bono too far, people might think that is the rule rather than the exception".

5.2.4 Delay in Legal Proceedings

Justice delayed is justice denied, is legal maxim meaning where a legal remedy is available for a party who has suffered some injury, but is not forth coming promptly, it is effectively the same as having no remedy at all. It is unfair for a victim to have to sustain injury with little hope for resolution. This is a very relevant factor that determines the response of victims of medical malpractice to litigation. Speedy trial is a rare occurrence in Cameroon judiciary. Justice cannot be said to be rendered if it is made within a long period of time. This is because beyond a certain time the decision taken by the court may lose their value.

In Cameroon, one sees ordinary cases of trespass and related dispute over land before the courts lasting for more than five years. In *Malafa Efungani v Ndive Mondoa*[724], the Court of Appeal nullified the decision of the lower court filed before the court in 2006, for lack of jurisdiction. The appeal which was filed in 2011 was only dismiss in 2014. Thus from 2006-2014, the matter was pending determination in court. It has become an accepted fact in Cameroon that cases must last several years in court before they are concluded.

These delays can be accounted for on a number of factors, nonappearance of lawyers, corruption, in which the judges may deliberately not delivered judgment, numerous adjournments, in order to elicit bribe from the litigants. Work overload also precludes magistrates from adjudicating cases on time. In Cameroon, judges cause list for a day may carry about twenty cases. Again, witnesses summon may fail to appear in court, thus months, years, and even decades may pass by, meanwhile the life of the victim becomes miserable during this long and never-ending fight for justice.

Delay in judicial procedure is in fact a problem in most African countries. The case of *Plateau State Health Services Management Board and Anor v Goshwe*[725] shows clearly how slow the system or wheel of justice can drag in Nigeria. In this case the plaintiff/Respondent suffered the injury in August 1990 whereupon he instituted an action against the hospital claiming damages but the case dragged on for 22yrs before the Supreme Court gave final judgment in respect of the matter in 2012. No litigant would want to spend money on litigation and wait for decades before getting his deserved judgment.

---

[724] Suit No CASWR/CC/02/2011

[725] (2012) LPELR-9830 SC

5.2.5 Burden of Proof

Burden of prove is generally considered as the "Legal obligation imposed on the party to persuade the tribunal of fact, to the required standard of prove and on the whole evidence of the truth of every essential fact at issue[726]." The onerous burden of prove lies on the plaintiff, and at times on the defendant in the case of reversal of burden of proof. Proving that loss or injury suffered is as a result of the negligence of a medical practitioner is a severe task on the claimant especially when such proof turns out to be technically complicated and expensive due to the requirement of expert opinion[727]. In Cameroon, it is sad to know that medical malpractice claims are frequently launched and advanced at trial without expert medical evidence. The plaintiff comes to court and gives his or her account of what occurred but fails to back up allegations of malpractice with coherent evidence from a medical expert. In such circumstances, it is no surprise that the Courts will heed the exculpatory evidence inevitably provided by experts on behalf of the defendant, and dismiss the claim.

According to traditional principles in the law of tort, the plaintiff must prove, on a balance of probabilities that "but for" the defendants tortuous conduct, the plaintiff would not have sustained the injury or damage[728]. If a plaintiff can hold that the damage would not have happened but for a particular fault, then that fault is in fact the cause of the damage; but if the plaintiff can say the injury would have occurred just the same, fault or no fault, then the fault is not the cause of the damage[729]. Due to the fact that allegation of negligence in the medical profession are serious, such that it may lead to the practitioner's name being deleted from the medical register and banned from medical practice, and the consequence damage to his reputation, a high standard of proof of negligence is required for liability so that the mere fact of a mishap, or error of clinical judgment does not in itself amount to negligence[730]. The onus lies on their colleagues to provide expert evidence

---

726 Fuah, C K., (2018), "Insurmountable Hurdles in the Proof of Causation in Pharmaceutical Product Liability in Cameroon: Perspective for Reform" *International Journal of Legal Developments and Allied Issues*, 4(5), p.508.

727 Commission Green paper: Liability for Defective Products, Brussels, Com 1999 396 (28 July 1999), summary P 2.

728 Lord Denning's statement in *Cork v Kirby Maclean Ltd*, 1952, 2 All ER 402.

729 *Ibid.*

730 Malemi, E., (2013), *Law of Tort*, 2nd Edition, Lagos, Princeton Publishing Company, p.362.

but most often the medical personnel are not willing to testify, a situation described as 'conspiracy of silence'[731].

Medical Experts are reluctant to openly criticize the professional conduct of their colleagues, moreover, it is difficult and expensive for a layman to produce evidence in such a technical domain which has to do with the skill and competence of a doctor, as such a victim of medical malpractice in Cameroon is not likely to succeed because expert witnesses are not willing to testify that the practices or procedures adopted by their colleagues should be stigmatized as negligent[732].

In the Cameroonian case of *The People of Cameroon v. Yilareng Elias Afoni*[733], the accused medical doctor was charged with assault occasioning death punishable under section 278(1) of the Cameroon Penal Code. All through the trial, the prosecution produced only one witness, who was an investigator. The court held that the evidenced adduced was grossly insufficient to buttress the charge, the accused medical doctor was able to produce expert witness who testify that on examination of the deceased, it was evidenced that the fetus in her womb was already death even before they got to the accused's clinic. On this score the accused medical doctor was discharged.

Again, in *Bwalya v Zambia Consolidated Copper Mines Ltd & Ors*[734], The plaintiff, a married woman, underwent a bilateral tubal ligation (BTL) in 1997 at the second defendant's hospital. In August 1999, she had a miscarriage. Further, in October/November 1999, after a thorough medical examination was found to be about five weeks pregnant. In June 2000, she gave birth to a child through a caesarean operation. She brought a claim in negligence against the defendants. She did not produce any expert medical witness in support of her claim. The Zambia Supreme Court based its conclusions, not surprisingly, on the evidence of the defendants' expert witness. In the absence of any evidence contradicting that of the defendants' expert witnesses, the plaintiff's claim inevitably failed.

The reasons for plaintiff's difficulties in discharging the burden of proof are many; medicine is practiced behind what is described as the 'fortress of

731 Emir, F., (2012), *Medical Law and Ethics in Nigeria*, Lagos, Malthouse Press Ltd, p.286.

732 This is so because of the duties they owe to their colleagues under the Code of Medical Ethics. Section 42(1) of Decree No. 83-166 of 12 April 1983, Cameroon Code of Medical Ethics, provides that "doctors must maintain good professional relations between themselves", and section 42(2) forbids a doctor from slandering or disparaging a colleague, or to repeat any remarks likely to harm him in the practice of his profession.

733 See Suit No HCK/15c/2020, (unreported).

734 20 April 2005 (Zambia SC).

Jericho walls'[735] as such it is not easy to identify breaches committed by health practitioners compared to other professionals. Members of the public do not easily access and assess the performance and quality of care delivered by health care givers. They equally have difficulty knowing if the injury suffered was as a result of the health practitioner's negligence. Again, poor knowledge of both the lawyer and the litigant on the relevant materials and evidence required to prove medical negligence compound the problem. There are also resource challenges, medical experts can be very expensive and beyond the means of impoverished plaintiffs. Moreover, it may be hard to find a doctor willing to give evidence criticizing the conduct of another doctor.

Since the duty of the law is to protect the weaker from the injustices of the strong and maintaining a balance between them, there is the need for a reversal of burden of proof. The reversal of burden of proof is equal to the shift of the risk of not being able to prove a certain fact unto someone else. Shifting the burden of proof may result in someone wining a case that would otherwise have been lost due to evidential difficulties. Reversal of burden of proof is a means of protection of the position of the victim because in medical liability, the victim is put under unreasonable difficulties due to, for instance, the technical and organizational complexity of the defendant's activities and as a result making the facts difficult to prove. There is also the need of channelling liability in a certain direction, the idea of promoting the preventive effects of habits, the need to prevent fundamental rights at stake, the wish to decrease the dependence of one party. This is a gap in the law that would need to be corrected for without the manner of operation of such a theory there would be practical difficulties in its application and causal difficulties would still remain. This theory needs to be put into practice. A Law must not only exist in principle but it has to be pragmatic.

5.2.6 Corruption of the Judiciary

Corruption is endemic in Cameroon even though punishable under Cameroon's penal legislation[736]. In fact, corruption in Cameroon has been called "Cameroon's worst-kept secret"[737]. It is rife in almost all the government sectors, most especially the judiciary. The corrupt nature of Cameroon's

[735] It is difficult to access and assess the activities of medical professionals as a layman.

[736] The Cameroon Penal Code, Section 134.

[737] G. Fominyen G., (2010), "Why Corruption is Cameroon's Worst-Kept Secret", *Thomson Reuters Foundation News*.

judiciary cannot be overstated. Transparency international[738] had way back in 1999 classified Cameroon as the most corrupt country in the world with the judiciary leading. In 2021, according to transparency international corruption perception index, Cameroon ranks 144 out of 180, even though there is an improvement in the score, it is still among the top 30 most corrupt countries in the world. Even the National Anti-Corruption Commission (CONAC)[739], an anti-corruption body set up the fight corruption in the country published its corruption index in Cameroon in 2016 indicating that the police and the judiciary were the most corrupt sectors in Cameroon.

Corruption is commonly defined as the misuse of public office or entrusted power for private gains. The paradigmatic image of judicial corruption is that of a judge taking bribes. However, judicial corruption is a lot more, it includes *all forms of inappropriate influence* that may damage the impartiality of justice, and may involve actors within the systems including lawyers and administrative support staff[740]. *C. Oputa JSC*[741] asserts that; "it is a calamity to have a corrupt judge, for money-its offer and its receipts corrupts and pollutes not only the channels of justice but the very stream itself. Honesty and judicial rectitude are therefore the very minimal requirement of the judicial office".

Corruption in the judiciary not only undermines the court's credibility in upholding justice, more generally, it erodes trust in the court's impartiality, harming all the core judicial functions, such as dispute resolution, law enforcement, protection of property rights and contract enforcement. In addition, it harms the broader accountability function that the judiciary is entrusted with in democratic systems; upholding citizens' rights, and sanctioning representatives of other branches when they act in contravention of the law[742].

In Cameroon, litigants pay to get their case through the system, to influence the outcome of their case, or to delay it. Bribes are paid to judges or registrars or lawyers to remove files or get their cases assigned to a particular judge. Judicial officers receive bribes in exchange for dropping charges,

---

738 Transparency international is a German registered non-profit association founded in 1993 by former employees of the World Bank, with purpose to combat corruption and prevent criminal activities. It's most notable publication is the corruption perception index.

739 Created by Decree No. 2006/088 of 11 March, 2006.

740 Gloppen, S., (2014), "Courts, Corruption and Judicial Independence", (2014) In Soreide, T and Williams, A., *Corruption, Grabbing and Development: Real World Challenges*, Cheltenham and Northampton, Edward Elgar Publishing.

741 A Retired Justice of the Nigerian Supreme Court.

742 See *supra* note 792.

reducing sentences, destroying evidence, and reduction in prison sentence[743]. The judiciary in Cameroon is inefficient, lacks adequate resources and expertise, and has an inadequate tracking system of cases, resulting in lengthy court procedures, vindicating the rights of patients in Cameroon is an uphill task. The process of dispute settlement is ineffective and oppressive as a result court being unreliable, very slow and selective in enforcing legislation.

All these create artificial barrier for ordinary citizens, like a victim of malpractice, to access the justice system besides, it erodes trust in the courts and distort the ability of the court to perform their function as impartial arbiters of dispute, guarantor of contracts and enforcers of law. The defaulting medical practitioner is well aware of all these; thus, he engages in malpractices with impunity knowing fully well that the victims cannot get justice for their cause. More so, victims of medical malpractices are left without effective recourse to justice when the malefactor has a strong political affiliate, just a phone call set him/her off the hook.

Insufficient implementation of anti-corruption legislation and the laws in general[744] coupled with impunity among public officials and lack of political will has exacerbated the levels of corruption in the country. Decree No 95/048 of 1995 on Status of Magistracy in Cameroon, sanctions corrupt magistrate; however, it is seldom implemented.

Corruption in Cameroon is associated with low income[745]. In Cameroon, per capita income is 1,520$ annually, which is extremely low by global standards. The cost of living is well below the global average, indicating massive socio-economic problems[746]. This partly accounts for high rate of corruption.

Apart from the above legal constraints, there are other constraints, not legal in nature which limits the effectiveness of the regulation of medical practice in Cameroon, with the result that medical service quality continues to deteriorate.

---

743 *Ibid.*

744 In FAKLA (Fako Lawyers Association) BULLETIN Vol. 1 p. 34, lawyers practicing within the jurisdiction of Fako castigate the corrupt practices of some magistrates/judges who had been collecting money from suspects and accused persons admitted to bail on grounds of fulfilment of condition for bail whereas bail in spite of the express provision of Law No 2005/007 of 27 July 2005 on the Criminal Procedure Code which states that bail is free. More to that, following the table of fees found with the Registrar in Chief of the High Court of Fako, criminal application for bail is filed tax and fee free.

745

746 Extent of Public Corruption in Cameroon, world data.info at https://www.worlddata.info. (accessed on 4th day of May 2022).

5.3 Extra-Legal Constraints to the Regulation of Medical Practice in Cameroon

Persistent, malpractices nullify all efforts and initiative taken to control and monitor the activities of doctors in Cameroon. Incessant acts, that constitutes gross flaunting of the professional code of practice, indulged in with impunity by medical practitioners in the face of weak and inefficient control by the medical council and inaction by the government, place a restraint on regulatory effort. This is the focus of this section.

The provision of medical services in health facilities in Cameroon is so terrible. Patients leave their homes for the hospital generally under very uncomfortable circumstances. When these patients approach a medical facility, they expect medical treatment and care given with all the knowledge and skill that will bring relief to their problems[747]. This expectation is a far cry in Cameroon. An increasing number of medical personnel are not providing the necessary care, consequently, patients particularly the financially vulnerable, experienced difficulties in accessing these health services[748].

5.3.1 Weak Regulatory Mechanisms

The self-regulatory nature of the medical profession is complex, and involves many levels of oversight aimed at guaranteeing the competence of the practicing physician. Regulation is aimed at enhancing the quality of health care services delivered to patients. Professional associations, as definers and guarantors of effective medical practice, have an implied contract with society to hold their members accountable[749]. The medical council sets out expected standards in relation to quality and accountability. It also highlights the duty a medical professional has to the profession, the wider community and the organization in which he/she is working. It empowers patients to pursue malpractice suits to hold health providers accountable. Overall, the regulator serves as the institutional structure of checks and balances of medical practice.

In a developing country like Cameroon, professional associations' capacity to fulfil these roles is relatively limited. Currently, there is a public

---

747 Ngeh, E N., *et al*, (2020). "Covid-19: Challenges and the Impact on Care in Clinical Settings in Cameroon", *Pan African Medical Journal*, 35(2), p.122.

748 *Ibid.*

749 Sylvia, C R. et al, (2000). "Professionalism: A Contract between Medicine and Society". *Canadian Medical Association Journal*, 162(5), *pp*.668-669.

perception that self-regulation has gone too far to protect the doctor. Regulatory bodies will always "in the last analysis put fairness to doctors ahead of patient protection"[750], that is, the professions tend to be protective of their members. When complaints do come in, the disciplinary process is self-serving; by doctors and for doctors. Members are at once players and referees in the field. Given the natural urge to protect one's own, and given the opportunity provided by self- policing, there is the likelihood that erring members would be left off the hook, based on the fellow-feeling theory[751]. The theory assumes that complaints against defaulters are likely to be treated lightly by other members, given that the non-erring members will exhibit a soft spot for their colleagues against whom complaints are lodged. Patients and the public seem to be ancillary, whereas they should be front and center. The domination of medical thought by men of the practicing profession, distort the pursuit of medical knowledge and block the development and delivery of medical care[752].

The Cameroon Code of Ethics forbids a doctor from criticizing a colleague or making any remark likely to harm him in the practice of his profession[753]. Thus, the Code enjoins them to protect each other's reputation. With this it becomes almost impossible to obtain genuine expert evidence during litigation. Enhanced investigation and discipline therefore seem to be a far cry; one is tempted to ask why investigation of problems or incidences should be confined strictly to self-regulated professional bodies. The tendency is for them to tilt in favour of their colleagues and come up with meaningless sanctions such as warnings, reprimand and even recommendation reports instead of disciplinary actions. A case in point is that of *Affaire Monique Koumateke* where the Commission of Inquiry (made up exclusively of medical professionals), set up by the Cameroon Medical Council in March 2016 to investigate the circumstances surrounding the death of *Monique Koumateke*, came up with report of recommendations to the government and the medical corps with no sanctions[754].

Monique Koumateke, was a pregnant woman who was disemboweled by her sister in a bid to safe her unborn babies in front of a public hospital

---

750 Smith, R., (2005), "The GMC: Expediency before Principle". *BMJ*. 330(7481), pp.1-2.
751 Jeffrey, B., (1975), *Profession and Monopoly*, Berkeley, University of California Press, p.88 .
752 *Ibid.*
753 Section 42(2).
754 ONMC, Rapport de la Commission d'enquete du Conseil de L'ordre National des Medecins du Cameroun sur L'affaire Monique Koumateke. Mars 2016.

in Douala, precisely the Laquintinin hospital. From the investigative report, there were instances of wanton neglect, carelessness and indifference towards the pregnant patient, which portray the malfunctioning of the Cameroon Health system. She was taken to two hospitals before finally brought to the Laquintinin hospital, where she was turned away by the hospital staffs stating she was dead. The family of the patient claimed that she was still alive when they got to the hospital, and that the real reason she was turned down was because they did not have enough money to pay her consultation fee. That all attempts to get the medical staff to attend to her was fruitless. Meanwhile, in a Press Conference the Minister of Public Health, refuting negligence on the part of the Hospital staff, gave a different version of the story, that the pregnant woman and her unborn fetus had been dead for four hours already before being brough to the hospital[755].

The Commission of Enquiry on its part, put up a scientific argument, relying on the three prenatal consultation report of the victim, stated that Monique Koumateke died at home hours earlier from eclampsia complications before being taken to Lanquantinine hospital, and that she refused to be hospitalized in the first health center she visited at PK13 in Douala[756]. That she carried a high-risk pregnancy and did not have any quality prenatal consultation. The family of Monique Koumateke made a complaint against the hospital for involuntary homicide, and failure to assist. They also denounce the Cameroon Medical Council for propagating false information, maintaining that *Monique* died in the hospital out of negligence and inhumane treatment from the hospital personnel[757].

Indeed, instead of sanctioning the reprehensible actions of the hospital management and its personnel, actions which poses a threat to the community, the commission of enquiry, made up exclusively of medical personnel, tends to shield their colleagues by bringing up scientific arguments to shift the blame on the victim. The report did not see any relationship between the dead of Monique and the indifference of the personnel of the hospital, the treatment received by the victim and her family, medical ethics, the refusal of hospitalization at PK13 and the cost of treatment. It hard to believe that the

---

755 "Pregnant Woman's Shock Death Puts Cameroon's Healthcare under Spotlight", *The Observer, France 24*, 15/3/2016 at http://observers.france24.com/en/20160315-pregnant-woman-cameroon-hospital-ceasarian. (accessed on 7th day of May 2021).

756 See *supra* note 809.

757 Azétsop, J. et al, (2018), "Morphologie du Quotidien, Souffrance Sociale et Parcours Individuels au Cameroun: La Mort De Monique Koumateke, Un Problème Social?", *African Sociological Review*, 22(1), pp68-69.

medical staff who consulted the deceased victim at PK13, knowing fully well that she had high risk pregnancy and was in danger of death, allowed her to go home when she refused hospitalization. The first mission of every health institution is to safe life, and where this mission is overlooked, the result is homicide.

The presence of non-experts in the regulatory commission has been advocated for; on the pretext that it will prevents members of a profession from speaking purely in their own language or acting strictly in the interests of the group. It helps keep an insular group connected to the public they serve. Though this is important, most doctors would be quick to point out there is still no substitute for technical expertise in the regulation process[758].

5.3.2 Absenteeism

Health personnel availability is a major problem in Cameroon public hospitals which needs to be addressed by effective regulation. This unavailability can be explained by the fact that private health facilities that accompany the government in the offer of health services to populations mostly have as promoters, medical doctors working in the public sector. These doctors spend most of their official working hours consulting in these private hospitals or in their homes. In fact, many patients who visit public health facilities are oriented by these doctors to their private health centres for medical care[759].

Indeed, this practice contravenes Article 13 of the Prime Ministerial Decree[760] on the Code of Ethics of care givers, which condemns diversions of users, (this consists in redirecting patients intercepted in public health facilities to private or informal care centres). However, owing to the unenforceability of laws in Cameroon, these predatory or unethical behaviours persist. For example, at the Lanquantinie Hospital in Douala, some young men called "les demarcheurs de maladies" or "tacleurs" or "racoleurs" were often posted at the entrance of the hospital, to divert the patients either to a specific doctor or to the private clinics.

---

758 Coller, R., (2012), "Professionalism the Privilege and Burden of Self-Regulation", *Canadian Medical Association Journal*, 184(14), Pp.1559-1560.

759 Yamb, B. & Bayemi, O., (2017), "Corruption and Discrimination in Douala Metropolis Public Hospitals of Cameroon", *Journal of Economics Library*, 4(4), p.505.

760 Decree No 2004/321 of 18/12/2004, Article 13 reads; are forbidden, any commission, or acceptance or sharing of clandestine money between practitioners and patients; the acceptance of commission for any medical act, including for examinations, drug prescriptions, appliances, sending to a specific clinic, station cure, or health home.

The redirection of patients from formal to informal health centres, are widespread practices in Cameroon hospitals. This unethical practice is mostly done by specialist doctors, who transform their homes into informal health care centres, and spend most of their work time in these centres regularly using materials diverted from public hospitals. Consequently, patients at the public hospitals, after paying the consultation fee and waiting for hours are later told that the doctor is not on sit[761].

This presupposes that the public practitioner has the discretional power which permits him/her to be absent from his official work and go to his private clinic or stay at home and receive patient during his contractual working period. The discretionary power held by the doctor allows him/her to reduce the quantity of service rendered, either by refusing to honour the appointment given to patients, or by simply refusing to serve them or even by discriminating them, and this is the most frequent case[762]. This he does without any fear of hierarchical authority.

One author[763] concluded that absenteeism of healthcare workers is ubiquitous because public hospitals do not have systems to monitor and sanction staffs who fail in their public responsibilities. The culture within public hospitals is highly tolerant towards absenteeism. A director's reluctance to confront doctors encourages other employees to also be absent during working hours[764]. As a result, high absenteeism and low productivity is widely reported in public hospitals[765]. In Cameroon, health-care providers in public hospitals justify their high rate of indolence on low salaries. Therefore; involvements in other economic activities during office hours or making use of possibilities for private gain through public health-care systems are everywhere[766].

---

761 Direct observation at the Regional Hospital Bafoussam on 13/10/2020, where some pregnant women upon paying the consultation fee to see the gynaecologist, were later told after several hours of waiting that she is not coming.

762 See *supra* note 777.

763 McPake, B. *et al.* (1999), "Informal Economic Activities of Public Health Workers in Uganda: Implications for Quality and Accessibility of Care", *Soc Sci Med,* 49, pp.849–65.

764 García-Prado, A. *et al* (2006), "The Impact of Hospital Management Reforms on Absenteeism in Costa Rica", *Health Policy Plan,* 21, pp. 91–100.

765 Lewis, M., (2006), "Governance and Corruption in Public Health Care Systems", *Center for Global Development,* Working Paper Number 78, at http://www.cgdev.org/publication/governance-and-corruptionpublic-health-care-systems-working-paper-78 (accessed on the22nd October 2020) .

766 Saskia, M. *et al,* (2015), "Corruption in Health-Care Systems and its Effect on Cancer Care in Africa", *Lancet Oncol,* 16, p.397.

5.3.3 Corruption

Corruption in Cameroon's public hospitals is severe. It is prevalent in services offered at the reception, hospitalization and hospital pharmacy[767]. These public hospitals are marked by racketeering, extortion, and theft[768]. Patients are forced to pay fees that have no official reference[769]. To see a specialist involves paying additional fees or financially motivating the secretary of the specialist (bribe)[770]. In order to receive emergency treatment, the care givers must be bribed if not the patient is allowed to languish in pain and eventually die[771]. Despite the public display of messages against corruption on all hospital notice boards, this ill prevails, and money has become the driving force in service provision in Cameroon. At such it is the patient's economic capital that counts. Patients without enough or sufficient financial resources wait long hours in corridors; some die in pain under indifferent gaze of the professionals who are supposed to take care of them, while financially viable patients are able to bribe care givers to attract their favours, skip the queue and obtain prompt, careful, and effective care[772].

Indeed, the Cameroon Penal Code[773] in its Section 134 criminalizes corruption, bribery, extortion. The government has also instituted ad hoc institutions to fight corruption, including the National Anti-Corruption Commission[774], the office of the Supreme State Audit, and the Special Criminal Court[775]. In hospitals the government installed anti-corruption units. These units have as objective to put a check on corrupt practices in hospitals; they control the rate at which medical doctors divert patients from public hospitals

---

767 Bayemi, O., (2018), "Corruption and Users in Douala-Cameroon Public Hospitals: An Evaluation of Determinants", *AERC Research Paper* 344, *African Economic Consortium*, Nairobi, p.6.

768 Bayemi, V., (2008), "Corruption et Crise des Hôpitaux Publics à Douala: le Schémas d'une Organisation Tripolaire", In Governing Health Systems in Africa, Dakar, *Council for the Development of Social Science Research in Africa* (*CODESRIA*), P.12-24.

769 That is; unregistered billing; extra-billing of real or presumed complementary services for their supposed rapidity or quality; payment for services which in fact have not been rendered; payments for services that are officially free of charge or subsidized such as mosquito nets and HIV screening and, the issuing of fake medical certificates.

770 Ntangsi, J., "An Analysis of Health Sector Expenditures in Cameroon Using a National Health Accounts Framework". at https://www.rad-aid.org/wp-content/uploads/Cameroon-Country-Report.pdf (accessed on 24 th day of October 2020).

771 Mougbaku, I B M., (2018) "Commodification of Care and Its Effects on Maternal Health in The Noun Division (West Region-Cameroon)", *BMC Medical Ethics*,19(43), p.72.

772 See *supra* note 814, pp. 502-513.

773 Law No. 2016/007 of 12 July 2016 relating to the Cameroon Penal Code.

774 Decree No. 2006/088 of 11 March 2006.

775 Law No. 2011/028 of 14 December 2011.

to their private clinics, and curtail the practices of doctors issuing fake medical certificates[776], amongst others.

In order to discourage corruption amongst health practitioners, Transparency International Cameroon (TI-C) in 2017 implemented an online whistleblowing platform for patients to report instances of corruption in health care service delivery[777]. It is envisioned for the reporting of corruption, particularly bribes and overcharging for health goods and services. Patients both literate and illiterate can avail themselves of this platform; they can log complaints online, by SMS, or by calling a local number. Their anonymity is maintained. The complaints are received by TI-C, and the anti-corruption unit of the target hospitals is given a means to view the complaints. The administration of the hospital then undertakes measures to address the situation at the facility level. These complaints are assessed by TI-C and shared directly to the Ministry of Health and other pertinent stakeholders to be dealt with. At its inception about six hundred victims and witnesses of corruption subscribed to the platform and it registered over two hundred cases of corruption[778]. This project was funded for six months by Transparency International - UK.

However, the problem of insufficient implementation of laws, coupled with impunity amongst public officials has exacerbated corrupt practice. Moreover, victims of corruption talk about it yet take no action to report it, this may be because the Cameroon legislator punishes both the person who solicit bribe and the giver of the bribe[779], however, the giver of the bribe shall not be prosecuted provided he reports the act to judicial authorities. However, most of these judicial authorities are also corrupt. In reality the victims of corrupt practices in the hands of medical doctors are helpless.

5.3.4 Inflated Hospital Bills

Exorbitant hospital bill is yet another disturbing issue that calls for the need of effective monitor and control of medical practices. The public health

---

776 Mbom, F T., (2012), "Government Install Anti-Corruption Unit at Limbe Hospital", *Cameroon Post*, at https://www.cameroonpostline.com. (accessed on the 22nd day of July 2022).

777 Prior, T. and Harris-Steingruber, S., (2017), "Corruption No Sisia: TI Cameroon Develops a Whistleblowing Platform for Health Care Patients", Transparency International Global Health, at https://tihealth.org/content/whistleblowing-platform-for-health-patient/ (accessed on the 22nd day of July 2022).

778 *Ibid.*

779 See *supra* note 828, Section 134 and 134-1.

sector in Cameroon is expected to provide the general population with cheap healthcare services and medications. However, what obtains is the reversed. Patients are given exorbitant bills, and immediate cash payment from patients for health services rendered is often demanded[780]. The government which is supposed to subsidize these services is failing in its obligation. Moreover, most of these exorbitant bills are unaccounted for, they go into the private pockets of the medical staff. In the Limbe Regional Hospital, it was reported that treatment in wards were haphazard, and patients complained of the unscrupulous bills the Regional Hospital is asking them to pay[781]. Patients were allegedly assigned to particular people from whom to buy drugs, spirit, and plaster or cotton. Nurses were reportedly collecting medical supplies from patients and not returning them. Patients were asked to clean their immediate surroundings to create an enabling environment before receiving the doctor who comes visiting at an unexpected time[782].

The national and international press has reported cases in cities such as Douala and Yaoundé where people were denied in hospitals because of their inability to pay their health care bills. In 2012, the BBC reported the case of a mother and baby who were detained for11months by a hospital in Yaoundé due to the mother's inability to pay her medical bill[783]. In 2018, it was reported[784] that the central hospital in the capital of Cameroon, Yaoundé, detained about a dozen mothers and their new-borns in a small room for about a month because they were unable to pay the hospital fees for the birth by Caesarean section. Eleven women gave birth in the hospital through caesarean section, the hospital gave them exorbitant bills which varies between 200.000-300.000frs CFA, not having the means to pay these bills within a time limit of 7 days, the hospital ask them to vacate their beds in the wards, they were later crammed like animals in one small room in the maternity section where they slept on the floor, and were treated like prisoners[785].

These public hospitals however, hold the best medical staff who are well trained and with vast experience. Private healthcare is also available in

---

[780] See *supra* note 753.

[781] *Ibid.*

[782] *Ibid.*

[783] Ngwa, F N., (2012), "Detained in Cameroon's Hospitals". *BBC News*, at http://www.bbc.co.uk/com/news/world-africa-20417377. (accessed on 2nd day of November 2020).

[784] Chouta P., (2018)," Denunciation-13 Women and 11 Babies Locked in a room in the Main Hospital in Yaoundé for Several Months like Prisoners", *The Observer*, at http://observers.france24.com/en/20180813-cameroon-hospital-mothers-babies-detained-fees (accessed on 24th day of October 2020)

[785] *Ibid.*

Cameroon; however, patients are expected to pay for all medical services used in private medical facilities, and the cost of treatment can be much higher than with equivalent procedures obtained through the public sector[786]. This is because they need to generate income to run the hospital and pay taxes, as such, only people who can afford private healthcare are entitled to services from this sector. This therefore makes health care services in Cameroon very expensive; Government needs to invest more resources to improve the quality of services by offering subsidize to the cost of treatment. Even though this is being done for the treatment of malaria for children age between 0-5 years, much more is needed.

5.3.5 Long Detention of Patients

This can be described as refusing release of either living patients after medical discharge is clinically indicated or refusing release of bodies of deceased patients if families are unable to pay their hospital bills[787]. The detention of patients is a common practice in Cameroon hospitals both in the public and private sectors. This is attributed to the over-commercialization of medical services coupled with inadequate regulation. Despite the prohibition of the confinement of indigent patients in public health facilities by the Cameroon Minister of Health, Malachie Manaouda[788], the practice persists. In a letter dated March 14, 2019, to the heads of public health facilities in Cameroon, the Minister urges the Directors of public hospitals to propose better adapted and less degrading solutions for the care of indigent patients as soon as possible. However, these are mere rhetoric with no implementation strategies. Normally, the managers of public health facilities will have to conduct, in conjunction

---

786 Pacific Prime, Cameroon Health Insurance, at http://www.pacificprime.com/country/africa/cameroon-health-insurance=pacific=prime-international/ (accessed on 10th day of October 2020).

787 Mostert, S. *et al*, (2015) "Hospital Detention Practices: Statement of a Global Taskforce". *Lancet*, 386(9994), p.649.

788 Andzongo, S., (2019), "Cameroon Health Ministry Forbids Public Hospital Services from Confining Indigent Patients due to their Inability to Pay Bills", *Business in Cameroon*, at http://www. businessincameroon.com/health/2603/8977-cameroonian-health-ministry-forbids-public-hospital-services-from-confining-indigent-patients-due-to-their-inability-to-pay-bills. (accessed on 27th day of October 2020). "I have the honour to prohibit as from date of signature of this letter the confinement of indigent patients in public health facilities", said the Minister in charge of Public Health, Manaouda Malachie. The minister said he noted that during his visit patients were being kept by force for failure to pay their hospitalization and care bills in total. "I would ask you to liberate all patients who may be held in your respective health facilities due to failure to pay bills, and let me know the cost involved", the Minister said.

with the competent services, social surveys to determine the indigence status of insolvent patients.

In fact, in Cameroon, eleven women and their babies were held for four months in a public hospital in Yaoundé for non-payment of hospitals bills. During this period, they were subjected to inhuman and degrading treatment. They were crammed in one room with their babies and some were forced to sleep on the floor. Some of them testified that they were not allowed to go out and that they were treated less than prisoners[789]. This violates the Cameroon Constitutional provision which provides that … "under no circumstances shall any person be subjected to torture, to cruel, inhuman or degrading treatment"[790].

Hospital detention practices are often very heavy handed, with medical staff or guards employed to watch over the detainees, and sometimes authorized to beat patients who attempt to escape. In some cases, security guards are supplied by outsourced companies that are paid a commission by the hospital for their ability to prevent escape[791]. What is even more astonishing is the fact that the authorities tend to view these detention cases as a private dispute and poor patients, not aware of their rights, are left to suffer[792].

This unethical practice of detaining patient for non-payment of medical fees, has attracted the attention of human rights groups, medical practitioners' organization and the media. Indeed, the position statement of an International Task Force of Pediatric Oncologist published in 2015 underscores that detention of patients in hospitals for lack of payment of medical bills violates international human rights standards, including the right to access to medical care[793].

Indeed, advocacy groups in Africa have challenged some of these detention cases in the courts. In 2015, two Kenyan women were awarded large financial settlements against a maternity hospital. The court held that the hospital had illegally detained the women and recognized that this abused was based on social and gender discrimination by the hospital authorities[794].

---

789 See *supra* note 838.

790 Preamble of the Cameroon1996 revised Constitution.

791 See *supra* note 844.

792 From Cameroon to Kenya Hospital Violate Patients Right Over Bills, 10/12/2017. at http//.www.camerounlink.com (accessed on 2nd day of November 2020).

793 Yastes, R. *et al*, (2017), "Hospital Detentions for Non-Payment of Fees: A Denial of Rights and Dignity", *Centre on Global Health Security, Chatham House, The Royal Institute of International Affairs*, p. 5.

794 Migiro, K., (2015), "Kenyan Moms Held and Abused in Hospital Win Court Verdict", *News 24*, at http//www.news24.com/Africa/news/Kenyan-moms-held-and-abused-in-hospital-win-court-

Again in 2018, a High Court in Kenya ruled that it was illegal to detained patients over unpaid bills[795].

In Cameroon this practice prompted the Minister of Health in March, 14, 2020 to prohibit illegal detention of patients over unpaid bills and to order for the release of all patients detained in hospitals for non-payment of medical bills[796], although no mention was made of any sanction for violating the order. Despite these pressures the practice persists in many hospitals in Cameroon. This is partly because most government officials do not consider detention of patients to be a human right violation, talk less of malpractice, thus they take no measures to make hospital staff halt the practice, nor do they punish them for continuing it.

5.3.6 Inappropriate Medical Care

The carelessness of medical practitioners leaves one wondering. Inaccurate diagnosis, poor attendance of patients at the emergency unit, medication errors, inappropriate or unnecessary treatment are frequent[797]. Whereas an accurate diagnosis of a patient's condition is a prerequisite for any treatment to be launched or medication given, as any error stemming from the diagnostic process may be fatal to the patient. Prompt diagnosis, with the greatest accuracy that medical knowledge and technology permit, is a requirement to any level of quality medical care, and medical professionals and institutions are responsible for ensuring that it occurs. This however is seldom obtained. This can partly be explained on the inadequate, obsolete and poor quality of medical equipment in Cameroon hospitals. It is heart-breaking to hear that Quadruplets born prematurely at the Yaoundé central

victory-20150918.(accessed on 23rd day of November 2020).

795 Ogemba, P., (2018), "It is Illegal to Detain Patient in Hospital over Bills, Court Rules", *The Standards*, at https://www.standardmedia.co.ke/nairobi/article/2001297635/holding-patients-over-hospital-bill-illegal-rules-judge (accessed on 2nd day of November 2020). Gideon Kilundo had sued the Nairobi Women's Hospital for detaining his father, Daniel Kilundo Mwenga, over non-payment of medical bill. Mr Mwenga was involved in a road accident on May 29 and taken to Nairobi Women's Hospita,l where he was admitted in the Intensive Care Unit. He was discharged on June 25 after gaining full recovery but was detained for failing to raise the required amount demanded by the hospital. His son Kilundu, filed the suit to secure his release, arguing that continued detention of his father was unconstitutional and an insult to his rights even after the family had made an undertaking to clear the bill. Justice Okwany agreed with his submissions and ordered the immediate release of Mwenga from the hospital.

796 See *supra* note 843.

797 Ndi and Tata, (2020). "Medical Errors in Health Care Institutions in Cameroon: Setting the Platform for Legal Intervention", *Indian Journal of Health & Medical Law*, 3(1), p.28.

hospital in May11, 2020, had to die due to insufficient incubators at the state-owned hospital[798].

The Covid-19 pandemic has exposed the under regulated medical practices in Cameroon. In the wake of this pandemic, patients presenting with episodes of cough and/or fever were easily over suspected as having Covid-19 without a proper clinical examination. Patients are not well interrogated and examined before a diagnosis is suspected or made. As a result, many are kept for long periods in the pre-isolation unit while awaiting results of the diagnostic test, a situation which can lead to all round psychological stress of these suspects[799]. Moreover, merging of potentially real Covid-19 cases and non-case in these units, which are generally poorly constructed and overcrowded for prolonged periods, lead to the spread of the diseases to non-Covid-19 cases.

5.3.7 Absence of Government Assistance

Primary Health care facilities in Cameroon have been making mandatory contribution to a Health Solidarity Fund since 1993. They contribute 10 per cent of their monthly revenue to a national health solidarity fund managed by the Ministry of Health[800]. This fund is intended to provide surge support during emergencies yet in the wake of the Covid-19 pandemic, this fund was not disbursed until the central African Director of Human Right Watch[801] had to call on the health minister to make this fund available to health care facilities in dire need of support[802]. A World Bank Report[803] sounded an alarm regarding lack of information on the fund, noting that it is still not clear what the solidarity fund is used for, and that there is still no legislation about its use. The report stated that transfers to the fund are key source of

798 See *supra* note 751.

799 Ngeh, E N. et al, (2020). "Covid-19: Challenges and the Impact on Care in Clinical Settings in Cameroon", *Pan African Medical Journal*, 35(2), p.122.

800 Human Rights Watch, Cameroon: Investigate, Distribute Health Fund", Published Information on emergency reserved use for Covid-19, June 2020.

801 Lewis Mudge, Director, Central Africa.

802 See *supra* note 855.

803 The World Bank, "Cameroon-public Expenditure Review: Aligning Public Expenditure with The Goals of Vision 2035", World Bank Report 2018, Washington, D.C. World Bank Group. at https://documents.worldbank.org/curated/en/412641543396425023/Aligninh-public-Expenditures-with-the-Goals-of-Vision-2035. (accessed on 6th day of May 2022).

'revenue-side inefficiency'; especially since primary care facilities are allotted a disproportionately small share of the health budget[804].

What is certain from the above is that the use of the health solidarity fund is not transparent, and this lack of transparency is problematic especially as the fund's revenues largely come from patient fees that drive up the cost of health services. In Cameroon about 70 per cent of total health expenditure is borne by patients[805], as a result, they should be able to rely on it to help them.

In the wake of the Covid-19 pandemic, the government asked citizens to contribute to the Special Fund of National Solidarity[806], which it established to provide additional support to efforts to curb the spread of Covid-19 and treat the sick. With the amount of money received into the fund, including the support fund received from the International Monetary Fund[807], health care facilities still lacked adequate resources to respond to the pandemic[808]. There were shortages in basic hospital equipment, including thermometers, disinfectants, medicine as well as ventilators and oxygen, protective gear for doctors and nurses, such as masks, gloves, and glasses. Patients also had to rely on out-of-pocket payments to cover health care costs related to Covid-19.

In fact, an independent local news agency[809] in the country reported that some public health institutions in Douala required Covid-19 patients to cover their health care costs. The news agency interviewed the spouse of a Covid-19 patient who, after spending approximately 200,000FCFA on tests and prescription drugs, turned to the use of free herbal medicine provided by the Archbishop of the Douala Metropolitan Archdiocese, His Lordship Samuel Kleda[810]. The country's Minister of Public Health, Dr. Malachie Manaouda, in a press release published on 16 April 2020, declared a ban on the systematic billing for screening tests, hospitalizations, and administration of prescription drugs. However, two weeks after the Minister's Press Statement, patients in Douala, for example, were still relying on out-of-pocket payments for Covid-19-related medical expenses[811].

---

804 *Ibid.*

805 *Ibid.*

806 Press Release From of 31st March 2020 from the Secretariat General of The Prime Minister Office.

807 International Monetary Fund Press Release No 20/205 of 4th May 2020.

808 There were only four testing laboratories, three located in Yaoundé. In the North West Region there were only three ventilators and lack of basic equipment.

809 Équinoxe TV—Journal 20H du Lundi, 27 Avril 2020, at https://www.youtube.com/watch?v=GqUGY4i0RT8. (accessed on 30th day of October 2020).

810 *Ibid.*

811 Cameroun Web. at https://www.camerounweb.com/CameroonHomePage/NewsArchive/Covid-19-les-mensonges-de-Manaouda-Malachie-sur-la-prise-en-charge-des-patients-508861.

5.4 Conclusion

The fight against medical malpractices through regulation is yet to achieve its desired result. In a country like Cameroon whose institutions are known for their failure of performance, effective regulation of medical malpractices is a long way off, reasons why deviant behaviours among health personnel persist in spite of numerous measures set up to fight the ill. The importunity of these malpractices is a source of restriction on the regulatory mechanisms put in place to censor these behaviours. If these negative practices are to be actually curtailed, there is an urgent need to bring in more stringent regulations coupled with effective implementation.

Medical practitioners in Cameroon, are able to commit a wrong and get away with it. One might be tempted to say it's because victims of these wrong doings are not reporting, but this is not wholly the case. These victims are tired of a system where even the laws put in place are unenforced. Hospitals have become lion dens where only financial prowess can liberate patients. Government assistance to hospitals is not felt. Indeed, it is reported that most of the funds made available for the management of the Covid-19 pandemic were diverted by top government officials, including money meant to purchase rapid covid-19 test[812]. It is therefore not surprising that patients had to bear the cost of their treatment.

The event of *Monique Koumetake* exposed the ineptitude of the Cameroon Medical Council and the Ministry of Public Health as regulatory bodies. When administrative and financial bureaucracy takes preeminence over lifesaving mission of hospitals and doctors, they lost their fundamental value and the effect is disastrous. Regulatory bodies are supposed to compel doctors to put up their best practices and to consider patient safety as primordial, but when the regulator begin to shield and cover up the malpractices of the regulated or feign ignorance, then it loses its privilege and public confidence, thereby promoting a culture of apathy amongst the regulated, hindering its proper functioning.

(accessed on 29th day of October 2020).

812 M. Songne, M., (2022), "Cameroon: IMF Awaits New Audit of Covid-19 Fund Management", *the Africa Report.*

CHAPTER SIX

General Conclusion and Recommendation

6.1 General Conclusion

Society entrusts the sacred duty of preserving the virtues of life and good health to medical professionals. Hence, only the most qualified individuals are permitted to engage in this profession[813]. Patients consign their fate and life to doctors because they blind-trust in the doctors' knowledge and skills. Even though, the Hippocratic Oath establishes principles and standards that must be complied with by medical doctors in the performance of their duties, over the years in Cameroon, doctors have engaged in malpractices of all sorts which are causing untold damages to patient's health.

The upsurge of medical malpractices in Cameroon may partially be explained by the presence of medical professionalism and doctor dominance. The doctor is seen as the health "guru" whose judgment is rarely to be questioned. He is placed on a pedestal by the patient and required to hand down decisions and treatment to the duly worshipful recipient. When things go wrong, the resulting injury is invariably seen by the patient as a mishap and there is little inclination to direct blame at the doctor and seek compensation from him. Patients are ignorant of their rights and doctors, aware of this ignorance, abuse these rights with impunity.

Regulation of medical practices which is aimed amongst others to protect the right to life and health of patients in Cameroon, is defective. The

[813] D. P. Angeles, (2011), "A Framework of Philippine Medical Malpractice Law", 85 *Phil. L.J.* 895, p. 1

government has not been effective in its obligation to respect, protect, and fulfil the right to health in fulfilment of its international commitment. It has not been able to adequately provide the necessary infrastructure and enabling environment for the medical practitioner to exercise his profession with less complexity. Indeed, doctors are faced daily with a workload of those whose conditions they must diagnose and then address. They are under constant pressure to proceed to treatment, and they must do so under conditions of complexity and uncertainty. Therefore, they run the risks of causing harm to individuals and, of course, on occasion, of causing their death. Human resources in the health sector are grossly inadequate, the doctor-patient ratio is far beyond standard, such that the practitioner is over burdened with work, reasons why there is too much error in output. All of these contribute to increase malpractice incident in the country, and necessitate the need to regulate medical practices.

Illegal health facilities keep springing up despite repeated efforts by the Ministry of Public Health and the Cameroon Medical Council to crack down on them. Most of these illegal clinics lack the required human and material facilities to operate. There are also nurses, pharmacists, medical laboratory scientists, technicians, as well as other health personnel, parading as medical doctors and rendering services, which only doctors are licensed to render, thereby causing considerable harm to patients.

The persistence of malpractices in Cameroon despite all measures taken to combat it keeps one wandering. It is as though there is absolutely no control and supervision of the activities of medical practitioners. Patients have horrible experiences in hospitals. Rudeness, negative attitudes, lack of care and compassion, absenteeism, inadequate response to request, are some of occurrences in hospitals. Commercialization and commodification of health services is the order of the day. Patients are treated like clients and services are accorded according to the financial power of the patient. Patients who are unable to pay their hospital bills upon discharge are held in the hospitals like criminals until the bill is settled, despite calls from the Minister of Health to abolish such practices.

Even though, both national and international legislative and regulatory instruments have established principles and standards that must be complied with by medical doctors in the performance of their duties, over the years in Cameroon, doctors have engaged in malpractices of all sorts in gross violation of these statutory texts, causing untold damages to patient's health. The laws and regulation in place to check adherence to these rules and principles of medical practices are not fully complied with by medical practitioners, and the mechanisms to ensure compliance are weak and inadequately implemented. Moreover, the self-regulatory nature of the medical profession is far from being efficient in ensuring compliance to rules of medical practices, because the tendency is for the profession to protect its interest rather than the interest of third parties or patients, as a result sanction for violation of medical practice by the Cameroon Medical Council is greatly ineffective. Also, the functioning of the Cameroon Medical Council in Cameroon is greatly hindered by the absence of political and financial autonomy. The result is persistent malpractices with patients being at the mercy of these doctors and losing their lives.

The assessment of professional competence is inadequately done. Medical professionals in Cameroon are license for life with no requirement of proof of up-to-date knowledge and skills as a condition of renewing their license. As a result, countless number of patients suffer in the hands of unskilled medical men and quacks. Manifestation of unprofessionalism is seen in hospitals everywhere both public and private. Illegal medical practice has become common place with the result that it is very difficult to distinguish a licensed medical professional from a quack.

Judicial regulation through prosecution and sanction is wanting. Recourse to legal redress in case of malpractices remains a challenge for victims of malpractices. Access to the courts is almost impossible because of the high cost involved. Filing a claim in Cameroon courts require a huge amount of money such that victims are discouraged from seeking redress in court. Lawyers are expensive to get, and some of the judges are corrupt to the core. Coupled to this is the usual delay in judicial proceedings in Cameroon. A case might take between three to five years before judgment is delivered. These judicial lapses, place a constraint on the effective regulation of medical malpractices in Cameroon. This discourages the prosecution of medical malpractice cases, thereby leaving victims without a remedy and malicious doctors are left free to continue with inflicting harm to patients.

To successfully hold a negligent medical practitioner civilly liable is a hard nut to crack. The burden of proof is correspondingly greater on the person who alleges negligence against a doctor. It is settled law that it is for the plaintiff to prove the negligence or deficiency in service, by adducing expert evidence or opinion, and this burden is a heavy one for the plaintiff to discharge. Mere allegation of negligence will be of no help to the plaintiff. In medical negligence cases, it is for the patient to establish his case against the medical professional and not for the medical professional to prove that he acted with sufficient care and skill. The true test for establishing negligence on the part of a doctor is, whether he is guilty of such failure as no doctor with ordinary skills would be guilty of if acting with reasonable care.

As per the law, a defendant charged with negligence can clear himself if he shows that he acted in accordance with the general and approved practice. It is not required in the discharge of his duty of care that he should use the highest degree of skill, since this may never be acquired. Even a deviation from normal professional practice is not necessarily evident of negligence. Proving the negligence of the doctor is very complex. Often, proving "causation" and adducing expert evidence is the most difficult part, especially in Cameroon where patients are not financially viable to sue a doctor, not to talk of getting another doctor to give expert evidence. As a result, most negligent doctors always get away because of these difficulties.

Moreover, the lack of high-performance equipment and means for treatment reduces the possibility to establish the responsibility of the doctor. How therefore can one prove the liability of a doctor restricted to the means of treatment at his disposal, and not on the dramatic result of his intervention, especially in our context where the said means are nowhere to be found and where found, are mostly outdated. The only possibility for a patient to be awarded compensation is through the principle of *Res Ipsa Loquitur.*

Until relatively recently, it was thought that informing patients about a poor prognosis, possible side effects, or the availability of alternative treatments would be likely to cause distress and confusion, and hence might jeopardize the patient's recovery. However, giving information to patients might help to redress the imbalance of knowledge and power within the doctor-patient relationship . It is the function of the law to redress the imbalance by imposing a duty on doctors to provide it[814]. The patient has the right to choose what is done to her body, and in order to exercise this choice, she needs information about what the doctor is proposing to do.

The duty to obtain the patient's consent prior to treatment is protected by the tort of battery. An action in battery will be successful only if the patient did not consent to the medical treatment that she received. The patient's consent will absolve a medical practitioner from liability in battery for unlawful touching as long as the consent is 'real', and to be real, the patient must have been told what the doctor is planning to do. If a patient consented

[814] Section 27 of Decree No 83/I66 of 12 April 1983 on Code of Medical Ethics in Cameroon

to a completely different procedure, an action in battery is possible. However, medical procedures incidental to the main operation are impliedly consented to by the patient and so no action in battery will lie when they are carried out.

The advantage of an action in battery is that it is not necessary to establish that any physical harm has been caused by the inadequate disclosure. It is no defense to a charge of battery that the doctor was acting in the best interests of the patient, or that the doctor exercised all reasonable care and skill. Given that obtaining consent prior to treatment is routine, it would be most unusual for a patient not to be told what is going to happen to her, and actions in battery are rare. In Cameroon actions in battery are rare not because obtaining prior consent is a routine but because patients rely on doctors to make decisions for them.

A medical practitioner can be contractually liable for malpractices. Once a doctor agrees to treat a patient and the patient submits to treatment by a doctor, a contract is inferred. This contract is mostly implied and hardly express. The contractual relationship is the basis for both party's rights and responsibilities which forms the term of the contract. In Heneberry v. Pharoan, the court held that to find a doctor contractually liable, it must be established that the physician gave a promise or warranty guaranteeing the outcome of a procedure, in addition to his agreement to perform a procedure. However, few doctors would ever choose to give such a warranty, and, the courts would be very unlikely to imply such a term into a contract for health care services, considering the unpredictability of medical results, and the differences in individual patients.

The level of negligence that the doctor must manifest in order to be criminally liable is considerably higher than that required for civil liability. To merit criminal prosecution, the negligence of the doctor must be of sufficient seriousness, and 'gross'. The 'amount of and degree of negligence' in determinative in a criminal prosecution was stated in the case of *Bateman*; gross negligence must show 'such disregard for the life and safety of others as to amount to a crime against the state and conduct meriting punishment. The burden of proof of gross negligence rest with the prosecution and he must discharge this burden beyond all reasonable doubt as per section 307 of the Cameroon Criminal Procedure Code. This is a difficult burden to discharge. There is need for expert evidence to be adduced to successfully prosecute a medical doctor for criminal negligence. Failure to adduced expert evidence will lead to the acquittal of the doctor. However, there is considerable difficulty in establishing the criminal negligence of a medical practitioner owing to the fact that a medical doctor summoned as an expert is not likely to give inculpating or incriminating evidence against his colleague.

The Cameroon Medical Council also sanctions defaulting medical practitioners, The principal objective for imposing sanctions for medical malpractice is to deter medical professionals from negligent acts and omissions in the performance of their tasks which may harm their patients, and thereby fostering good practice. The Law regulating the practice of medicine in Cameroon outlines four sanctions that may be impose by the CMC on a medical doctor found guilty of medical malpractice. These are warning, reprimand, suspension from practice, and striking off the roll of the medical profession, depending on the gravity of the offence. The courts on their parts are empowered to order an imprisonment term, a fine, confiscation of equipment, closure of establishment and a ban on occupation as possible sanctions for medical malpractice.

Compensation to victims of medical malpractices is mostly an award of specific and general damages which are intended to compensate a claimant for losses suffered as a result of the doctor's wrongful conduct. The basic rule, under common law formulation, is that a claimant is entitled to 'that sum of money which will put the party who has been injured, or who has suffered, in the same position as he would have been in if he had not sustained the wrong for which he is now getting his compensation or reparation[815]. However, the quantum of damages is at the discretion of the court, and most often is inadequate. Again, the injured party may agree to an out of court settlement with the negligent doctor, during which an amount of compensation is agreed to be paid by the medical practitioner to the injured patient for the injuries sustained and other losses suffered as a result of his negligent act.

Again, an injured party may need just an apology from the medical practitioner who inflicted injuries to him as a result of his negligent act. Such an apology must be sincere, recognizing the wrong and be willing to make reparation for the wrong suffered. However, the traditional culture of medicine is one in which medical errors are commonly not disclosed to patients by doctors and hospitals, due in part to the hospital's fear of malpractice litigation. They believed that offering an apology is acceptance of liabilities, thus the tendency is to avoid apologizing.

815 *Livingstone v. Rawyards Coal Co* [1880] 5 App Cas. 25 at 39, Quoted in McGregor, H., (2017), *McGregor on Damages,* 20th ed. London, Sweet & Maxwell, Section 2-002.

None the less, the practice of medicine, is such a technical and complicated domain, and if it is properly executed, it secures great benefits to individuals and the society as a whole, whereas if it is improperly done. it brings about great harms. Thus, in prosecuting a medical practitioner, the Courts always strife to secure a balance between, the benefits of the doctor's services, which is of enormous value, both to the individuals treated and to the general health of society, and the need to punish him/her for malpractices.

The compromise between medical practitioners' liability and the rights of patients with regards to ensuring safety and quality of medical services is echoed by Lord Denning in *Roe vs. Minister of Health*[816] thus:

> *It is so easy to be wise after the event and to condemn as negligence that which was only a misadventure. We ought always to be on our guard against it, especially in the cases against the hospital and doctors. Medical science has conferred great benefit on mankind, but these benefits are attended by considerable risks. We cannot take the benefits without taking the risks. Every advance in technology is also attended by the risks. Doctors, like the rest of us, have to learn by experience; and experience often teaches in a hard way. Something goes wrong and shows up a weakness and then it is put right*[817].

Protection of doctors is therefore seen as essential to ensure that their primary role of treating their patients is not interfered with. The threat of "defensive medicine" with all its perceived inhibiting qualities for doctors and the practice of medicine looms large in the minds of the courts and steers them towards a conservative view of the liability of doctors. As Lord Denning puts it in 1954 in *Hatcher v. Black*: 'A doctor examining a patient, or a surgeon operating at a table, instead of getting on with his work would be forever looking over his shoulder to see if someone was coming up with a dagger'. There is therefore, need for caution and to ensure that justice is seen to be done not only to the victims but also to the medical practitioners who deserves all legal protection in the exercise of their professional duties.

Medical malpractice lawsuits are a global phenomenon and Cameroon is slowly catching up with this phenomenon. There is a rising awareness of patients' rights and expectations in relations to health care providers that is

816 (1954) 2 All ER 131; (1954) 2 QB 66
817 *Ibid.*, at p. 137

why there are a few rising numbers of law suits against doctors in Cameroon, but again, the possibility of success of such lawsuits are slim.

6.2 Recommendations

This work has critically analysed the regulation of medical practice in Cameroon. The importance of medical practitioners in life saving mission, and safeguarding the right to health makes it imperative for the state and other actors to regulate the activities of medical practitioners through laws and regulatory organs. In the course of the work, we discovered that medical practitioners most often fail to comply with the standards of the profession in the performance of their duties, thereby causing injury and harm to patients. It was further revealed that the supervision and control of medical practitioners through legislation and regulatory organs is fraught with procedural hurdles, irregularities, weak monitoring mechanisms, thereby rendering the whole process ineffective. To compound the problem, the government has failed to fulfil its responsibility by not providing the needed human, material and financial resources needed to enable medical practitioners perform their duties effectively. In order to overcome these shortcomings, this work has provided some recommendations which will go a long way to guarantee effective regulation of medical practice in Cameroon. These are discussed hereunder.

1. Instituting an Efficient Quality Control System

Medical practitioners in the country are involved in all types of illegal activities with ensuing negative consequences on patients. Government has made some efforts to curb the illegal activities of medical personnel, yet they persist. This indicates that there is a problem with the control mechanism. There is need to provide more efficient control mechanism to limit these malpractices. This can be achieved by the creation of independent sub-supervisory bodies at the hospitals to supervise the activities of medical practitioners. The Cameroon Medical Council should institute a system to compel doctors to document precisely and adequately their diagnosis process and procedures which will generate complete medical records in order to make medical quality auditing effective.

The Ministry in charge of Public Health together with the Cameroon Medical Council should closely monitor the activities of private health facilities by creating Regional and Divisional Monitoring Committee to control the activities of these health facilities to ensure that they comply with the requirements to function.

Control at the borders need to be tightened to fight against the influx of illegal and contraband drugs that are ravaging the segment of the population who rely on drug vendors for health services.

2. Encourage Continuous Medical Education

Continuous Medical Education should be encouraged. Regular training through seminars and conferences should be organized by the Cameroon Medical Council and participation should be made compulsory, this will enhance the competence of medical practitioners and reduce medical errors.

3. Compel Compliance to Ethical Standard

Violation of professional ethics in health facilities is at its peak in Cameroon. The Cameroon Medical Council should make adherence to the ethics of the profession more rigorous; the Disciplinary Board of the Council should be ready to severely punish violation of medical ethics. This will deter ethical violations. Frequent seminars should be organized by the CMC to refresh practitioners on the need to comply with ethical standards. This will enhance quality of medical services, and instil confidence in practitioners.

Practitioners should be made aware of the laws and statute governing medical practice at an early stage of their career, preferably in medical school, considering the specificity of such regulation and its consequences for themselves and for the patients.

Private Medical Educational Institutions should be effectively monitored to ensure that their school curriculum reflect the standards set by the law and regulatory bodies.

4. Revision of the Code of Medical Ethics

The Cameroon Code of Medical Ethics is a 1983 instrument and needs revision to reflect the current international guidelines and standards of medical practice. It should adopt some of the provision of the International Code of Ethics, especially the requirements of doctors to report colleagues who are incompetent, and those engaged in unethical practices. This will go a long way to guarantee quality services.

5. Increase of National Budget allocation for Health

Cameroon has a fragile health care system. The existing health system is faced with several challenges ranging from the lack of resources, to poor management of the available resources. There is shortage of healthcare professionals, poor infrastructure, inadequate social services, and poor institutional and political leadership. These greatly affect medical services rendered. This work recommends an increase in the National Budget allocation for health care which will go a long way to improve health care system in Cameroon.

Inefficiency in the performance of medical practitioner is associated with absence of good working condition. The lack of available infrastructure, manpower, and basic equipment in hospitals reduces quality services. The adequate provision of these facilities will go a long way to create a conducive working environment for practitioners to exercise their profession. Developing new health care policies that will eliminate health related disparities is also imperative.

6. Improve Access to Medical Services

Access to medical service is a challenge in Cameroon. The quality of medication, the attitude of hospital staff, the constant unavailability of doctors and other health personnel, and scarcity of medication in health care facilities, especially in rural areas, impede access to medical care.

This study recommends increase training and recruiting of more health personnel and improving their condition of work. It also recommends the utilization of community nursing programs where healthcare practitioners travel to rural communities at least once a week to conduct check-ups and alleviate the need for patients to travel long distances to get to hospitals. Government should ameliorate infrastructures in rural areas by providing electricity, portable water and good housing. This will encourage medical professionals to take up residence in the areas when posted.

7. Creating Awareness of Redress for Medical Malpractices

Most patients, victims of medical malpractice suffer in silence because they are not aware of the available avenues of redress for such occurrences. This could be achieved through workshops, seminars and conferences organized by health planners, non-governmental organization, and jurists, to keep patient abreast of their rights, and of the duties and responsibilities of medical practitioners.

Creation of forums (e.g., by dialling a toll-free number) to lodge medical malpractice complaints immediately they occur within health facilities is also recommended.

The laws, necessarily, should help to create conditions congenial to the advance of medicine, to the benefit of the patient, to the protection of the doctor and to the good of the community. So, the laws should also be clear, comprehensive, balanced, flexible and facilitating.

8. Improve Access to Legal Redress

Medical malpractice persists partly because medical practitioners are yet to fill the impact of the hammer of the law on them. Victims are unable to vindicate their wrong and assert their rights because they find it difficult to access the courts and lodge a medical malpractice compliant. It is recommended that the filing fees be made less costly and the stamp duty fee required during filing should be eradicated. The conditions precedent to be granted legal aid should be made less stringent.

9. Institute a Strategic Legal Aid Program

This consists of promoting legal literacy, and organizing legal aid camps. Legal literacy will enable the poor to have strength and confidence to fight, and help them avoid needless difficulties arising from ignorance. Legal aid camps will carry legal services to the doorsteps of the rural poor. Voluntary associations, social action groups, journalists and even advocates can render services to educate the people about the laws and their rights. The government can assist these voluntary associations financially to operate the legal aid program in its widest and, most comprehensive sense.

10. Intensify the fight against Corruption

Corruption is a canker worm that is eating deep into the fabrics of the Cameroonian society. This evil is manifested in all the sectors in Cameroon especially in the health and judicial sectors

This work recommends the implementation of more rigorous measure to fight corruption. Anti-corruption units exist in these sectors but they are failing in their function partly because most of the members of these units are answerable to higher authorities who are themselves corrupt. The anti-corruption unit should be revived by creating an enabling environment for them to operate. They should be accorded some independence free from bureaucratic bottlenecks.

Victims of corruption should be encouraged to speak up, by educating them on the harmful effect of corruption, and providing protection for those who speak up.

An improvement in the material condition of judicial personnel will go a long way to reduce corruption. There should be increase transparency in the different types of transactions (assigning of cases to judges, filling of cases), and procedures that reduces the scope for individual discretion; this will reduce the opportunities for both judges and court registrars to conveniently lose files and destroys exhibits. Until such time that judges begin to prosecute their own for violating the laws they are expected to enforce, citizens will continue to view the courts with skepticism,

Moreover, the salary scale of the judicial and medical core should be revised to reflect their status in the society. There should be an increase in their salaries, this will discourage them from seeking side gains to meet up with the high living standard.

11. Shifting the Burden of Proof

Claims for medical malpractice under the tort of negligence are the most common avenue for redress. However, victims end up without compensation or inadequately compensated because they find it difficult to discharge the burden of proof. It is one thing to know that a mistake was made and another thing to prove it. Generally, medical expert evidence is required. This is a daunting task for victims because it is not only difficult to find medical practitioners who are willing to testify against their colleagues, but it is also very expensive. The burden of proof on the victim produces results that are intuitively and strikingly unjust. As a result, this work proposes that medical liability be subject to different rules. This is because a patient cannot be expected to prove that the doctor has actually committed a fault in the performance of his duties since he has little or no knowledge about the intricacies of medical science, on the other hand the medical practitioner cannot be expected to guarantee the results of the treatment, and the rules of strict liability would in all probability, impede the medical profession by requiring a standard of excellence that could not be attained.

This work recommends the shifting of the burden of proof from the patient to the doctor, as done in France since 1997 in the *Hedreul case*[818] where it was held that the doctor had to adduce evidence that he gave all the information to the patient and administered what should be considered as the best treatment at the moment just like the ''reasonable man'' he is supposed to be.

12. Enforce Control of the Judiciary

The activities of Magistrates and judges should be effectively monitored. In so far as the judge is independent and guided by the law and his conscience, many at times they ignore their consciences and indulge in practices that are reproachable. Ethical control of the judicial core should be instituted such that the profession can regulate the activities of its own. This will revive the consciences of those judges and magistrates whose consciences are dead and are involved in partiality in the administration of justice.

13. Strict Enforceability of Legal Instruments

The problem of malpractices in Cameroon as has been identified is not the lack of laws and regulation, but the absence of willingness to effectively implement these laws. It is so disheartening that these laws end up only on papers. It is recommended that laws enacted be appropriately implemented in all the sectors in the country. Laws should not only be promulgated, but they must be enforced. Where the laws are not enforced to the latter, the system becomes non-functional, a situation giving rise to all types of miscreant behaviours, including medical malpractices.

---

818 Arrêt *Hedreul*, Cassation Civile 1ère, Arrêt n° 426, 25 Février 1997.

BIBLIOGRAPHY

BOOKS

Alghrani A. *et al*, *Bioethics Medicine and The Criminal Law Volume 1: The Criminal Law and Bioethical Conflict: Walking the Tightrope*. (Cambridge University Press,2013)

Ayangwe C., *Criminal Law in Cameroon: Specific Offences*, (Bamenda, Langaa Research and Publishing CIG, 2011.)

Beauchamp, T L. and Childress J F., *Principles of Biomedical Ethics*, 4th Edition (New York, Oxford University Press, 1994)

Bentham J., *An Introduction to the Principles of Morals and Legislation*, A New Edition, (Oxford, The Clarendon Press 1789)

Boma A L., *Principles of Consumer Protection Law*, (Bafoussam, Ultranet, 2021)

British Medical Association, *The Medical Profession and Human Rights: Handbook for a Changing Agenda*, (London, Zed Books Ltd, 2001)

Black M A, *Black's Law Dictionary*,4th Edition Rev, (St Paul, Minn, West Publishing Copyright, 1968)

Bryan A Garner, *Black's Law Dictionary*, Abridged, 9th Edition, (West, June 11 2010)

Clarke D., "*Law, Regulation and Strategizing for Health*". *Chapter 10 In*: *Strategizing National Health in the 21st Century*: A Handbook. Geneva: World Health Organization; 2016.

Elliot A.K., *Death of the Guilds. Professional, States, and the Advance of Capitalism, 1930 to the present* (Yale University Press, 1999)

Emir F., *Medical Law and Ethics in Nigeria* (Lagos, Malthouse Press Ltd, 2012)

Ese Malemi, *Law of Tort*, 2nd Edition (Lagos, Princeton Publishing Company, 2013)

Fleishacker S., *A Short History of Distributive Justice* (Harvard University Press)

Galega S D., and Fuah C K., *The Law on Pharmaceutical Product Liability in Context*, (Ibadan, University Printery, 2018)

Gidney R D et al, *Professional Gentlemen: The Profession in the Nineteenth Century Ontario,* (Toronto, UTP, 1914)

Gough, J W., *The Social Contract: A Critical Study of its Development*, (Oxford: Clarendon Press, 1936)

Henry Campbell Black, M.A., *Black's Law Dictionary*, 4th Ed. Rev. (St. Paul, Minn., West Publishing Company. 1968)

Howlett M., et al, *Studying Public Policy: Policy Cycles and Policy Subsystems.* (Toronto, Oxford University Press, 2003).

Irvine D., *The Doctor's Tale: Professionalism and Public Trust.* (Abington, UK: Radcliffe Medical Press; 2003).

Jackson E., *Medical Law: Text, Cases, and Materials*, (Oxford University Press,2016)

Jeffrey B., *Profession and Monopoly*, (Berkeley: University of California Press, 1975)

Kant I., *The Metaphysical Elements of Ethics,* (Start Publishing LLC, 2013)

Kruglanski A W. and Higgins E T., Social Psychology: Handbook of Basic Principles, 2nd Edition (New York,The Guilford Press, 2007)

Markesinis B S. Deakin S F., *Tort Law*, 4th Edition, (Oxford, Clarendon Press, 1999)

Martindu G M., *L'appel du Cameroun*, (Paris, Flamarion, 1939)

McMahon & Binchy., *Law of Torts*, 4th Edition, (Bloomsbury Professional Ltd, 2013)

Mills J S., *Utilitarianism, Liberty, and Representative Government* (Wildside Press, 1863)

Mingshu H., *Study of Roman Contract System and Modern Contract Law*, 1st Edition (China Procuratorial Press, 1996)

Pollock S. .F.,Bart, *Principles of Contract :A Treatise on the General Principles Concerning the Validity of Agreement in the Law of England*, 7th Edition (London, stevens and Sons Limited, 119&120 Chancery Lane Law Publishers, 1902).

Ries N M., "*Health Professionals and the Organization of Health Care*", (Routeledge Handbook of Medical Law and Ethics, August 2014).

Schmets G. et al., *Strategizing National Health in the 21st Century*: A Handbook. Geneva: World Health Organization; 2016.

Smith, A., *An Inquiry into the Nature and Causes of the Wealth of Nations*, Vol 1, (W Strahan and T. Cadell, London, 1776)

Soreide T. and Williams A., *Corruption, Grabbing and Development: Real World Challenges*, (Cheltenham and Northampton, Edward Elgar Publishing, 2014)

Tavuchis N., *Mea Culpa*: *A Sociology of Apology and Reconciliation*, (Stanford CA: Stanford University Press; 1991)

Umerah, B.C., *Medical Practice and the Law in Nigeria* (Longman Nigeria limited, 1989)

Xinhua Y., *Freedom of Contract*, 1st Edition (China Legal Publishing House, 2004)

ARTICLES

Abbassi, I. N., (2014), "Protest of Doctors: A Basic Human Right or an Ethical Dilemma", *BMC Med Ethics*, 15(24), pp.1-5.

Agarwal A. K., (2011) Medical Negligence: Law and Interpretation", *Indian Institute of Management Working Paper No-03*, pp. 1-15

Agarwal S. S., (2009), "Medical Negligence. Hospital's Responsibility". *J Indian Acad Forensic Med. 31*, pp.164–170.

Ajong A B., et al, (2016), "Knowledge of Women in Family Planning and Future Desire to Use Contraception: A Cross Sectional Survey in Urban Cameroon". *BMC Res Notes*, 9(347), pp.1-6

Aldridge S., (2008), "The Regulation of Health Professionals: An Overview of the British Colombia Experience", *Journal of Medical Imaging and Radiation Sciences,* 39(1), pp.4-10.

Angeles D P., (2011), "A Framework of Philippine Medical Malpractice Law", 85 *Phil. L.J.* 895, pp. 926-927

Anup N, et al, (2014), "Knowledge, Attitude & Practices Regarding Ethics & Law Amongst Medical and Dental Professionals in Rajasthan—A Questionnaire Study", IOSR *Journal of Dental and Medical Sciences* (IOSR-JDMS), 13(5), pp.102–109.

Andzongo S., (2019), "Cameroon Health Ministry Forbids Public Hospital Services from Confining Indigent Patients Due to their Inability to Pay Bills", *Business in Cameroon.*

Arrow K J., (1963) "Uncertainty and the Welfare Economics of Medical Care", *American Economic Review,* 53(5), pp.941-973.

Asanga I. N., (2020), "Access to Justice and Legal Aid in Cameroon: A Critical Analysis", *Journal of Legal Studies and Research,* 6 (1), pp. 240-260.

Atiyah P S., (1986) "Medical Malpractice and the Contract/Tort Boundary", *Law and Contemporary Problems,* 49(2), pp. 287-303

Awati A. M. et al, (2014) "Professional Liability in Medical Practice: A 20 Years Retrospective Study At District Consumers Forum Gulbarga (1991-2011)", *J NTR Univ Health Sci,* 3(1), pp. 15-18.

Azétsop J. et al, (2018), "Morphologie du Quotidien, Souffrance Sociale et Parcours Individuels au Cameroun: La Mort De Monique Koumateke, Un Problème Social?", *African Sociological Review,* 22(1), pp.68-69.

Bal, B. Sonny, (2009), "An Introduction to Medical Malpractice in The United States", *Clinical Orthopaedics and Related Research,* 467(2), pp. 339-347.

Baldwin D J. et al (1998), "Unethical and Unprofessional Conduct Observed by Residents during their first year of Training", *Acad Med,* 73(11), pp.1195–1200.

Bandura, A., (1991) "Social Cognitive Theory of Self-Regulation", *Organizational Behaviour and Human Decision Processes,* 50, pp. 248-287.

Bauer, A., (2014) "Illegal Health Clinics in Cameroon", *Borgen Magazine*

Baumeister, R F and Vohs K D., (2007), "Self-Regulation, Ego Deletion, and Motivation", *Social and Psychology Compass*, 1(1), p.1.

Bayemi O.V., (2018), "Corruption and Users in Douala-Cameroon Public Hospitals: An Evaluation of Determinants", *AERC Research Paper* 344, African Economic Consortium, Nairobi, p.6

Bayemi O. V., (2008), "Corruption et Crise des Hôpitaux Publics à Douala: le Schémas d'une Organisation Tripolaire", In Governing Health Systems in Africa, Dakar, *Council for the Development of Social Science Research in Africa* (*CODESRIA*), pp.12-24.

Begum H.,, (2004), "Poverty and Health Ethics in Developing Countries". *Bioethics*,15(1), pp.50-56.

Beisecker A E., (1990), "Patient Power in Doctor-Patient Communication: What Do We know?" *Health Commun.*, 2(2), pp.105-122.

Bending Z J., (2015), "Reconceptualising the Doctor-Patient Relationship: Recognizing the Role of Trust in Contemporary Health Care", *Bioeth Inquiry*, 12, pp.189-202

Berlinger N., (2005), "After Harm: Medical Error and the Ethics of Forgiveness". *Johns Hopkins University Press,* 31, pp.61–62

Bertoli P. and Grembi V., (2017) "Medical Malpractice: How Legal Liability Affects Medical Decisions", *Health Econometric (Contributions to Economic Analysis,* 294), pp.235-236

Binchy & Komolafe, .(2011), "Patients, Contributory Negligence and Medical Negligence Litigation" *Quarterly Review of Tort Law*,4(2), p.21

Blake V., (2012), "When is a Patient-Physician Relationship Established?", *AMA Journal of Ethics*,14(5) , pp.403-406

Brecher, R., (1985), "Striking Responsibilities", *Journal of Medical Ethics*,11, pp.60-9

Carlson D. and Thompson J N., "The Role of State Medical Boards", Virtual Mentor,7(4), (2005): pp.311-314.

Carol B. Bonebrake, (1974), "Contractual Liability in Medical Malpractice - Sullivan v. O'Connor", *DePaul L. Rev.*, 24(1), pp.212-226

Chichom-Mefire A. et al, (2014) “Compliance of District Hospitals in the Center Region of Cameroon with WHO/IATSIC Guidelines for the Care of the Injured: A Cross-Sectional Analysis”, *World Journal Of Surgery*, 38(10), pp.2525-2533

Chouta P., “Denunciation - 13 Women and 11 Babies Locked in a Room in the Main Hospital in Yaoundé for Several Months like Prisoners” *The Observer*, 08/13/2018.

Chrenkoff, A., (1996), ‘Freedom of Contract: A New look at the History and Future of the Idea’, *Australian Journal of Legal Philosophy*, 21, p. 37.

Chukwuneke, F N., (2015), “Medical Incidents in Developing Countries: A Few Case Study from Nigeria”, *Nigerian Journal of Clinical Practice*, 18(7), pp.20-24.

Cohen J I., (1996), “An Awesome Responsibility for Medical Educators”, *Acad Physician Sci.*, 71(1), p56

Cruess S.R., (2006) “Professionalism and Medicine’s Social Contract with Society”, *Clin. Orthop. Relat Res.*, 449, pp.170-176

Cruess S.R. et al, (2005), “The Medical Profession and Self-Regulation: A Current Challenge”, *AMA Journal of Ethics Virtual Mentor*, 7(4), pp.320-324

Cullian K., (2021), Universal Health Coverage: Only Half of Africans Have Access to Health Care, *Health Policy Watch.*

Curran, (1959), “Professional Negligence-Some General Comments”, *Vand. L. Rev.* 12(3), p.535-547

Deshpande S P., et al, (2006), “Factors Impacting Ethical Behaviors in Hospitals” *Journal of Business Ethics*, 69(2), pp.207-216.

Djoko C., “Comprendre la Corruption au Cameroun”, *Le Grand Soir*, Octobre 3, 2010 .

Don S Smith, (1967) “Battery in Medical Torts”, *Cleveland Marshall Law Review*, 16(1), pp.22-38.

Edie G.E.H.E et al, (2015), “Perceptions of Antenatal Care Services by Pregnant Women Attending Government Health Centers in the Buea Health District, Cameroon: A Cross Sectional Study”. *Pan African Medical Journal*, 21(45), pp.48-58.

Edwards S. L., (1970), "Failure to Inform as Medical Malpractice", *Vanderbilt Law Review*,23(4), p.754-774.

Enang A E., (2019), "An Appraisal of the Evolution of Medicine in Cameroon", *2nd International Conference on Research in Social Science*, p. 86.

Fokwen M., "Acute Staff Infrastructure Shortage Hits Kumba District Hospital", *Cameroon Post*, February 10, 2015.

Fominyen G., "Why Corruption is Cameroon's Worst-Kept Secret", *Thomson Reuters Foundation News*, 2010.

Fongwa Marie N., (2002) "International Health Care Perspectives: The Cameroon Example", *J Transcult Nurs* 13(4), pp. 325-330.

Fuah C K., (2018), "Insurmountable Hurdles in the Proof of Causation in Pharmaceutical Product Liability in Cameroon: Perspective for Reform" *International Journal of Legal Developments and Allied Issues*, 4(5), p.496-521.

Funwie B. N., "Border Protection: Officials Delve On the Issue of Smuggling", *Cameroon Radio Television*, 2019,

Gallagher T H. et al, (2003), "Patients' and Physicians' Attitudes Regarding the Disclosure of Medical Errors", *JAMA*. 289, pp.1001–1007

García-Prado A. et al, (2006), "The Impact of Hospital Management Reforms on Absenteeism in Costa Rica", *Health Policy Plan,* 21, pp. 91–100.

Geest S V D., (1988) "The Articulation of Formal and Informal Medicine Distribution in South Cameroon", *The Context of Medicines in Developing Countries. Culture, Illness, and Healing,* 12, pp.131-148

Gittler G J. and Goldstein J C., (1996), "The Elements of Medical Malpractices: An Overview", *Medicolegal Case Reviews,* 23, pp.1152-1155.

Gostin L. O., (2015), "The future of the World Health Organization: Lessons Learned from Ebola". *The Milbank Quarterly*, 93(3), pp.475–479.

Goudkamp J. and Nolan D., (2016), "Contributory Negligence in The Twenty-First Century: Empirical Study Of First Instance Decisions", *The Modern Law Review*,79(4), pp. 575-622.

Gutman, T., (2013), "Theories of Contract and the Concept of Autonomy", Working *Papers of The Centre for Advance Study in Bioethics*, 55. p.3

Guyer P., (2003), "Kant on the Theory and Practice of Autonomy", *Soc Philos Policy,* 20(2), PP.70-98.

Gwangudi M I., (2002), "Problems Militating against Women's Access to Justice in Nigeria", *University of Maiduguri Law Journal,* 5, pp.13-14.

Hanson L R. and Stromberg E R., (1969), "Hospital Liability for Negligence", *Hasting Law Journal*, 21(1), pp.1-35.

Herman N Y S., (2005), "Report on Medical Liability in Council of Europe Member States: A Comparative Study of the Legal and Factual Situation in Member States of the Council of Europe", *European Committee on Legal Cooperation*, 3(1), pp.1-28.

Hogan D., (1983), "The Effectiveness of Licensing: History, Evidence and Recommendations", *Law Hum Behav*, 7, pp.117-136.

Howell C D., (1981), "Reform and the Monopolistic Impulse", *Acadienst,* 11(1), pp.3-22.

Hutchins, H B., (1906), "What is the Practice of Medicine", *Minch. L. Rev*., 4, pp.373-9.

Iserson K V., (1999), "Principles of Biomedical Ethics", *Emergency Medicine Clinics of North America*, 17(2), pp.283-9.

James T C., (1996), "The Patient -Physician Relationship: Covenant or Contract?" *Mayo Clin Proc*, 71, pp.917-918.

Jerrold L., (2020), "Medical Malpractice or Breach of Contract", *American journal of Orthodontics and Dentofacial Orthopedics, Litigation and Legislation*, 157(2), pp. 278-279.

Joga Rao, S V., (2009), "Medical Negligence Liability under the Consumer Protection Act: A Review of Judicial Perspective", *Indian Journal of Urology*, 25(3), pp. 362-363.

Jonathan C., et al, (2013). "Human Rights in Patient Care: A Theoretical and Practical Framework", *Health and Human Rights Journal*, 15(2), pp.7-19.

Kaldjian L C. et al, (2006) "An Empirically Derived Taxonomy of Factors Affecting Physicians' Willingness to Disclose Medical Errors. *J Gen Intern Med*. 21, pp.942–948.

Kale A., et al, (2012), "Adverse Drug Events Caused by Serious Medication Administration Errors,", *BMJ Quality &Safety*, 21(11), pp. 933-938

Keith Somerville, "Africa's Borders: Porous, Unprotected and Blocking Trade and Economic Development", African Arguments, 2013.

Kessler P D. and McClellan B M., (1997), "The Effects of Malpractice Pressure and Liability Reforms on Physicians' Perceptions of Medical Care", *Law and Contemporary Problems*, 60(1), pp.81-106

Kibu O., (2019), "Health System Decentralisation as a Critical Deriver for Better Care", *Nkafu Policy Institute*, p. 2

Kindzeka M. E., (2016), "Death of Pregnant Woman Provokes Debate on Cameroon's Health Care", *VOA News.*

Kindzeka M. E., (2021), "Cameroon Hospitals Accused of Preventing Insolvent Patients from Leaving", *VOA News*

Kindzeka, M E., (2015), "Cameroon Medical Council Calls for Closure of Illegal Hospitals", *VOA News*

King Jr. J. H., (2004), "Pain and Suffering, Noneconomic Damages, and the Goals of Tort Law", *S.M.U. Law. Review*,57(1), pp.163-175

Lee Y K., (1967), "Professional Secrecy and the Law", *Singapore Medical Journal,* vol.8(2), p.87-101.

Lewis M., (2006), "Governance and Corruption in Public Healthcare Systems", *Center for Global Development*, *Working Paper Number*78.

Loudon I S., (1982), "The Origin of the General Practitioner", James Mackenzie Lectures, *JR Coll Gen Pract,* 33(246), pp13-23.

Mah E. M., et al, (2017), "Birth Injuries in Neonates at a University Teaching Hospital In Cameroon: Epidermiological, Clinical And Therapeutic Aspects", *Open Journal Of Pediatrics*, 7, pp.51-58

Maina Peter C., (2008), "Access to Justice: Creating a Role for Paralegal in the Administration of Justice in Africa", *Recht in Africa*, 11(1), pp.101-129.

Mandal J., et al, (2016), "Utilitarian and Deontological Ethics in Medicine", *Trop Parasitol* 6(1), pp.5-7.

Mathers C D. et al, (2009), "Global and Regional Causes of Death", *British Medical Bulletin*, 92(1), pp.7-32

Mathur M C., (2020), "Professional Medical Indemnity Insurance- Protection for the Experts, by the Experts", *Indian Journal of Ophthalmology*, 68(1), pp.3-5.

Maybelline Martez, "Illegal Hospitals In Cameroon", *Voice Of America*, World Health Organization, 2014

Mbom F.T., "Government Install Anti-Corruption Unit at Limbe Hospital", *Cameroon Post*, April 2012.

McCoid A H (1957), "A Reappraisal of Liability for Unauthorized Medical Treatment', 41 *Minnesota Law Review*, 41, pp.381-435.

McPake B. et al. (1999), "Informal Economic Activities of Public Health Workers in Uganda: Implications for Quality and Accessibility of Care", *Soc Sci Med* , 49, pp.849–65.

"Medical Negligence in Uganda", *Uganda Law Reform Commission, Issues Paper*, Nov. 2017, pp.1-35.

Mello M. M. et al, (2020), "Malpractice Liability and Health care Quality, A Review", *JAMA*, 323(4), pp. 352-366.

Miech R P., (1995), "The Doctor Patient Relationship: Friend or Adversary", *The Linacre Quarterly*, 62(2), pp.13-18

Migiro K., "Kenyan Moms Held and Abused in Hospital Win Court Verdict", *Africa News* 24, 18 September 2015.

Miller, A J., (1953) "The Contractual Liability of Physicians and Surgeons", *Washington University Law Quarterly*, 4, pp. 413-438.

Mock C. et al, (2004), "Global Strengthening of Care for the Injured", *Bull World Health Organisation*, 82(4), p.241

Monkaree, K A., (1999-2000) "Remedies for Medical Practitioners Liability", *Amadu Bello University Law Journal*, 17-18, pp. 16-27.

Morales L. S., et al, ,(2002) "Socio Economic, Cultural And Behavioural Factors Affecting Hispanic Health Outcomes", *Journal Of Health Care For The Poor And Underserved*, 13, pp. 477-503.

Mostert S. et al, (2015) "Hospital Detention Practices: Statement of a Global Taskforce". *Lancet*, 386(9994), p.649.

Moungbakou I B M., (2018), "Commodification of Care and Its Effect on Maternal Health in the Noun Division (West Region Cameroon)", *BMC Medical Ethics*, 19(43), pp.71-79.

Ndi R. and Tata K. E., (2020). "Medical Errors in Health Care Institutions in Cameroon: Setting the Platform for Legal Intervention", *Indian Journal of Health & Medical Law*, 3(1), p.28.

Ndong O., (1995), « Le Droit Camerounais a la Protection de la Sante et de la Salubrité Publique de 1916 à 1978 », Tome 1 : Les Administrations Sanitaires, p.13.

Ngeh E. N. et al, (2020). "Covid-19: Challenges and the Impact on Care in Clinical Settings in Cameroon", *Pan African Medical Journal*, 35(2), pp.122-123

Ngwa A. C. et al, (2020), "British Southern Cameroons Health Services as an Appendage to Nigerian Health Sector, 1922-1961, *International Journal of Scientific Research and Management*, 8(3), p.638.

Ngwa Keziah, "Illegal Drugs :Cameroon Suffers Tax Losses, Health Threats" *Cameroon Radio Television*, February 2022.

Ngwa F. N., "Detained in Cameroon's Hospitals". BBC News, 29 Nov. 2012.

Nsom K Y., "Medical Council Flays Tchiroma", Cameroon Postline, May 7 2010.

Nzouedja T A., (2021), "Access to Justice and Human Rights Protection in the Common Law Jurisdiction in Cameroon: Problems and Prospects", *Zien Journal of Social Sciences and Humanities*, 1(1), pp.200-210

Obah N G., et al,(2020), "Porous Borders and National Integration in Africa", *Journal of African Foreign Affairs*, 7(3), pp.89-111.

Obame A., et al, (2003) 'La Migration du Personnel de la Sante Qualifie Dans la Region Afrique : Le Cas Du Cameroun', *Health Science& Disease*, 4, pp.22-27.

Ogemba P., (2018) "It is Illegal to Detain Patient in Hospital over Bills, Court Rules" *The Standards*, October 3rd,

O'Hara E A.& Douglas Yarn, (2002), "Note & Comment, On Apology and Consilience", *Wash. L. Rev.*, 77, pp.1121-1122.

Ojong N., (2020), "The COVID-19 Pandemic and the Pathology of the Economic and Political Architecture in Cameroon", *Healthcare*, 8(2), pp. 1-16.

Ojong, T., (2016) "The Liability of Medical Doctor Towards Patients in Cameroon", University of *Buea Journal of Applied Social Sciences,* ix(1), pp. 63-82

Oludamilola A. A. et al, (2020) "Legal Perspectives on Liability for Medical Negligence and Malpractices in Nigeria", *Pan African Medical Journal*, 35(44)

Oral T., (2011), "The Definition of the Legal Relationship between a Patient and Physician", *Ankarah Bar Review*, 4(1), pp.21-32

Payne, (1977), "Recent Development Affecting a Hospital's Liability for Negligence of Physicians", *TEX. L. J*, 18 S. pp. 389,390.

Pefok J D., "Ministers Decision to Shut Down Douala Health Unit Sparks Controversy, Hon. Nintcheu calls on Health Minister to Resign", *Cameroon Postline*, 2022

Pemunta N. V., et al, (2020), "Self-Medication within the Context of Medical Pluralism in Yaounde, Cameroon", *Pan African Medical Journal*, vol.37(14).

Pheage T., "Dying From Lack of Medicines", *Africa Renewal*, March 2017

Pituru S. et al, ,(2015), "Malpractice and Professional Liabilities of Medical Personnel", *Farmacia*, 63(2), pp.318-324.

Prillaman H L., (1990), "A Physician's Duty to Inform of Newly Developed Therapy", *Journal of Contemporary Health Law and Policy*, 6, pp.43-58.

Prior T. and Harris-Steingruber S., (2017), "Corruption No Sisia: TI Cameroon Develops a Whistleblowing Platform for Health Care Patients", *Transparency International Global Health.*

Raach J. H., (1944), "English Medical Licencing in the Early Seventeenth Century", *Yale Journal of Biology and Medicine*, 16(4), pp.267-288.

Rice J., "Strong Health Professional Associations 2020: Promoting the Long-Term Viability of Health Professional Associations (Hpas) In Sub-Saharan Africa", *Discussion Paper. Management Sciences for Health* – LMG Project, (2013).

Richards T., (1994), "The World Medical Association: Can Hope Triumph over Experience?", *British Medical Journal* 308(6923), pp.262-266.

Roberts M.J.D., (2009), "The Politics of Professionalization: MPs, Medical Men, and the 1858 Medical Act", *Med Hist*, 53(1), pp.37-56.

Ruger J. P. et al, (2009), "The Global Role of The World Health Organization", *Glob Health Gov*, 2(2), pp. 1-11

Sama, N J., (2005), "Providing Legal Aid in Criminal Justice in Cameroon: The Role of Lawyers", Access to Justice in Africa and Beyond, Making the Rule of Law a Reality. *Penal Reform International and Bluhum Legal Clinic of the North western University School of law.* pp. 153-162.

Samanta A. and Samanta J., (2004), "Regulation of the Medical Profession: Fantasy, Reality and Legality", *Journal of The Royal Society of Medicine,* 97(5), *pp.*211-218

Sanders J., (2008), 'Reforming General Damages: A Good Tort Reform", *Roger Williams University Law Review,*13(1), pp.115-153.

Saskia M. et al, (2015), "Corruption in Health-Care Systems and its Effect on Cancer Care in Africa", *Lancet Oncol,* 16, p.397.

Sawicki, N N., (2010), "Character, Competence, and the Principles of Medical Discipline", *Journal of Heath Care Law and Policy,*13(2), pp.285-320.

Scher S J. and Darley J M., (1997), "How effective are the things people say to apologize? Effects of the realization of the apology speech act", *J Psycholinguistic Res.* 26, pp.127–140

Shelton D., (2009) "Common Concern of Humanity", *Environmental Law and Policy,* 39(2), pp. 83-86.

Shelton D., (2007), "Human Rights, Health and Environmental Protection: Linkage in Law and Practice", *Hum. Rts.& Int'l Legal Discouse,* 1, pp.9-30.

Shepherd J., (2014), "Uncovering the Silent Victims of the American Medical Liability Systems", *Vanderbilt Law Review*, 67(1), pp.151-195.

Sina, K N., "Public Health: Over 35000 Health Care Workers Needed", *Cameroon Radio Television News,* July 2020.

Smith, R., (2005), "The GMC: Expediency before Principle". BMJ. 330(7481), pp.1-2.

Soh M., (2013), "Access to Health Care Vis a Vis Women's Reproductive Health in Cameroon", *Journal of International Women's Studies*, 9(1), pp. 117-134.

Songne M., "Cameroon: IMF Awaits New Audit on Covid-19 Fund Management ", *The Africa Report*, March 2022.

Sylvia R C., et al. (2000), "Professionalism: A Contract between Medicine and Society", *Canadian Medical Association Journal,*162(5), pp.668-669

Tamblyn R., (1994), "Is the Public Being Protected? Prevention of Sub-Optimal Medical Practice through Training Programs and Credentialing Examinations," Evaluation of Health Professionals, 17(2), pp. 198 –221.

Tegna E M., (1989), « Historique de la Politique de Sante au Cameroun : De la Promotion Sanitaire Allemande au Politique Sectorielle Actuel », *Review Scientifique de l'école des Science de la Sante de l'université catholique d'Afrique Centrale*, No.4, p,145

Tinyami E. et al, (2015), "Cameroon Public Health Sector: Shortage and Inequalities in Geographic Distribution of Health Personnel", *International Journal for Equity in Health*, 14(43), pp. 2-12.

Tita A. T., et al, (2005) "Evidence-Based Reproductive Health Care in Cameroon: Population-Based Study of Awareness, Use and Barriers", *Bulletin Of The World Health Organization*, 83, pp.895–903.

"Theories for Imposing Liability upon Hospitals for Medical Malpractice: Ostensible Agency and Corporate Liability",(1985),*William Mitchell Law Review*,11(2), pp.561-583.

Uyo Yenwong-Fai, "Border Porosity and Boko Haram as a Regional Threat", *Institute For Security Studies*, May 2012.

Villas M E., (2015), "The Right and Duty of Secrecy, as a Patient Protection", *Rev. Bioet.* 23(3), pp.511-521.

Vinard P. and Djateng F., "Anti-corruption Strategy and Governance Indicators in the Health Sector in Cameroon: Mission of March 24-April 12 2007", Washington, D.C.: World Bank Group, pp.2-57

Walker R. D., (1994), "Medical Practice Guidelines", *Western Journal of Medicine*, 161(1), pp.39-44.

Wang, Zhan, et al, (2017), "Records of Medical Malpractice Litigation: A Potential Indicator of Health-Care Quality in China", *Bulletin of the World Health Organization*, 95(6), pp.430-436.

Wei M., (2007) "Doctors, Apologies, and the Law: An Analysis and Critique of Apology Laws", *J Health Law*. 40, pp.107–159

Weisz G.and Nannestad B., (2021), "The World Health Organization and the Global Standardization of Medical Training, A History", *Weisz and Nannestad Globalization and Health*, 17(96), pp. 1-13.

WhiteW. D., (2014) "Professional Self-Regulation in Medicine"., *AMA Journal Of Ethics* 16(4): pp.275-278.

Yam C. et al, (2016) "Medical Regulation: Ten Key Trends Emerging From an International Review", *JMed Regul*, 102 (1), pp.16-27

Yamb B. & Bayemi O., (2017), "Corruption and Discrimination in Douala Metropolis Public Hospitals of Cameroon", *Journal of Economics Library*, 4(4), pp.501-513.

Yastes R. et al, (2017),"Hospital Detentions for Non Payment of Fees: A Denial of Rights and Dignity", *Centre on Global Health Security, Chatham House, The Royal Institute of International Affairs*, pp.1-16.

Yule J., (2011) "Defences in Medical Negligence: To What Extent has Tort Law Reform in Australia Limited the Liability of Health Professionals?" *Journal of the Autralian Law Teachers Association*, 4(1&2), pp.53-63.

Zamo-Akono C., et al, (2013), "Institutions and Hospital Efficiency in Cameroon: A Data Envelopment Analysis" *Journal of African Development* 15(1), pp.45-71.

THESES AND DESRTATIONS

Amani A., "The Health Workers Crisis in Cameroon", Masters Thesis, Institute of Public Health, Georgia State University 2010

Ambe, H A., "The Regulation and Control of Retail Pharmaceutical Drugs in Cameroon", Unpublished PhD Thesis, Faculty of Law and Political Science, University of Bamenda, Cameroon. 2017.

Assoumou R S, La Responsabilité Pénale du Médecin Traitant dans le Système Pénal Camerounais, DEA Mémoire, Faculté de Science Juridiques et Politique, Université de Douala, 2006

Forkusam A L., The Evolution of Health Services in the Southern Cameroons under British Administration 1916-1945, DES Dissertation in History, University of Yaoundé, 1978.

Kontchou L F., Evolution des Politiques Sanitaires au Cameroun (1919-2000) : Approche Historique, Mémoire en vue de l'obtention d'un DEA, Université de Yaoundé 1, 2008-2009

Obafemi K A R., "Medical Negligence Litigation in Nigeria: Identifying the Challenges and Proposing a Model Law Reform Act", unpublished PhD Thesis, School of Law, Trinity College Dublin, Ireland, 2017

Obasi E. Z., "A Review of the Barriers and Socio-Cultural Factors Influencing the Access to Maternal Health Care services in Nigeria", unpublished Masters Thesis., Helsinki Metropolia University of Applied Sciences, Helsinki, Finland. 2013

Nzima Nzima, V. "Health Sector Strategy and Economic Development in Cameroon: History, Challenges and Perspectives", unpublished Masters Theses, Georgia State University, Atlanta, GA. 2014.

Shu C A., "Public And Private Hospitals In Cameroon: Service Quality And Patients' Choice Of Hospitals", unpublished Masters Thesis, Institute of Graduate Studies and Research, Eastern Mediterranean University, North Cyprus, 2010,

Tchuinguem G., 'Ampleur, Couts, Facteurs Personnels Et Occupationnels De L'absentéisme Dans la Fonction Publique Hospitalière Au Cameroun', unpublished Masters Thesis, Université De Montréal, 2009.]

REPORTS

Commission d'enquête, chargée d'élucider les circonstances de la mort du Dr NGO KANA survenue le 10 janvier 2016 à 4h55 à l'HGD.

Institute Nationale de la Statistique 2eme enquête sur le suivi de Dépense Publiques et le niveau de satisfaction des bénéficiaires dans les Secteurs de l'éducation et de la Sante au Cameroun (PETS 2) : Rapport Principal, volet Sante, 2010.

Ministry Of Public Health Cameroon, Department Of Human Resource. General Census Report of Health Personnel, Yaoundé 2012.

ONMC, Rapport de la Commission d'enquête du Conseil de L'ordre National des Medecins du Cameroun sur L'affaire Monique Koumateke. Mars 2016.

Rapport d'inspection et de Supervision MINSANTE 1er semestre2015

Report of the Special Rapporteur on the Right of Everyone to the Enjoyment of the Highest Attainable Standard of Physical and Mental Health". United Nations General Assembly. Human Rights Council. Thirty-second Session. A/HRC/32/32.4 April, 2016.

Transparency International, Corruption Perception Index 2020

World Health Organisation Global Report on Traditional and Complementary Medicine 2019,

World Health Organisation, "Diagnostic Errors : Technical Series On Safer Primary Care" (2016)

WEBSITES

Access to health in Cameroon @ www.Worldbank.Org/En/Country/Cameroon/Publication/Better-Health-Care-Access-For-All-Cameroonians. visited: 29th April 2022

access to medical services in Cameroon @ www.panafrican-med-Journal.com/ content/article/21/45/full. visited: 2nd May 2022

apologies in medical malpractice litigation @ www.natlawreview.com/article/you-had-me-i-m-sorry-impact-physicians-apologies-medical-malpractice-litigation visited: 25th May 2021

Cameroon profile @ www.rad-aid.org/wp-content/uploads/Cameroon-Country-Report. pdf visited: 24th October 2020

Closure of marie o polyclinic @ http//cameroonpostline.com/ministers-decision-to-shut-down-douala-health-unit-sparks-controversy-hon-nintcheu-calls-on-health-minister-to-resign/%E2%. Visited: 9th March 2021.

Collusion of medical practitioners @ http//Briefing_Paper10-Collusion_among_Health_Service_Providers_in_India.pdf visited:11th May 2021

corruption in Cameroon @ www.cgdev.org/publication/governance-and-corruptionpublic-health-care-systems-working-paper-78 visited: 22nd October 2020

Corruption in Cameroon @ www.cgdev.org/publication/governance-and-corruptionpublic-health-care-systems-working-paper-78. visited: 8th November 2020

corruption in hospitals in Cameroon @ https://tihealth.org/content/whistleblowing-platform-for-health-patient/visited: 22nd July 2022

Corruption index @ www.Transparency.Org. visited :4th May 2022

Criminal sanction of medical doctors in Cameroon @ www.medcamer.org/en/doctor-illegal-arrest-in-kumba/. visited:11thApril 2021.

Detention of patience in hospitals @ www.news24.com/Africa/news/Kenyan-moms-held-and-abused-in-hospital-win-court-victory-20150918. visited: 23rdNovember 2020

Detention of patients in Cameroon hospitals @ https://observers.france24.com/en/20180813-cameroon-hospital-mothers-babies-detained-fees.. Visited: 24th October 2020

Detention of patients in Cameroon hospitals @ www.businessincameroon.com/health/2603/8977-cameroonian-health-ministry-forbids-public-hospital-services-from-confining-indigent-patients-due-to-their-inability-to-pay-bills. visited: 27th October 2020

detention of patients in hospitals @ www.camerounweb.com/CameroonHomePage/NewsArchive/Covid-19-les-mensonges-de-Manaouda-Malachie-sur-la-prise-en-charge-des-patients-508861. Visited: 29th October 2020

Health Professional Regulation in Historical Context: Canada, the USA and the UK @http://doi.org/10.1186/s12960-020-0050-y. Visited 6th December 2024.

http://www.healthpolicy-watch.news visited: 11th July 2022.

https://documents.worldbank.org/curated/en/412641543396425023/Alignh-public-Expenditures-with-the-Goals-of-Vision-2035. Visited: 6th May 2022

https:// mcwilson.com visited: 2nd May 2022)

https://africama.net/cont_professional_dev.htm. visited: 17th March 2021

Illegal clinics in Cameroon @ www.borgenmagazine.com/illegal-health-clinics-cameroon/ visited: 19th April 2022

Illegal hospitals in Cameroon @ borgenproject.org/Illegal-Hospitals-Cameroon/ visited: 19th April 2022

Illegal hospitals in Cameroon @ www.Voanews.Com/Africa/Cameroon-Medical-Council-Calls-Closure-Illegal-Hospitals. Visited: 14th April 2021

Illegal sale of drugs in Cameroon @ www.Panafrican-Med-Journal.Com/Content/ Article/37/14/Full. visited: 2nd May 2022

Infrastructural deficiencies in Cameroon hospitals @ https://cameroonpostline.com/acute-staff-infrastructure-shortage-hits-kumba-district-hospital/%E2%80%8B. visited: 25th April 2022

International code of medical ethics @ www.wma.net/policies/WMAInternational code of medical ethics. Visited: 23rd July 2022

Literacy rate in Cameroon @ www.macrotrends.net/countries/CMR/Cameroon/literacy-rate>Cameroom Literacy Rate 1976-2022. visited: 16th July 2022

Medical confidentiality @ https://cameroonpostline.com/medical-council-flays-tchiroma. Visited: 1st June 2021

Medical negligence @ www.panafrican-med-journal.com/content/article/35/44/full. Visited:22nd January 2022

Medical professional insurance @ www.pacificprime.com/country/africa/cameroon-health-insurance=pacific=prime-international/ visited: 10th October 2020

Ministry in charge of public health in Cameroon @ www.minsante.cm. visited: 12th May 2022

negligence in Cameroon hospitals @ http://newspittsburghcourier.com/020/07/08/ quadruplets-die-in-government-run-hospital/. Visited: 2nd November 2020

negligence in Cameroon hospitals @ http://observers.france24.com/en/20160315-pregnant-woman-cameroon-hospital-ceasarian. Visited: 7th May 2021

Operation of illegal hospitals in Cameroon@ www.journalducameroun.com/en/2000-illegal-hospitals-uncovered-cameroon/ visited: 14th April 2021

Patient safety @ www.who.int/news-room/fact-sheets/detail/patient-safety. visited: 3rd November 2020)

Porous borders @ www.Crtv.Cm. visited: 1st May 2022.

Professional sanctions of medical practitioners in Cameroon @ www.journalducameroun.com/en/cameroon-5-medical-personnel-of-garoua-regional-hospital-suspended/ visited: 16th May 2021

Regulation @ www.who.int/teams/regulation-prequalification/regulation-and-safety. visited: 13th March2021.

Right to health @ http://www.ohchr.org/EN/Issues/Health/Pages/AnnualReports. aspx. visited: 23rd October 2020.

Right to health @ www1.umn.edu/humanrts/africa/comcases/74-92.html. visited: 1st October 2020

Righttohealth@file:///C:/Users/the%20eye%20informatique/Documents/Human_Rights_Health_and_Environmental_Protection.pdf. Visited: 19th February 2021.

Roadside medication @ www.journalducameroun.com. visited: 30th May 2022

sanctions of medical practitioners in Cameroon @ www.Journalducameroun. Com/En/Cameroon-Two-Nurses-Suspended-For-Posting-Pictures-Of-Patient-On-Social-Media/. Visited:1st June 2021

Surgical errors @ www.hardball-law.com/practice-areas/medical-malpractice/ surgical-errors-as-medical-malpractice/ visited:28th April 2022

Use of the Hippocratic or other Professional Oath in the UK Medical Schools in 2017 @ http//10;777 doi.org/10.1186/s13104-017-3114-7 Visited: 6th December 2024

Violation of medical ethics in Cameroon @ www.journalducameroun. com/en/cameroonminister-suspends-three-nurses-for-filming-dying-student-in-douala-hospital/ visited: 16th June 2021

World health organization @ www.who.int/publications/who-guidelines, visited: 16th March 2021

World medical association @ www.wma.net/policies-post/declaration-on-euthanasia-and-physician-assisted-suicide/ visited: 29th March 2021

World medical association @ www.wma.net/who-we-are/about-us/ visited: 6th January 2021

www.jdsupra.com/legalnews/resolving-medical-malpractice-matters-44779/ visited: 13th June 2021

www.thehealthlawfirm.com/resources/health-law-articles-and-documents/ patient-abandonment.html. Visited: 6th May 2022

APPENDICES

Appendix A: Decree No 83 166/ 12 April 1983 on the Code of Medical Ethics in Cameroon

Appendix B: Law No 90/036 of 10th August 1990 on the Organization and Practice of Medicine in Cameroon

Appendix C: The WMA International Code of Medical Ethics

Appendix A: Decree No 83/166 of 12 April 1983 on the Code of Medical Ethics in Cameroon

United Republic of Cameroon
République Unie du Cameroun
Code of Medical Ethics
Code de Déontologie des Médecins
Decret N°83-166 of 12 April 1983
Décret N°83-166 du 12 Avril 1983
/p. 31/
Decree No. 83-166 of 12 April 1983
Code of Medical Ethics
The President of the Republic,
Mindful of the Constitution,
Mindful of Law No. 80-6 of 14 July 1980 to regulate the practice of Medicine;
Mindful of Law No. 80-7 of 14 July 1980 to organize the Medical Association;
Upon the recommendation of the Council of the Medical Association. Hereby decrees as follows:

Part I – General obligations of doctors

1. Respect for life constitutes in every instance the primary duty of a doctor.
2. (1) The doctor must tend ail sick persons with the same diligence, whatever their status, nationality, religion, reputation and the feelings he may have concerning them.
   (2) In no case shall the doctor exercise his profession under conditions prejudicial to the quality of medical care and attention.
3. (1) Whatever his official duties or special field may be, every doctor must, except in the case of force majeure, give help urgently to a sick per-son in immediate danger, unless he has ensured that other medical care likely to ward off the danger has been given to him.
   (2) He may not leave his patients in the event of public danger, except upon an order issued in writing by the competent authority.
4. Professional secrecy shall be binding on ail doctors, unless otherwise provided by law, provided that in ail conscience it is not harmful to the interests of the patient.
   /p.32/

5. In their relations, the doctor and the patient shall each have the following guarantees:
   - freedom for the patient to choose his doctor;
   - freedom for the doctor to make prescriptions;
   - payment of fees by the patient.

6. (1) A doctor shall not relinguish his professional independence in any way whatsoever.
   (2) He must refrain, even outside the practice of his profession, from any action that could bring it into discrepute.
   (3) He may not, while practising medicine, perform any other activity incompatible with the dignity of the profession.

7. The medical profession shall not be exercised like a trade. For this reason :
   (a) Any form, direct or indirect, of publicity or advertisement, and any spectacular occasion concerning medical matters but not having exclusively a scientific or educational purpose shall be forbidden.
   (b) The only observations which a doctor is authorized to enter on his prescriptions or in a year book are :
   - those which facilitate his relations with his patients;
   - such titles, duties, qualifications that are officially recognized and are related to the profession;
   - scientific honours related to the profession.

   c) The only information that a doctor is authorized to put up on the door of his consulting room are the surname, names, titles, qualifications, the days, times for consultation and the floor, where applicable.
   Such information must be displayed with due restraint according to the custom of the liberal professions. The plate on which they are to be inscribed must not be larger than 25 cm by 30 cm.
   In the event of possible confusion, the medical association may require that first name(s) be mentioned.
   /p.33/

8. Unauthorized assumption of titles or use of those not authorized by the Council of the Association and all practices intended to mislead the public shall be forbidden.

9. Practice under an assumed name shall be forbidden.

10. A doctor must exercise his profession under conditions allowing him regular use of premises and the technical facilities necessary for his profession.

11. It shall be forbidden for a doctor to entrust the running of his consulting room to a colleague, except in the case of replacement.
12. The exercise of medicine in fairs or markets shall be forbidden.
13. The following shall be forbidden:
    - any act that may enable that patient to obtain unjustified or illegal material gain;
    - any refund in cash or in kind made to a patient;
    - any payment, acceptance or secret sharing of money between practitioners;
    - any commission to any member of the staff; and
    - acceptance of a commission for any medical act whatever, and in particular in respect of examinations, prescriptions of drugs or appliances, or consignments to a specific consulting room or clinic, a sanatorium or nursing home.
14. It shall be forbidden for doctors to grant any facilities to persons indulging in illegal medical practice.
15. (1) Any collusion between doctors and pharmacists, medical assistants and any other persons shall be forbidden.
    (2) No doctor shall be allowed to give consultation in commercial premises where medicines or medical appliances are on sale, or in annexes to the said premises.
    /p.34/
16. Every doctor shall be forbidden to exercise any other trade or profession permitting him to increase his profits by giving prescriptions or his professional advice.
17. Any doctor holding an elective or administrative office shall be forbid-den to use his position in order to increase his clientele.
18. Any deceiptful practices likely to discredit the profession and in particular charlatanism, shall be forbidden.
19. It shall be a serious offence to mislead practitioners or patients by proposing as beneficial or harmless a new or insufficiently tested procedure for' diagnosis or treatment.
20. (1) In medical practice, the doctor may issue certificates, attestations or documents in due form.
    (2) Any certificate, attestation or document issued by a doctor must bear his signature, his name and address.

21. It shall be a serious offence to issue a tendentious report or a certificate as a favour.

Part II - Duties of doctors towards their patients

22. A doctor, from the moment he is called to give attention to a patient and agrees to do this, shall be bound:
    - to give the patient ail the necessary medical care withing his power, either personally or with the help of qualified third parties;
    - to always act correctly and courteously towards the patient and to show himself sympathetic towards him.
23. (1) A doctor must always formulate his diagnosis with the greatest care, regardless of the time that this work may cost him.
    (2) After having made his diagnosis and prescribed treatment, the doctor must endeavour to ensure that this treatment is carried out, especially if the patient's life is in danger.
    /p.35/
24. (1) A doctor must always prescribe treatment within the limits imposed by the conditions of the patients. He must in good faith not prescribe very costly treatment for a patient until the patient or his family have been informed of the sacrifices which this would entail and the benefit which they may derive from it.
    (2) A doctor must never give treatment to a patient with a view to profiting therefrom.
25. (1) A doctor called upon to give medical attention in a particular family or place must take ail necessary prophylactic measures. He shall inform the patients and their relatives, etc., of their responsibilities towards themselves and their neighbours. He must, in particular, ensure the respect for rules of hygiene. In the absence of hygienic conditions, the doctor must instruct the patient to arrange for transport to a health establishment.
    (2) He must avoid getting involved in the affairs of the family or place concerned.
26. When ca lied urgently to consult a minor or any other incapable person and when it is impossible to obtain the consent of the legal representative of the latter in time, a doctor must give ail medical care necessary.
27. (1) A serious prognosis may lawfully be concealed from the patient.

(2) A fatal prognosis may not be divulged to him except with the greatest prudence; it must normally be divulged to his family, unless the patient is already so aware or if he has appointed a third party to be informed.

28. Except in an emergency and where he would be shirking his human responsibilities, a doctor may refuse his services for professional or personal reasons, provided that :
    - he does not, by doing this, do harm to the patient;
    - he ensures that medical treatment is continued and supplies the necessary information for this purpose.

29. (1) Any practice or act of abortion shall be forbidden.
(2) Therapeutic abortion may however be performed if such action is the only way of safeguarding the mother's life.
/p.36/
In such a case, the doctor must perforce obtain the opinions of two doctors, one of whom shall be chosen from the civil court list of experts and the other a member of the council of the Association who will give a written attestation that the life of the mother can only be preserved by such therapy.
The consultation report shall be drawn up in three copies, one of which shall be given to the patient, the other two shall be kept by the consulting physicians.
Moreover a report of the decision taken, not containing the patient's name, must be sent by registered mail to the President of the Council.
(3) In areas where there is only one doctor, or where the opinion of two colleagues cannot easily be obtained, the decision to induce therapeutic abortion shall be at the discretion of the doctor in charge, who must forthwith send a circumstantial report to the Minister of Public Health and to the President of the National Council of the Medical Association.
(4) A doctor must if necessary accept the refusal of the patient, who has been duly informed. There shall be no exception to this rule, save in the case of extreme urgency, and where the patient is not in a fit state to give her consent.
(5) If the doctor cannot, because of his convictions, practise abortion, he may withdraw his services, ensuring that treatment is continued by a qualified colleague.

30. During difficult or prolonged labour, the doctor must consider himself as the sole judge of the respective interests of the mother and child, without let-ting himself be influenced by considerations of a family nature.

31. (1) A doctor must establish his own fees. He may not refuse to give explanations on these fees to his patient.
(2) He may offer his service free of charge if his conscience so dictates.

32. (1) A fixed fee for the duration of a course of treatment shall be forbidden, except in the case of childbirth, surgical operation, physical therapy, treatment in a sanatorium or nursing home.
(2) Fixed payment for the effectiveness of treatment shall be forbidden under any circumstances.
/p.37/

33. (1) Any sharing of fees between a practitioner on the one hand and a consultant, surgeon, or specialist on the other hand, at the time of a consultation or operation, is strictly forbidden. Each physician must submit his own bill.
(2) acceptance, solicitation, or offer to share fees, even if not followed up, shall be a serious professional offence.

34. (1) A surgeon shall have the right to select his own assistant or operation assistants, as well as the anaesthetist. The latter persons may either claim their fees directly from the patient, or add such fees to the surgeon's bill to the patient.
(2) Nevertheless, when the surgeon deems it advisable to entrust the duties of operation assistant or anaesthetist to the medical practitioner, the latter must claim his own fees separately.

35. The presence of the practitioner at a surgical operation shall give him the right to separate fees if his presence has been requested or accepted by the patient or his family.

Part III – Duties of doctors in matters of social medicine

36. (1) The doctor shall, bearing in mind his age, health and specialized field, as the case may be, give his assistance with regard to work undertaken by the competent authorities for the protection of health and organization of health care on a permanent basis.
(2) Doctors must inform the Public Health Services of contagious diseases, and must also supply statistical data needed by the public health services.

37. (1) Practitioners engaged as labour medical officers by industrial or commercial undertakings must transmit their contract or engagement to the Ministry in charge of Public Health and to the Council of the Association within one month preceding their assumption of duties.
(2) Private doctors who do not own their equipment or the premises in which they practise must send in the contracts relating thereto under the conditions fixed by the preceding paragraph.
/p.38/

38. Any doctor who, while practising curative medicine, carries out preventive medical treatment in a community or gives a public consultation for detecting disease, shall be forbidden to make use of such activities to increase his private clientele.

39. (1) No one may be both specialist and general practitioner for the same patient, except in the event of absolute necessity due to lack of doctors in the area.
(2) Unless the parties otherwise agree, a doctor must not agree to undertake an assessment when the interests involved concern one of his patients, friends, relatives or group which calls upon his services.
The same shall apply when his personal interests are involved.

40. A specialist must, before undertaking any operation of assessment, inform the person he is to examine of his mission.

41. (1) When entrusted with his mission a specialist must decline to give an opinion if he considers that the questions put to him are not relevant to medicine properly speaking.
(2) In his report, the specialist must only reveal the information necessary to serve as replies to the questions asked in the decision appointing him and must not reveal any other information he might have learnt.

Part IV – Duties of colleagues

42. (1) Doctors must maintain good professional relations between themselves. They owe each other moral support.
A doctor having a professional disagreement with a colleague must first attempt to come to an agreement with him; if he does not succeed, he must inform the President of the Council of the Association of the matter.
(2) It shall be forbidden to slander or disparage a colleague, or to repeat any remarks likely to harm him in the practice of his profession.

(3) Defense of a colleague unjustly criticised shall be deemed good professional conduct.
/p.39/

43. It shall be forbidden to attract and attempt to attract the patients of another doctor.

44. A doctor called to a patient who is being tended by one of his colleagues must respect the following rules:
  - if the patient intends to dispense with his first doctor: the second doctor must obtain the patient's express wish and advise his colleague;
  - if the patient simply wanted to ask an opinion without changing his doctor ; the second doctor must suggest a joint consultation and withdraw after having given only the emergency treatment necessary.

  In the case where, for a valid reason consultation seems impossible or inappropriate, the doctor may examine the patient, but shall reserve for his colleague his opinion on the diagnosis and treatment ;
  - if the patient has, owing to the absence of his usual doctor, called upon him, he must give him all treatment necessary until his colleague returns and give him all necessary information.

45. Subject to the provisions of Article 57, a doctor may receive any patient at his surgery, whoever their usual doctor.

46. (1) A Doctor treating a patient must suggest a consultation with a specialist whenever circumstances so require.
(2) He must accept a consultation requested by the patient or his friends and relations.
(3) In both cases the doctor shall propose the consultant whom he deems most qualified, but he must take the patient's wishes into account and agree, in principle, save for any serious reasons to meet any other doctor. He shall be responsible for organizing the procedure for consultation.
(4) If the examining doctor considers that he should not agree to the choice made, he may withdraw and shall not be obliged to explain his refusal.

47. (1) At the close of consultation between two or more doctors, their conclusions shall be drawn up jointly and in writing, then signed by the examining doctor and countersigned by the consulting doctor or doctors.
(2) When conclusions are not drawn up in writing the consultant is deemed to be fully in agreement with the opinion of the doctor.
/p.40/

48. When, during a consultation between doctors, the opinions of the consultant and the examining doctor basically differ, the examining doctor shall be free to case treatment if the consultant's opinion prevails.

49. Except in an emergency, a doctor who has been called for consultation must not return to the patient he examined with his colleague, in the absence of the examining doctor or without his approval, during the illness which necessitated the consultation. In this case, the examining doctor must be notified as quickly as possible.

50. (1) A doctor may only have himself replaced temporarily in respect of his patients by a colleague, a student or doctor whose name does not appear on the Roll of the Association; the Council, which must compulsorily and immediately be informed, shall decide whether the substitute satisfies the necessary moral conditions.
(2) During the period of replacement, the student or doctor shall be under the disciplinary jurisdiction.

51. (1) A doctor who, during or after his studies, has replaced a colleague for a period of more than three months, shall not, within two years after such replacement, set himself up in an establishment, where he could be in direct competition with the doctor whom he replaced, unless they have reached an agreement which shall be notified to the Council of the Association.
(2) When such agreement cannot be obtained, the case must be submitted to the Council of the Association.
(3) A doctor may not be replaced by a government doctor, a doctor serving the State under technical assistance or a colleague serving a missionary agency, unless there is a shortage of private doctors.

52. No doctor shall set himself up in a building in which a colleague of the same speciality practises.

53. (1) Any associations or partnership between doctors must form the subject of written contract respecting the professional independence of each doctor.
(2) Draft contracts must be submitted to the Minister in charge of Public Health and to the Council of the Association.
/p.41/

54. Any doctor practising on an individual basis shall be forbidden, in the normal, customary and organized practice of his profession, to obtain the

assistance of a doctor practising on his behalf, except in an emergency and for a maximum period of fifteen days.

Part V - Duties of doctors towards members of paramedical professions and auxiliary medical staff

55. In their relations with members of paramedical professions, particularly pharmacists and dental surgeons, doctors must respect the independence of such persons. They must avoid any unjustified action likely to harm them in the eyes of their clientele and they must behave courteously towards them.

56. A doctor must be courteous and benevolent towards auxiliary medical staff refrain from inconsiderately causing them prejudice.

57. Any proposal of contract, association or partnership having a professional object, between one or more members of one of the professions mentioned in Articles 55 and 56 above, must be submitted to the Council of the Association for approval.

Part VI - Miscellaneous provisions

58. (1) Any infringement of the provisions of the present Code shall fall within the jurisdiction of the Council of the Association sitting as the Disciplinary Board in conformity with the law.
(2) The initiative to refer a matter to this Board shall be jointly taken by the Association and the Minister in charge of Public Health.

59. Except in unavoidable circumstances or where a requisition concerns a spouse, an ascendant or a descendant, the summoned medical practitioner must comply with the requisition as soon as possible.
/p.42/

60. (1) In order to suspend a practitioner in the event of physical disablement or of a pathological condition rendering the practice of the profession. dangerous, three experts shall be empowered to draw up the report.
(2) The said experts shall be appointed as follows:
   - the first by the person concerned or his family;
   - the second by the Council of the Association;
   - the third by the first two experts.

In the case where the first two fail to agree on the choice of the third, the latter shall be appointed by the authority in charge of Public Health.

61. (1) When a matter is referred to the Council of the Association in all the cases referred to in the present Code, the Council shall give its ruling within 30 (thirty) days after the matter has been referred to it.
(2) Where it is deemed necessary to carry out an investigation, such period shall be extended for a further period of not more than two months.
(3) Upon the expiry of these different periods, the recommendation of the Council shall be deemed favourable.

62. Every doctor shall, at the time of enrolment in the Association, declare before the Council of the Association that he has cognisance of the present Code of ethics and shall undertake, under oath and in writing, to abide by it.

63. Any doctor who discontinues practice shall be bound to notify the Council of the Association thereof. The latter shall give official notice of its decision and where the person concerned expressly requests it, his name shall be struck off the roll. The Minister in charge of Republic Health shall be notified of such decision.
/p.43/

Part VII – The General Assembly

Chapter I – Organisation and functioning of the General Assembly

64. The General Assembly shall comprise all doctors inscribed on the Roll of the Association. It shall be made up of three divisions:
   - Division A: medical practitioners engaged in private practice or those employed by enterprises;
   - Division B: medical practitioners employed by missionary agencies;
   - Division C: Government medical practitioners.

65. (1) When convened in constituent assembly, the General Assembly shall be presided over by the oldest medical practitioner, assisted by two young colleagues.
The functions of such interim officers shall terminate as soon as the officers of the Council are elected.
(2) The ordinary or extraordinary sessions shall be presided over by the President of the Council or, if he is unable to attend, by the Vice-President.

66. (1) The quorum of the General Assembly shall be two-thirds of the members of each division.

(2) Members who are unable to attend may be represented by proxy. Each medical practitioner shall give only one proxy. Such proxies shall be registered by the officers of the General Assembly at the start of the session.
(3) Where the quorum has not been attained, the authority who convened the General Assembly shall again convene the Assembly within not less than 15 days and not more than a month. The deliberations of the General Assembly shall then be valid whatever the number of members present and represented.
(4) Only members who have paid all their contributions shall take part in the vote.
/p.44/

Section 2 - Functioning of the General Assembly

67. (1) The convening of the Constituent General Assembly shall fall within the jurisdiction of the authority responsible for Public Health.
2) Ordinary or extraordinary meetings of the General Assembly shall be convened by the President of the Council.
(3) Notices of meetings shall be forwarded together with the agenda, to members one month before the appointed date for the session.

68. (1) The decisions of the General Assembly shall be taken by simple majority. In the event of a tie, the President shall have the casting vote.
(2) The vote shall be open.

69. During extraordinary sessions, the Assembly shall discuss only the items on the agenda.

Chapter II - Election and replacement of members of the council

70. When the General Assembly meets in order to elect the members and officers of the Council, the quorum shall be two-thirds of the members of each division.

71. (1) The members of the Council shall be elected by the General Assembly according to division.
Voting shall be for a single candidate and by simple majority.
(2) Each division shall propose its candidates. The substantive and alternate members shall be elected individually, one after the other.

72. The officers shall be elected by the General Assembly from among the members of the Council.
Voting shall be for a single candidate and by absolute majority.
/p.45/

73. (1) In the event of death or duly established default of a member of the Council, the alternate member shall automatically replace him until new elections are held in the General Assembly.
(2) Where an officer of the Council is concerned, he shall be replaced by elections within the Council.

Part VII – Final provisions

74. All previous provisions, in particular Decree No. 66-DF-311 of July 1966: Code of Medical Deontology, are hereby repealed.

75. This decree shall be registered and published in the Official Gazette in English and French.
Yaoundé, 12 April 1983.
Paul Biya, President of the Republic.
/p.46/

Appendix B: Law No. 90/036 of 10August on the Organisation and Practice of Medicine in Cameroon

Law relating to the Organization and Practice of Medicine
Law No. 90-036 of 10th August 1990

Section1.

This law and the implementation instruments thereof shall govern the organization and practice of medicine

PART I. - PRACTICE OF MEDICINE

CHAPTER I. - CONDITIONS OF PRACTICE OF MEDICINE

Section 2.

(1) Persons engaged in the practice of medicine in Cameroon shall be subject to registration with the Medical Association.
(2) However, physicians of foreign nationality who fulfil the following additional conditions may engage in the practice of medicine in Cameroon;

- Nationals of a country with a reciprocity agreement with Cameroon;
- Physicians who have not been struck off the roll in their countries of origin or in any other country where they had practised medicine;
- Physicians recruited on contract or under a co-operation agreement exclusively for the Administration, a religious body or benevolent Non-Governmental Organization (NGO);
- Physicians serving an approved private undertaking.

Section 3.

The physician himself shall perform professional acts of an administrative and legal nature and draft and issue documents relating thereto either in the normal exercise of his duties or in the carrying out of a special mission assigned to him. He shall be bound in this connection to comply with any instructions given to him.

Section 4.

A physician in service in the Administration or in the private sector shall be bound by:

- Professional secrecy;

- The Code of Ethics adopted by the Cameroon Medical Association and approved by the supervisory authority;
- The statutory provisions of the Association.

CHAPTER II. – PRACTICE OF MEDICINE ON A PRIVATE BASIS

I. – Conditions of practice of medicine on a private Basis

Section 5.

(1) The practice of medicine on a private basis shall be subject to an authorization issued by the Council of the Association under the terms and conditions laid down in this law.
(2) The Council of the Association shall also rule on applications for change of professional domicile or place of activity and resumption of activity after interruption following a disciplinary measure under conditions laid down by regulations.
(3) Authorizations granted by the Council of the Association must comply with the health map established by regulations.
Authorizations granted in violation of the health map shall be null and void.

Section 6.

Persons engaged in the practice of medicine on a private basis shall be subject to the following conditions:

- be of cameroonian nationality and enjoy their civic rights;
- be registered with the Medical Association;
- have completed five years of effective practice in a public service or a private body within the national territory or abroad;
- produce a letter of discharge in principle where they are gainfully employed or assist a colleague who is practising on a private basis;
- be of good conduct;
- produce an insurance policy covering occupational hazards
- have paid all their contributions to the Association.

Section 7.

Except in the case of a reciprocity agreement, a foreign physician may not engage in the practice of medicine on a private basis in Cameroon.

Section 8.

(1) Applications for approval shall be deposited in two copies with the Council of the
Association against a receipt.
(2) The Council of the Association shall decide on the application forwarded to it within a period of thirty days with effect from the date of deposit thereof.
(3) The decision of the Council of the Association shall be subject to prior approval by the supervisory authority from the first working day following that decision. The supervisory authority shall rule on the decision within a period of thirty days. After this period, the decision of the Council of the Association shall be enforceable. It shall be notified to the applicant.
(4) In any case, after a period of 90 (ninety) days with effect from the date of deposit of the application, silence by the Council of the Association shall imply acceptance of the application and the applicant may open his surgery.
(5) Every rejection decision shall set out the reasons on which it is based.

Section 9.

(1) The decisions of the Council of the Association on approval applications may, within thirty days of their notification, be appealed against before the Appeal Board of the Council of the Association by the applicant when it is a rejection decision or by any aggrieved member of the Association if it is an approval decision.
(2) The appeal shall not bar enforcement of the decisions except where it concerns an approval decision.
(3) The Board of Appeal shall give its ruling within a period of two months after the matter has been referred to it. Its decisions shall be notified as provided for by this law and any appeals against them may only be lodged with the Supreme Court in accordance with ordinary law procedure.
(4) After the period of two months, silence by the Board of Appeal shall be considered as a favourable decision on the application.

Section 10.

(1) No surgery or clinic shall remain open in the absence of its licence unless he has arranged to be replaced in due and proper form.
(2) In the absence of a physician, he may be replaced at his surgery by a colleague practising on a private basis or by an additional physician. The Council of the Association shall be informed forthwith about the replacement.

Section 11.

(1) The physician may be assisted by one or more colleagues.
(2) The remuneration of the additional physician shall be determined by mutual agreement.
The Council of the Association shall be notified accordingly.

Section 12.

(1) In the event of the death of a physician operating on a private basis the period during which his heirs may have the surgery managed by a locum tenens may not exceed five years; such period may be renewed once.
(2) Where during the above-mentioned period, one of the children of the deceased is studying medicine, the said surgery may be reserved for him.
(3) The conditions of replacement shall be the same as those for approval to practise medicine on a private basis.

II. Incompatibilities

Section 13.

Subject to special enactments, civil servants and government contract employees who are in active service or employed persons in general shall not be authorized to practise medicine on a private basis.

III. Partnerships of physicians

Section 14.

Physicians operating on a private basis in the same place may enter into an association and carry out their practice in the form of a partnership whose organization and functioning shall be laid down in separate instruments.

IV. Obligation to take out an insurance policy

Section 15.

(1) Every physician or partnership of physicians shall be bound to take out an insurance policy from an approved national insurance company to cover his or its occupational hazards.

The receipt of the insurance policy shall be deposited with the Council of the Association at the beginning of each calendar year.
(2) Failure to take out an insurance policy shall, on the instructions of the Council of the Association or the supervisory authority, lead to the temporary closure of the establishment.
Such establishment may be re-opened only on presentation of the receipt showing payment of the insurance policy.

CHAPTER III. – UNLAWFUL PRACTICE OF MEDICINE

Section 16.

The following shall be guilty of unlawful practice of medicine.
(1) any physician who practises under an assumed physician name or who grants consultations in business premises where some of the apparatus he prescribes or uses are sold;
(2) any unauthorized person who, even in the presence of a physician, habitually or under supervision, provides diagnosis or treatment for diseases on a personal basis by consultation or by any other procedure;
(3) any physician who exercises his profession in violation of the provisions under section (1) above or who offers his assistance to persons who are not authorized to practise;
(4) any physician who exercises his profession while on temporary or permanent suspension.

Section 17.

(1) Without prejudice to the application of more severe administrative, disciplinary or penal sanctions, any person found guilty of unlawful practice of medicine shall be punished with imprisonment of from 6 (six) days to 6 (six) months or with fine of from 200 000 (two hundred thousand) to 2 000 000 (two million) francs or with both such imprisonment and fine.
(2) The court may, where applicable rule that the equipment used in the commission of the offence be confiscated and the establishment be closed.
(3) Any person who violates the provisions of this law shall cease his activity with immediate effect. Furthermore, the closure of his surgery or clinic may be ordered by the Council of the Association, irrespective of any court judgment.

Section 18.

The Council of the Association may refer the matter to the Legal Department or the trial court or, where necessary, be a civil party in any action taken at the instance of the Legal Department against any per-son guilty of unlawful practice of medicine.

PART II. — CAMEROON MEDICAL ASSOCIATION

Section 19.

The Cameroon Medical Association hereinafter referred to as the Association, established in Section 1 of law No. 80/7 of 14 July 1980, shall comprise all physicians practising their profession in Cameroon.

Section 20.

(1) The Association shall ensure compliance with the principles of moral conduct and devotion essential to the practice of medicine as weil as observance of the rules prescribed by the Code of Ethics.
(2) The Association shall equally carry out any duty assigned to it under this law or other separate instruments.
(3) The Association shall have legal personality. Its headquarters shall be in Yaounde. The Association shall be under the supervision of the authority in charge of public health.

CHAPTER 1. — THE ORGANIZATION OF THE CAMEROON MEDICAL ASSOCIATION

Section 21.

The Association shall carry out the duties assigned to it through the following two bodies
- the General Assembly; and
- the Council.

Section 22.

(1) The General Assembly shall comprise all physicians registered on the Roll of the Association.
(2) It shall meet every year in ordinary session when convened by its President and, where necessary, in extraordinary session at the request of the absolute

majority of its members, or of the Council of the Association or of the supervisory authority to:

- elect members of the Council of the Association;
- elect six (6) members for the Appeal Board;
- rule on the progress report of the President of the Council of the Association;
- lay down the guidelines for the smooth running of the profession;
- adopt the Code of Ethics of the profession and the Internal Regulation of the Association.

(3) The General Assembly shall elect the President of the Council of the Association and an Auditor for a term of three (3) years. They shall be eligible for re-election.

Section 23.

(1) The agenda of the General Assembly sessions shall comprise only items relating to the practice of the profession. It shall be drawn up by the President of the Council of the Association to whom questions may be referred one month before the session by members of the Association or by the supervisory authority.
(2) The agenda of every General Assembly session shall be forwarded at least 15 (fifteen) days before the session to the supervisory authority who shall send a representative to the General Assembly deliberations.
(3) The supervisory authority may prohibit the holding of an ordinary or extraordinary session of the General Assembly if the agenda is not in conformity with the provisions of the preceding subsection.

Section 24.

The organization and functioning of the General Assembly shall be defined by internal Regulations.

The Council of the Association

Section 25.

(1) The Council of the Association shall be the executive body of the Association. It shall comprise 12 members elected for a period of three years as follows:

- four substantive Division A members and one alternate member (civil servants) ;
- four substantive division B members and one alternate member (non-religious) .
- four sustantive division C members and one alternate member (religious).

(2) All physicians registered on the roll of the Association shall be electors and eligible for election. The members of the Council shall be eligible for re-election.

(3) The procedure for electing members of the Council and the rules relating to their replacement in case of default shall be laid down by the Code of Ethics.

Section 26.

In addition to the President elected by the General Assembly, the Council of the Association shall elect its Bureau for a period of three (3) years comprising:

- a Vice-President
- a Secretary-General
- a Treasurer.

Section 27.

(1) After each election, a report thereof shall be forwarded on the working day following the election to the supervisory authority.

(2) Disputes arising from the elections may be referred to the Administrative Bench of the Supreme Court by any physician entitled to vote, within fifteen days following the elections.

The supervisory authority shall be notified of such action.

Section 28.

Membership within the Council of the Association shall cease;

1 - When the term of office expires;

2 - In case of unjustified absence from three consecutive meetings of the Council of the association;

3 - in case of a permanent disablement or death ;

4 - in the event of duly established resignation ;

5 - when the officer is struck off the roll of the Association.

Section 29.

The quorum of the Council of the Association shall be three-fifths of its members. Its sessions shall be presided over by its President or, in his absence by the Vice-President or the oldest member of the Council of the Association.

Section 30.

(1) The Council of the Association shall meet in ordinary session twice a year when convened by its President. It may, where necessary, meet in extraordinary session on the initiative of its President or at the request of not less than half of its members or of the supervisory authority.
(2) The President shall fix the date venue and time of the meetings.
(3) Every member of the Council shall be entitled to vote. The decisions of the Council of the Association shall be taken by a simple majority of the members present.
(4) The deliberations of the Council shall be held in camera. Howerer, the President may invite any person of his choice in view of his competence to attend the meetings of the Council in an advisory capacity.

Section 31.

(1) Under Section 20 (1) and (2) and Section 21 above, the Council of the Association shall:
- rule on applications for enrolment and re-enrolment with the Association and the election of the members of the Council;
- approve applications to practise medicine on a private basis as well as applications for establishment, locum tenens, change of professional domicile or place of practice and resumption of practice after interruption following a disciplinary measure;
- exercise any powers entrusted to it by this law or special instruments;
- examine any matters referred to it by the supervisory authority;
- take disciplinary measures against defaulting members of the Association under the conditions laid down by this law.

(2) Under no circumstances, shall the Council take into consideration political or religious acts, leanings and beliefs of the members of the Association.

Section 32.

The Council of the Association shall fix the amount of contributions of members of the Association which shall be compulsory under pain of disciplinary measures.

Section 33.

The President of the Council shall represent the Association in all civil matters and before the Courts. He shall manage the property of the Association by delegation of the Council.

CHAPTER II. — ENROLMENT IN THE ASSOCIATION

Section 34.

Persons engaged in the practice of medicine in Cameroon shall be subject to prior enrolment in the Association.
The roll of the Association shall be kept up-to-date by the Council. The supervisory authority, Senior Divisional Officers, Council and the Legal Department shall be notified regularly of such roll.

Section 35.

Applicants for enrolment with the Association shall fulfil the following conditions.
(a) be of Cameroonian nationality and enjoy their civic rights.
(b) have attained maturity.
(c) hold a State or University diploma of doctor of medicine or any other equivalent diploma recognized by the competent authority at the time of submission of the application.
(d) have not been convicted for any act contrary to honour or morality (theft, false pretence, misappropriation of public funds, forgery and use of forged documents);
(e) neither have been declared bankrupt nor liquidated by court order.

Section 36.

(1) The application for enrolment in the Association shall be deposited with the Council of the Association in two copies against à receipt.
(2) The Council shall decide on the application for enrolment within 30 (thirty) days following the submission of the application.

(3) Decisions of the Council on applications for enrolment with the Association shall be submitted for prior approval by the supervisory authority on the first working day following the day the decision was made. The supervisory authority shall rule on the decision within a period of thirty days. After this time-limit, the decision of the Council shall be enforceable. It shall be notified to the applicant.
(4) In any case, after a period of 90 (ninety) days following the submission of the application, silence by the Council of the Association shall imply acceptable of the application and the applicant's automatic enrolment with the Association.
(5) Every rejection decision shall set out the reasons on which it is based.

Section 37.

(1) Decisions of the Council of the Association on applications for enrolment or re-enrolment with the Association may, within 15 (fifteen) days of notification thereof, be appealed against before the appeal Board of the Council by the applicant in the case of a rejection decision or by any aggrieved member of Association in the case of enrolment or re-enrolment.
(2) In any case, where the Appeal Board fails to take decision within a period of two months from the date such appeal was brought before it the applicant shall be enrolled with the Association.
(3) The appeal shall not have an interlocutory effect save in the case of an acceptance decision.

Section 38.

(1) Without prejudice to the provisions of Section 18 and 36 above, decisions, proceedings, resolutions or any act of the General Assembly or of the Council of the Association shall be null and void unless they are submitted for the prior approval of the supervisory authority on the first working day following the day on which they were made.
(2) The supervisory authority shall rule thereon within a period of thirty days. After this period, the decision shall be automatically enforceable.

Section 39.

In the event of cessation of activity, the person concerned shall, within a period of 15 (fifteen) days, notify the Council thereof. The Council shall strike him off the roll of the Association.

Section 40.

(1) The Secretary General of the Council shall keep the roll of the Association.
(2) Only professional diplomas and qualifications recognized by the competent authority of the country where they were obtained shall figure on the roll of Association. However, titles and decorations conferred on the physician by the State may be mentioned on the Roll.

CHAPTER III. — DISCIPLINE

Section 41.

(1) The Council shall exercise disciplinary jurisdiction at the first instance within the Medical Association. In this capacity, it shall appoint amongst its members a Disciplinary Board.
(2) The Disciplinary Board which shall be presided over by the president of the Council shall comprise four others members elected form within the Council. The President may be replaced in case of his exclusion and objection or absence.

Section 42.

(1) A matter may be referred to the Disciplinary Board by the supervisory authority, the Legal Department or any physician enrolled with the Association who has an interest at stake.
(2) Only the authority responsible for Public Health or the Council of the Association after consultation with the supervisory authority may bring a physician serving the State before the Disciplinary Board for acts committed in the performance of his duties.
The supervisory authority shall take a decision within 30 (thirty) days from the date a matter is referred to it. After this time-limit, if the supervisory authority does not reply it shall be considered as upheld.
(3) The quorum of the Disciplinary Board shall be three-fifths of its members.

Section 43.

Matters that may be referred to the Disciplinary Board shall include;
- any conviction for any offence of a nature to discredit or jeopardize the reputation of the profession committed within or outside the national territory;
- any conviction for professional misconduct.

Section 44.

The Disciplinary Board may, at the request of the parties or on its own initiative, order an inquiry into any facts the findings of which it deems useful for its proceedings. The decision to order an inquiry shall indicate the matters to be investigated and shall prescribe, according to the circumstances whether it is to be conducted before the Disciplinary Board or pressed on by a member of the Board who shall visit the place of occurrence of the matter.

Section 45.

(1) Any physician accused of an offence may be assisted by a defence counsel of his choice.
(2) He may exercise the right of exclusion and objection in accordance with ordinary law procedure.

Section 46.

(1) The Disciplinary Board shall keep records of its proceedings.
(2) Minutes shall be drawn up after each meeting and signed by all members.
(3) The minutes of cross-examinations or hearings shall likewise be drawn up and signed by the persons concerned.

Section 47.

(1) No disciplinary sanction may be pronounced unless the physician accused has been heard or summoned to appear before the Board within a period of 30 (thirty) days following receipt of the summons with acknowledgement of receipt.
(2) Where the accused physician fails to appear before the Disciplinary Board after a duty notified summons, the Board may make its rulings.

Section 48.

(1) The Disciplinary Board may pronounce any of the following disciplinary sanctions;

- warning
- reprimand
- suspension from practice from three months to one year, depending on the seriousness of the offence committed;
- striking off the Roll of the Association.

(2) The first two sanctions shall entail ineligibility for membership of the Council of the Association for 2 (two) years with effect from the date of notification of the sanction. The third sanction shall tail ineligibility for 3 (three) years with effect from the date of notification of the sanction.

Section 49.

(1) The decision of the Disciplinary Board shall set out the reasons on which they are based.
(2) They shall be notified on the first working day following the date, which they are taken to the supervisory authority, the Public prosecutor and the accused physician who shall acknowledge receipt thereof.

Section 50.

(1) Where the decision is delivered by default, the accused physician may raise objection there to within a period of 10 (ten) days with effect from the date he was personally notified of the decision with acknowledgement of receipt.
(2) Where he is not personally notified of the decision, the time-limit for objection shall be 30 (thirty) days with effect from the day notice was served at his professional domicile.
(3) The objection shall be in the form of a simple declaration submitted to the Secretariat of the Council of the Association which shall issue a receipt therefor.

Section 51.

(1) Where the decision is made after full argument on both sides, the accused physician may, within 60 (sixty) days with effect from the date of notification of the decision of the Disciplinary Board lodge an appeal before the Appeal Board referred to in Section 52 below.
(2) After this time-limit, the decision shall be final and enforceable.

Section 52.

The Appeal Board shall comprise the following Chairman.

- a Judicial and Legal Office of the Supreme Court designated by the President of the said Court;

members:

- a physician designated by the supervisory authority;
- three members of the Association elected within the General Assembly who did not hear or decide on the matter in the first instance.

Section 53.

(1) Without prejudice to the provisions of Section 9 and 37 above, the Appeal Board shall hear appeals against decisions of the Council concerning discipline.
(2) The decisions of the Board shall be taken by simple majority of the members present.

Section 54.

(1) Appeals shall be in the form of an explanatory motion lodged at the Secretariat of the Council of the Association against a receipt.
(2) The appeal may be lodged by the physician concerned, the supervisory authority, the Department of Public prosecutions or any member of the Association with an interest at stake within 30 (thirty) days following notification of the decision of the Disciplinary Board.
(3) Appeals shall not bar enforcement of the decisions.

Section 55.

(1) The Appeal Board shall give its ruling within 2 (two) months from the date the matter is referred to it. Its decisions shall be taken and notified as provided for in Section 53 above and may be appealed against only before the Supreme Court according to ordinary law procedure.
(2) After a 2 (two) months period, a decision taken in the first instance shall automatically be suspended.

Section 56.

(1) Where a physician is struck off the Roll of the Association, he may, after a period of 5 (five) years apply to the Council of the Association for resumption of practice.
(2) Should the request be rejected, he may re-apply only after another period of 2 (two) years.

Section 57.

The exercise of disciplinary action as provided for hereinabove shall not bar;
- any proceedings instituted by the Legal Department, private individuals or by the Association before the courts in accordance with ordinary law procedure, or - any disciplinary action that the supervisory authority may take against a medical Officer.

PART III. — TRANSITIONAL AND FINAL PROVISIONS

Section 58.

The following shall be authorized to continue to practise medicine:
(1) physicians approved under farmer regulations.
(2) physicians recruited to serve exclusively the Administration.
(3) foreign physicians exercising their profession in Cameroon or recruited an a contract basis prior to the publication of this law.

Section 59.

All physicians legally practising their profession on behalf of the Administration, private undertakings or on a private basis on the date of enactment of this law shall be automatically enrolled in the Association in accordance with the previsions of this law.

Section 60.

Files being studied on the date of enactment of this law shall be subject to the conditions and procedures provided for by this law.

Section 61.

The conditions of implementation of this law shall, as and when necessary, be laid dawn by regulations.

Section 62.

All previous provisions repugnant hereto, in particular Laws Nos. 80/7 of 14 July 1980 to set up the National Medical Association and 80/6 of 14 July 1980 to regulate the practice of medicine are hereby repealed.

Section 63.

This law shall be registered, published according to the procedure of urgency and inserted in the Official Gazette in English and French.
Yaoundé, 10 août 1990

Paul Biya, President of the Republic

Appendix C: The WMA International Code of Medical Ethics

WMA INTERNATIONAL CODE OF MEDICAL ETHICS

Adopted by the 3rd General Assembly of the World Medical Association, London, England, October 1949 Revised by the 22nd World Medical Assembly, Sydney, Australia, August 1968, the 35th World Medical Assembly, Venice, Italy, October 1983, the 57th WMA General Assembly, Pilanesberg, South Africa, October 2006 and by the 73rd WMA General Assembly, Berlin, Germany, October 2022

PREAMBLE

The World Medical Association (WMA) has developed the International Code of Medical Ethics as a canon of ethical principles for the members of the medical profession worldwide. In concordance with the WMA Declaration of Geneva: The Physician's Pledge and the WMA's entire body of policies, it defines and elucidates the professional duties of physicians towards their patients, other physicians and health professionals, themselves, and society as a whole.

The physician must be aware of applicable national ethical, legal, and regulatory norms and standards, as well as relevant international norms and standards.

Such norms and standards must not reduce the physician's commitment to the ethical principles set forth in this Code.

The International Code of Medical Ethics should be read as a whole and each of its constituent paragraphs should be applied with consideration of all other relevant paragraphs. Consistent with the mandate of the WMA, the Code is addressed to physicians. The WMA encourages others who are involved in healthcare to adopt these ethical principles.

GENERAL PRINCIPLES

1. The primary duty of the physician is to promote the health and well-being of individual patients by providing competent, timely, and compassionate care in accordance with good medical practice and professionalism.

   The physician also has a responsibility to contribute to the health and well-being of the populations the physician serves and society as a whole, including future generations.

The physician must provide care with the utmost respect for human life and dignity, and for the autonomy and rights of the patient.

2. The physician must practise medicine fairly and justly and provide care based on the patient's health needs without bias or engaging in discriminatory conduct on the basis of age, disease or disability, creed, ethnic origin, gender, nationality, political affiliation, race, culture, sexual orientation, social standing, or any other factor.
3. The physician must strive to use health care resources in a way that optimally benefits the patient, in keeping with fair, just, and prudent stewardship of the shared resources with which the physician is entrusted.
4. The physician must practise with conscience, honesty, integrity, and accountability, while always exercising independent professional judgement and maintaining the highest standards of professional conduct.
5. Physicians must not allow their individual professional judgement to be influenced by the possibility of benefit to themselves or their institution. The physician must recognise and avoid real or potential conflicts of interest. Where such conflicts are unavoidable, they must be declared in advance and properly managed.
6. Physicians must take responsibility for their individual medical decisions and must not alter their sound professional medical judgements on the basis of instructions contrary to medical considerations.
7. When medically appropriate, the physician must collaborate with other physicians and health professionals who are involved in the care of the patient or who are qualified to assess or recommend care options. This communication must respect patient confidentiality and be confined to necessary information.
8. When providing professional certification, the physician must only certify what the physician has personally verified.
9. The physician should provide help in medical emergencies, while considering the physician's own safety and competence, and the availability of other viable options for care.
10. The physician must never participate in or facilitate acts of torture, or other cruel, inhuman, or degrading practices and punishments.
11. The physician must engage in continuous learning throughout professional life in order to maintain and develop professional knowledge and skills.

12. The physician should strive to practise medicine in ways that are environmentally sustainable with a view to minimising environmental health risks to current and future generations.

DUTIES TO THE PATIENT

13. In providing medical care, the physician must respect the dignity, autonomy, and rights of the patient. The physician must respect the patient's right to freely accept or refuse care in keeping with the patient's values and preferences.
14. The physician must commit to the primacy of patient health and well-being and must offer care in the patient's best interests. In doing so, the physician must strive to prevent or minimise harm for the patient and seek a positive balance between the intended benefit to the patient and any potential harm.
15. The physician must respect the patient's right to be informed in every phase of the care process. The physician must obtain the patient's voluntary informed consent prior to any medical care provided, ensuring that the patient receives and understands the information needed to make an independent, informed decision about the proposed care. The physician must respect the patient's decision to withhold or withdraw consent at any time and for any reason.
16. When a patient has substantially limited, underdeveloped, impaired, or fluctuating decision-making capacity, the physician must involve the patient as much as possible in medical decisions. In addition, the physician must work with the patient's trusted representative, if available, to make decisions in keeping with the patient's preferences, when those are known or can reasonably be inferred. When the patient's preferences cannot be determined, the physician must make decisions in the patient's best interests. All decisions must be made in keeping with the principles set forth in this Code.
17. In emergencies, where the patient is not able to participate in decision making and no representative is readily available, the physician may initiate an intervention without prior informed consent in the best interests of the patient and with respect for the patient's preferences, where known.
18. If the patient regains decision-making capacity, the physician must obtain informed consent for further intervention.

19. The physician should be considerate of and communicate with others, where available, who are close to the patient, in keeping with the patient's preferences and best interests and with due regard for patient confidentiality.
20. If any aspect of caring for the patient is beyond the capacity of a physician, the physician must consult with or refer the patient to another appropriately qualified physician or health professional who has the necessary capacity.
21. The physician must ensure accurate and timely medical documentation.
22. The physician must respect the patient's privacy and confidentiality, even after the patient has died. A physician may disclose confidential information if the patient provides voluntary informed consent or, in exceptional cases, when disclosure is necessary to safeguard a significant and overriding ethical obligation to which all other possible solutions have been exhausted, even when the patient does not or cannot consent to it. This disclosure must be limited to the minimal necessary information, recipients, and duration.
23. If a physician is acting on behalf of or reporting to any third parties with respect to the care of a patient, the physician must inform the patient accordingly at the outset and, where appropriate, during the course of any interactions. The physician must disclose to the patient the nature and extent of those commitments and must obtain consent for the interaction.
24. The physician must refrain from intrusive or otherwise inappropriate advertising and marketing and ensure that all information used by the physician in advertising and marketing is factual and not misleading.
25. The physician must not allow commercial, financial, or other conflicting interests to affect the physician's professional judgement.
26. When providing medical care remotely, the physician must ensure that this form of communication is medically justifiable and that the necessary medical care is provided. The physician must also inform the patient about the benefits and limitations of receiving medical care remotely, obtain the patient's consent, and ensure that patient confidentiality is upheld. Wherever medically appropriate, the physician must aim to provide care to the patient through direct, personal contact.
27. The physician must maintain appropriate professional boundaries. The physician must never engage in abusive, exploitative, or other inappropriate relationships or behaviour with a patient and must not engage in a sexual relationship with a current patient.

28. In order to provide care of the highest standards, physicians must attend to their own health, well-being, and abilities. This includes seeking appropriate care to ensure that they are able to practise safely.

29. This Code represents the physician's ethical duties. However, on some issues there are profound moral dilemmas concerning which physicians and patients may hold deeply considered but conflicting conscientious beliefs.

    The physician has an ethical obligation to minimise disruption to patient care. Physician conscientious objection to provision of any lawful medical interventions may only be exercised if the individual patient is not harmed or discriminated against and if the patient's health is not endangered.

    The physician must immediately and respectfully inform the patient of this objection and of the patient's right to consult another qualified physician and provide sufficient information to enable the patient to initiate such a consultation in a timely manner.

DUTIES TO OTHER PHYSICIANS, HEALTH PROFESSIONALS, STUDENTS, AND OTHER PERSONNEL

30. The physician must engage with other physicians, health professionals and other personnel in a respectful and collaborative manner without bias, harassment, or discriminatory conduct. The physician must also ensure that ethical principles are upheld when working in teams.

31. The physician should respect colleagues' patient-physician relationships and not intervene unless requested by either party or needed to protect the patient from harm. This should not prevent the physician from recommending alternative courses of action considered to be in the patient's best interests.

32. The physician should report to the appropriate authorities conditions or circumstances which impede the physician or other health professionals from providing care of the highest standards or from upholding the principles of this Code. This includes any form of abuse or violence against physicians and other health personnel, inappropriate working conditions, or other circumstances that produce excessive and sustained levels of stress.

33. The physician must accord due respect to teachers and students.

DUTIES TO SOCIETY

34. The physician must support fair and equitable provision of health care. This includes addressing inequities in health and care, the determinants of those inequities, as well as violations of the rights of both patients and health professionals.

35. Physicians play an important role in matters relating to health, health education, and health literacy. In fulfiling this responsibility, physicians must be prudent in discussing new discoveries, technologies, or treatments in non-professional, public settings, including social media, and should ensure that their own statements are scientifically accurate and understandable.

    Physicians must indicate if their own opinions are contrary to evidence-based scientific information.

36. The physician must support sound medical scientific research in keeping with the WMA Declaration of Helsinki and the WMA Declaration of Taipei.

37. The physician should avoid acting in such a way as to weaken public trust in the medical profession. To maintain that trust, individual physicians must hold themselves and fellow physicians to the highest standards of professional conduct and be prepared to report behaviour that conflicts with the principles of this Code to the appropriate authorities.

38. The physician should share medical knowledge and expertise for the benefit of patients and the advancement of health care, as well as public and global health.

DUTIES AS A MEMBER OF THE MEDICAL PROFESSION

39. The physician should follow, protect, and promote the ethical principles of this Code. The physician should help prevent national or international ethical, legal, organisational, or regulatory requirements that undermine any of the duties set forth in this Code.

40. The physician should support fellow physicians in upholding the responsibilities set out in this Code and take measures to protect them from undue influence, abuse, exploitation, violence, or oppression.